FROM BYZANTIUM TO ITALY

From Byzantium to Italy

Greek studies in the Italian Renaissance

N.G. Wilson

The Johns Hopkins University Press · Baltimore

Printed in Great Britain

Published in the United States of America by
The Johns Hopkins University Press
701 West 40th Street
Baltimore, Maryland 21211-2190

Library of Congress Cataloging-in-Publication Data

Wilson, Nigel Guy
   From Byzantium to Italy : Greek studies in the Italian Renaissance
/ N.G. Wilson.
      p.   cm.
   Sequel to: Scholars of Byzantium.
   Includes bibliographical references and index.
   ISBN 0-8018-4563-7
   1. Greek philology—Study and teaching—Italy—History.   2. Italy—
Civilization—Greek influences.   3. Renaissance—Italy.   4. Humanists—
Italy.   I. Title.
PA78.I8W54   1992
480′.0704509024—dc20   92-22678

Contents

This book is dedicated to
ALESSANDRO PEROSA
whose Oxford lectures of 1965
introduced me to these studies

But it is in Italy, in the fifteenth century, that the
interest of the Renaissance mainly lies – in that
solemn fifteenth century which can hardly be
studied too much.

Pater

Preface

This book is a sequel to *Scholars of Byzantium* (London 1983), in which I described the preservation of the classical heritage and the use made of it by the intellectuals of Byzantium. It was the story of a long struggle against great odds, with as many defeats as victories. Relief came only just in time, but when it came it was effective. What the Byzantines had preserved was transmitted to a vigorous culture; the fate of the Greek legacy in territories occupied by the Ottomans makes an eloquent contrast. But though it is a commonplace, repeated in every book about the Italian Renaissance, that the Greek influence was a significant factor, no one has tried to chronicle the stages by which a lost culture was recovered and so to make clear how its effects began to be felt in various fields. If the narrative were continued beyond the death of Aldus Manutius, this last point would assume greater significance, because it was in the following decades that Italian science and mathematics reached the stage where Greek texts could be more fully used as a stepping-stone to further discoveries. But after a good deal of thought I came to the conclusion that 1515 marks the end of an era and is a less artificial terminal date than others which might have been chosen. Perhaps at some time in the future I shall turn to the task of describing developments in the middle of the sixteenth century. In the meantime the present volume is a sketch and a challenge. It is a sketch because a full treatment of the subject, even with the chronological limit imposed as it has been, would entail postponement of publication for many years, and there is much to be said for offering a provisional account. It is a challenge to others to continue the inquiry in order to see whether the conclusions put forward retain their validity.

One deliberate omission should be mentioned: there is no attempt to describe the early stages of archaeology in Greece, partly because it made so little impact in intellectual circles in the period under discussion – it was Roman ruins that inspired architects – and partly because Roberto Weiss's book *The Renaissance discovery of classical antiquity* is a good account, now available in revised form.

In *Scholars of Byzantium* I was very sparing with bibliographical references in the footnotes. In this book I have again tried not to overload the reader. My failure to cite such-and-such an article should not automatically be taken as proof of ignorance; it may simply mean that the article did not seem to offer a real contribution to the point I wished to argue.

Lincoln College, Oxford   N.G.W.

Abbreviations

Abh	*Abhandlungen*
BibHumRen	*Bibliothèque d'humanisme et Renaissance*
BICS	*Bulletin of the Institute of Classical Studies*
BullJRL	*Bulletin of the John Rylands Library*
BZ	*Byzantinische Zeitschrift*
CP	*Classical Philology*
CR	*Classical Review*
GRBS	*Greek, Roman and Byzantine Studies*
GSLI	*Giornale storico della letteratura italiana*
IMU	*Italia medioevale e umanistica*
JÖB	*Jahrbuch der Oesterreichischen Byzantinistik*
JWCI	*Journal of the Warburg and Courtauld Institutes*
PG	*Patrologia graeca*
REG	*Revue des études grecques*
RevHistTextes	*Revue d'histoire des textes*
RGK	*Repertorium der griechischen Kopisten 800-1600*
RhMus	*Rheinisches Museum*
RivFil	*Rivista di Filologia*
RivStudBiz Neoell	*Rivista di studi bizantini e neoellenici*
SB	*Sitzungsberichte*
SIFC	*Studi italiani di filologia classica*

1

The beginnings

(i) Precursors

In western Europe during the middle ages Greek was not generally known. On rare occasions from the ninth century onwards attempts were made to increase knowledge of the language and produce translations of a variety of ancient texts. It was usually Aristotle, Galen and some early fathers of the church who claimed attention. Few of these enterprises had an outstanding or enduring success. The earliest of any note are due to Henricus Aristippus in Norman Sicily in the twelfth century and his contemporary Burgundio of Pisa. Their efforts resulted in a product which was judged very crude by later generations. In the meantime some Greek works, in particular Ptolemy's *Almagest* and various Aristotelian writings, found an alternative and roundabout route to the West: in Toledo during the second half of the twelfth century translations were made from Arabic versions into Latin. A rather more successful attempt to tackle the original texts was made in the thirteenth century by the Dominican William of Moerbeke. In 1260 he made quite a good job of Aristotle's *Politics*, and he also tried to deal with the very difficult treatises of Archimedes and the Neoplatonist Proclus. Yet he does not appear to have established a school.

The immediate predecessors of the famous humanists fared little better than their medieval counterparts. This negative judgement seems to apply even to a group of translations of undoubted importance which has still not been fully investigated, the medical texts rendered by Nicholas of Reggio for the Neapolitan king Robert of Anjou (1308-1345). The latter had received as a gift from the Byzantine emperor Andronicus III a copy of Galen which apparently included some unique texts, and as that precious volume can no longer be traced Nicholas' versions assume a much greater significance than they might otherwise have deserved.[1] But even his work, praiseworthy in intention and valuable to his contemporaries, not to mention its value to modern students of Galen, was not continued by others. A court circle in the south of Italy seems not to have been able to exploit the advantage of its close proximity to the Greek communities of Calabria, Apulia and Sicily, which were still quite substantial.

1

The same inability is observable for a time in the wealthier and more developed cities of the north. A recent discovery has demonstrated that in the Padua of the so-called pre-humanists at the turn of the thirteenth and fourteenth centuries one learned man had obtained a copy of the *Moralia* of Plutarch (Ambr. C 126 inf.), manufactured recently for Maximus Planudes, the leading Byzantine scholar of the day who had served on a diplomatic mission to Venice in 1296. Yet Pace of Ferrara (*fl. c.* 1299 – *post* 1317) probably never learned Greek at all. Certainly he believed that Sophocles was the author of both the *Iliad* and the *Odyssey*. His best chance of learning the language would have been through Pietro d'Abano, then resident in Padua, who had been to Constantinople and was able to translate Galen and other scientific works. But there is no sign that contact between them, if any took place, was beneficial.[2]

The episode is puzzling. So is another curious story from Padua a little later in the fourteenth century. During a court case someone cited Homer; indeed it seems that he did so twice. The report comes from Leonzio Pilato, of whom more in a moment. He says that he was in Padua at the time, and the date must be shortly before 1358-9. The passage or passages in question must almost certainly have been among the ten quotations from Homer found in the *Digest*. Pilato says that the Greek, badly written, was shown to the court. One wonders how the lawyer obtained his text, since ordinary copies of the *Digest* omitted all passages of Greek.[3]

(ii) Petrarch, Boccaccio and Pilato

Every schoolboy knows, or did so in the days when Macaulay coined the phrase, that Petrarch wished to learn Greek. He owned a copy of the *Iliad* (now identified as Ambr. I 98 inf.)[4] and of Plato (perhaps Paris gr. 1807),[5] and suffered the frustration of never being able to read them, despite having taken lessons with the Greek scholar and diplomat Barlaam (d. 1348). Another chance seemed to present itself some ten years later when Petrarch was in Padua and came across Leonzio Pilato, a man from Calabria whose education and culture were more Greek than Latin. In 1359 he must have discussed with Boccaccio the idea of obtaining a complete translation of Homer from Pilato. It is notable that such a plan should have been the joint initiative of the leading poet and the leading prose writer of Italy. Pilato is soon after found in Florence, teaching under the auspices of Boccaccio, who later held the chair of Dante studies there. Homer was not the only author to be lectured on; Pilato also found time to begin work on Euripides. Although no record survives of any stipend paid to him, the minor humanist Domenico Silvestri tells us that he gave public lectures,[6] and so it is no longer strictly true to say that Chrysoloras' appointment in 1397 marks the beginning of the teaching of Greek in the Renaissance.

Pilato's brief stay in Florence from 1360 to 1362 has recently been studied carefully and shown to possess a greater significance than was previously attributed to it. He had already given Petrarch a small specimen of his Homer translation; during his stay in Florence he managed to produce versions of both the epics, which after some delay found their way into Petrarch's hands.[7] They were studied carefully by the poet in his last years, as is evident from the many notes he made in the margins of his books. Although Pilato's work now seems crude and mediocre, it has been said in his defence that when allowance is made for the limited resources available to him and the traditions in which he had been educated, he did as well as could be expected.[8] This is fair comment, especially if his task was purely and simply to take each word in turn and render it for the benefit of a class of beginners. But if it was clear that other readers could be envisaged, men of letters like Petrarch who had to rely wholly on a translation, Pilato's achievement looks more modest. It is perhaps rather surprising that it did not prove possible to find someone from the Italo-Greek communities of southern Italy with a better command of Latin than Pilato possessed, and if some members of his Florentine audience felt a measure of disappointment at his performance, one can sympathise with their feelings. On the other hand, the existence of several manuscript copies of each version suggests that they met a need. Two very brief specimens will serve to give an impression of them.

Here are the first few lines of the *Odyssey*:

Ἄνδρα μοι ἔννεπε, Μοῦσα, πολύτροπον, ὃς μάλα πολλὰ
πλάγχθη, ἐπεὶ Τροίης ἱερὸν πτολίεθρον ἔπερσε·
πολλῶν δ' ἀνθρώπων ἴδεν ἄστεα καὶ νόον ἔγνω,
πολλὰ δ' ὅ γ' ἐν πόντῳ πάθεν ἄλγεα ὃν κατὰ θυμόν,
ἀρνύμενος ἥν τε ψυχὴν καὶ νόστον ἑταίρων.

which were rendered as follows by the Victorian novelist Samuel Butler in 1900:

Tell me, O Muse, of that ingenious hero who travelled far and wide after he had sacked the famous town of Troy. Many cities did he visit, and many were the nations with whose manners and customs he was acquainted; moreover he suffered much by sea while trying to save his own life and bring his men safely home.

Pilato's Latin is:

Virum mihi pande, Musa, multimodum, qui valde multum
erravit, ex quo Troiae sacram civitatem depredatus fuit;
multorum hominum vidit urbes et intellectum novit,
multas autem hic in ponto passus fuit angustias proprio in animo,
redimens propriam animam et reditum sociorum.

Similarly with the *Iliad* one sees immediately the word-for-word approach adopted by Pilato. The opening lines are

Μῆνιν ἄειδε, θεά, Πηληϊάδεω ᾿Αχιλῆος
οὐλομένην, ἣ μυρί᾽ ᾿Αχαιοῖς ἄλγε᾽ ἔθηκε,
πολλὰς δ᾽ ἰφθίμους ψυχὰς ῎Αϊδι προΐαψεν
ἡρώων, αὐτοὺς δὲ ἑλώρια τεῦχε κύνεσσιν
οἰωνοῖσί τε πᾶσι, Διὸς δ᾽ ἐτελείετο βουλή,
ἐξ οὗ δὴ τὰ πρῶτα διαστήτην ἐρίσαντε
᾿Ατρεΐδης τε ἄναξ ἀνδρῶν καὶ δῖος ᾿Αχιλλεύς.

The slightly archaic version made by Walter Leaf in 1882 runs as follows:

Sing, goddess, the wrath of Achilles, Peleus' son, the ruinous wrath that brought on the Achaeans woes innumerable, and hurled down into Hades many strong souls of heroes and gave their bodies to be prey to dogs and all winged fowls; and so the counsel of Zeus wrought out its accomplishment from the day when first strife parted Atreides king of men and noble Achilles.

Here is Pilato's attempt to convey the force of the original:

Iram cane dea Pelidis Achillis
pestiferam, quae innumerabiles Graecis dolores imposuit
multas autem fortes animas inferno antemisit
heroum, ipsosque cadavera praeparavit canibus
avibusque omnibus – Iovis autem perficiebatur consilium –
ex quo iam primitus diversimode litigaverunt
Atridesque imperator virorum et divus Achilles.[9]

Pilato added explanatory notes, mostly drawn from the ancient and medieval commentaries. This material was taken up enthusiastically by Boccaccio, who collected information about classical mythology for his *Genealogia deorum gentilium*, a large reference book used by many generations of students.

The Euripides version is a mere fragment, consisting of no more than the first 466 verses of the *Hecuba*, written between the lines of the Greek exemplar (Laur. 31.10) and then copied with revisions by Pilato himself into a fresh book (San Marco 226). The Latin is again of very poor quality. There are notes which display some knowledge of Homer and of Lycophron's *Alexandra*, a curious riddling poem in which Cassandra makes prophecies to Priam. This mediocre production of a Hellenistic poetaster was quite well known in Byzantium, and it is not surprising to find Pilato acquainted with it. It was also perfectly natural for him to choose to begin work on the *Hecuba*, since that was the first play in the selection normally read in Byzantine schools. What could not have been taken for granted, however, is that instead of using a manuscript recently transcribed and likely to offer an inferior text, Pilato hit on an earlier copy dating from *c.* 1175. Although it does not rank as one of the key witnesses to the text, it is not neglected by modern editors.[10] How Pilato found it remains a mystery. It is one of a collection of books produced by two scribes, mostly of considerable importance for the texts that they transmit, and part of the collection passed through the hands of the medieval translator Burgundio of Pisa (1110-1193); but in the present case there is no evidence of Burgundio's ownership. At all events Pilato was using a fairly good source, and it is greatly to be regretted that he was not capable of doing justice to it. Nevertheless Boccaccio was able to acquire some more information about Greek mythology.[11]

Another minor product of Pilato's residence in Florence is a version of a miscellany of strange and mainly false information which circulated as part of the Aristotelian corpus (*De mirabilibus auscultationibus*). Once again Boccaccio was responsible, his thirst for such information evidently being insatiable.[12] A much more important recent discovery is that Pilato studied the Greek texts in the *Digest*, using the copy now known as the Florentine Pandects.[13] This famous treasure was still in Pisa at the time, and the most likely reconstruction of the sequence of events is that a Pisan lawyer heard of Pilato's presence in Florence and arranged for him to come and perform the task. Since Pisa and Florence were on very bad terms and safe-conducts had to be issued before anyone could travel from one city to the other, the Pisans deserve credit for their enterprise. As Lord Lytton said

> Beneath the rule of men entirely great
> The pen is mightier than the sword.

It can hardly be said that they were appropriately rewarded. The Greek passages in question had been translated once before, by the most eminent Pisan of the middle ages, Burgundio, and while his rendering is literal to the point of being unidiomatic or unintelligible – it earned him the epithet of 'indoctus aliquis' from Politian – examination of Pilato's attempt to replace it shows that on the whole there was no improvement. Although a few flashes of intelligence can be seen, there are also mistakes, and in some places he seems to have been unable to decipher correctly the uncial script. To modern readers such a failure is very strange, because a capital letter script appears simple when compared with the minuscule or cursive that replaced it. But it is clear that in the late Byzantine period educated men were not at ease with uncial hands, as is proved by a slightly later case, the disfigurement of the beautiful illuminated Vienna Dioscorides, in which the uncial text was recopied into blank spaces *c.* 1400 by John Chortasmenos in his ordinary script.

This work on the Pandects, although not of a high standard, is an early sign that Greek was not always valued for purely literary reasons, even though it was originally the Florentine literary circle which made it possible for the lawyers to aim at a better understanding of part of the *Digest*. A fashionable modern interpretation of the history of classical scholarship accords a vital role to poets in the periods of revival and success.[14] In the present instance lawyers stand alongside poets among the pioneers.

Boccaccio took note of Pilato's efforts. In Book 14 of the *Genealogia deorum gentilium* he mentions the quotations from Homer in the Pandects, where the poet is described as the father of all the virtues, which is why it was thought appropriate to cite his authority in a legal context. But the lawyers were not yet satisfied, and further attempts were made to learn the exact meaning of the Greek passages in the *Digest*. Half a century later, shortly after the Pandects had passed into Florentine possession as a result of the conquest of Pisa in 1406, the Venetian Francesco Barbaro expressed an interest in the question and approached Niccolò Niccoli. Incredible as it may seem, Niccoli was unable to gain access to the book for him, as it was guarded like a sacred relic. Ambrogio Traversari, in explaining to Barbaro that his request could not be granted, states that the magistrates had powers to permit inspection of the book and that the uneducated public thought of it as something special. The implication is that the magistrates would not dare to let anyone tamper with the talisman. It is as well to remember that fifteenth-century Florence, like fifth-century Athens, was not a society composed exclusively of rational educated men. Serious work on the Pandects had to wait until Politian was able to exploit his privileged position.

When Pilato left Florence he had made his mark, but it was not a permanent imprint. The most eager recipient of the knowledge he could transmit was in no position to become in turn the teacher of others. One cannot expect rapid progress from a man in his late forties learning a difficult language in conditions far from ideal, and Boccaccio's linguistic competence never took him beyond the rank of a beginner. There are mistakes in his application of Pilato's information,[15] and his attempt to deal with an epigram in elegiac couplets shows him unable to appreciate metrical considerations.[16] Although the rules of scansion are not quite the same as in the corresponding Latin metre, a pupil under the direction of a better teacher would have been able to master them.

There is now a gap in the story, punctuated for a moment in 1381-2, when Simon Atumanus, the Greek bishop of Gerace in Calabria, being in Rome for a short time, taught Greek to Radulf de Rivo, later dean of Tongres. He had earlier translated Plutarch's essay *De cohibenda ira*, but so badly that Salutati felt impelled to redraft his Latin. Atumanus' version does not strictly belong to our story because it was done in Avignon at the papal curia in 1372. He serves to remind us that there were flickerings of interest in Greek outside Italy.[17]

All the episodes narrated so far, however distinguished the main actors, have in common a failure to produce a continuing tradition of teaching and scholarship. In this respect they are no more than repetitions of what had occurred from time to time during the middle ages. In 1397 that was to change.

2

Chrysoloras: methods of learning
the language

The stimulus for a new initiative can be traced back to 1390-1, when Manuel Chrysoloras, a Byzantine diplomat making his first visit to Venice, gave some lessons to a certain Roberto Rossi, who reported his experience to Coluccio Salutati, the chancellor of Florence. Salutati arranged for Jacopo Angeli da Scarperia to go to Constantinople with instructions to learn Greek from Chrysoloras, bring him back to Florence if possible, and to buy books.[1] The chancellor made it clear what kind of texts he wished to acquire. The historians head the list. In second place, although Salutati was not himself a poet, come the poets and the writers who have dealt with the legends found in poetry. As an aid to reading poetry metrical treatises will be required. After them he mentions the complete works of Plato and dictionaries. The latter, like the metrical handbooks, are a recognition of practical needs and difficulties. One would like to know whether Plato was thought of as a potential counterweight to Aristotelianism or more narrowly as a source of political theory. That the former view is correct would be a natural inference from the wide range of translations undertaken at his suggestion by Leonardo Bruni (1370-1444), the historian of Florence who was also from 1427 chancellor of the city.

All the books mentioned so far must have been intended for some public or university library, since Salutati continues with some requests on his own account: Plutarch, Homer and a writer on mythology. His taste for Plutarch has already been noted. A book on mythology indicates interests akin to those of Boccaccio. The Homer is to be 'grossis litteris et in pergameno'. The mention of parchment may imply that he was after a luxury article. As to the capital letters, he may well have felt that one of the great difficulties in learning Greek was the protean nature of minuscule script, and perhaps he hoped to overcome it by acquiring a text in the alternative uncial lettering, not realising how rare such copies were and how unwilling contemporary scribes would be to produce a fresh one.[2]

The supply of texts was still a mundane but vital concern after Chrysoloras' arrival. The wealthy Florentine nobleman Palla Strozzi, who had taken a leading part in the negotiations leading to Chrysoloras' appointment, knew that nothing can be done without books and put himself to great expense by ordering a large number from Greece. In his short biography of Palla Vespasiano da Bisticci tells us that they included an illustrated 'Cosmografia', which is Ptolemy's *Geography* (now Urb. gr. 82), but Palla himself says that this volume was in fact Chrysoloras' own property, brought by him to Florence in 1397.[3] Other titles mentioned by Vespasiano are the *Lives* of Plutarch, Plato, and the *Politics* of Aristotle. The last of these was allegedly the copy that served as the basis for Bruni's translation. If this detail is correct, we may infer that Palla's purchases continued over a long period of years, because the version of the *Politics* was one of the last works by Bruni.

The plan to secure Chrysoloras' services matured slowly. In a letter of 28 March 1396 the Florentine Studio invited Chrysoloras to take up a ten-year contract to teach 'grammaticam et litteras graecas' at a stipend of 100 florins payable in two half-yearly instalments. He was not to be allowed to charge any fee for instruction but might accept offerings from pupils without deduction from his stipend. If he did not arrive by the following 1 January, the offer was to lapse. In fact he arrived on 2 February, but far from being penalised he received an improved contract, being offered 150 florins with a tenure of five years. The following year the figure rose again to 250.[4] It has been suggested that the changes were made in order to fend off competition from Giangaleazzo Visconti, who would have liked to lure him to the Milanese university at Pavia, and this seems likely, since he actually went to Pavia on leaving Florence in 1400.[5]

Although his stay was shorter than intended, Salutati and the university had achieved their object. In the short space of three years the Byzantine diplomat was able to do what Pilato had failed to do. The secret of Chrysoloras' success perhaps lies in his ability to simplify the traditional grammar books, removing the bewildering complexities inflicted on Byzantine schoolchildren. A comparison of his textbook *Erotemata* with a late Byzantine work of the same title by Manuel Moschopoulos reveals that the categories of the noun have been reduced from fifty-six to ten.[6] Although the language was still far from easy, Chrysoloras may well have brought it within the reach of a fair number of keen and gifted students. His *Erotemata* were soon provided with a Latin translation and abbreviated by Guarino, and it is tempting to infer that this revised edition of his manual was highly valued, because it appeared in print remarkably early, *c.* 1471.[7]

The title means 'questions', and the book is to some extent cast in question-and-answer form. However, this does not reflect the practices of the schoolroom in the way that might be expected, in other words by showing how the master questioned the pupils. Instead the questions are of the type that a reader might approach a reference book with, e.g. 'How many declensions of the noun are there?', and the arrangement is systematic, not that of a course book or reader. In fact there are occasional examples of sentences, but no texts for reading, and one gets no impression of how the teacher combined the elementary linguistic introduction with the process of bringing pupils to the point of being able to read continuous prose or verse. In the case of Guarino we know, on the authority of his son, that he thought it necessary for the teacher to question the pupils incessantly in order to make sure that they were mastering the grammar. In easy stages they could be introduced to original texts, prose authors coming before poetry. Among the poets Homer came first, after which they could graduate to other epic writers, tragedy and comedy. Some of the best pupils achieved a degree of competence within a year.[8]

The *Erotemata* are not only a proof of Chrysoloras' effectiveness with his students in Florence but also a pointer to the problems of the student elsewhere, who might have to learn by himself. Although the book was helpful, it was only one of the necessary tools. It is worth pausing for a moment to consider how the humanists approached the task. Reliable reports indicate that it was common practice to learn from bilingual texts.[9] The best evidence comes from Aldus Manutius' letter to Alberto Pio of Carpi which serves as the preface to the third volume of his Aristotle, issued in 1497. This contains the zoological works, which Aldus recommends as a text for study both for its varied subject matter and 'the elegant and felicitous style of the divine Aristotle', the latter phrase indicating that Aldus' literary taste was less well developed than his sales technique. Alberto Pio is invited to compare the Greek with the version made by Theodore Gaza with great success. The process will allow an appreciation of the different character of the two languages. Then follows the interesting assertion: 'Believe me, there is no Greek book from which our fellow-countrymen can learn Greek better, thanks to Theodore. That is how Ermolao Barbaro, Pico, Hieronymus Donatus and Politian learned Greek'. Aldus appears to be saying not merely that the method used by the humanists was to set the Greek text alongside a Latin version, but that Gaza's translation of the zoological books was the work they used for the purpose. While these examples belong to the second half of the fifteenth century, the practice goes back further, and we have a valuable account by Traversari of his own experience.[10] He is replying to a correspondent who had sent a young relative to him for advice on how to learn Greek. Traversari regrets that he does not have a spare copy of any text by Plutarch or the other pagan authors or even of Scripture which contains both the Greek and a Latin translation.[11] Then he recalls his own progress as a student of the language. He had owned a Greek copy of the Psalter, a text which he knew well because he was a monk. By comparing it with the Latin he gradually made out the sense.

After that he went on to read the Gospels, Acts and Pauline Epistles. He remarks of the versions that 'they are all faithfully, accurately and not inelegantly translated', a judgment which would have attracted the scorn of Lorenzo Valla. Finally he satisfied his ambition to read pagan texts but he did not find them easy to understand. He nevertheless recommends this method rather than the employment of a tutor, unless a very good one can be found, and explicitly states that his own experience with a tutor had not been happy.[12]

Chrysoloras' other achievement was that a number of Latin versions of Greek texts began to appear, and these versions were intended to be true to the spirit of Latin idiom, whereas previous attempts had in general failed badly in this respect, even when the translator had a good understanding of the original. Chrysoloras' attitude is summed up by his pupil Cencio de' Rustici, who had accompanied him to the Council of Constance and in 1416 wrote: 'Let me say something about the character of the translator: Manuel, without any doubt a man of divine quality, used to say that a word-for-word rendering into Latin is quite inadequate. He claimed that it was not merely absurd, but that at times it entirely falsified the meaning of the Greek. Instead he said that one needed to translate according to the sense, on condition that those performing the task should impose on themselves the requirement not to change in any way the idiom of the Greek. For if anyone did change the Greek idiom in order to speak more clearly or openly to his audience, he would be performing the duty of the commentator, not the translator.'[13] This last concept, the contrast between the translator and the commentator, had medieval precedent, being found in John Scotus Erigena's preface to pseudo-Dionysius the Areopagite.[14] It is well known that Bruni's views were similar, and he expressed them in various prefaces and an essay.[15] He is probably indebted to Chrysoloras, but one should not forget Salutati's reworking of a version made in the medieval style by Atumanus, to which reference has already been made. From this one might infer that the credit is to be shared between the two men who influenced Bruni.

One must also pose the question whether the advice which could have been obtained from a brief treatise by the most famous of all previous translators was overlooked: St Jerome, especially in his 57th letter, stated principles which could have put the Italians on the right track.[16] But if Bruni and his circle were acquainted with what Jerome had to say on the subject, they chose not to draw attention to it, giving the credit instead to the teacher who had presumably given them practical instruction in the translator's art. Theoretical questions apart, the liveliest indication of what the new attitude meant in practice is to be seen perhaps in some remarks made by Bruni when he was at work on the *Phaedo*: 'I am keeping close to Plato. I call up a vision of him, one that speaks Latin, so that he may judge, and I will ask him to bear witness to the translation of his own work. I translate him in a way that I understand will give him most pleasure. So first of all I preserve every statement without the least deviation from its meaning; then if a word-for-word rendering is possible without oddity or absurdity, this is most welcome; when it is not possible, I am not so timid as to fear accusations of lèse-majesté if I depart a little from the wording while preserving the sense, always avoiding absurdity. This is what Plato by his speeches obliges me to do; being the most elegant of writers in the Greek, he will not wish to appear lacking in taste in Latin.'[17]

Chrysoloras did remain long enough in Florence to transplant a Byzantine curriculum on Italian soil. But when he went back to Constantinople he was followed by Guarino, who lived there from 1403 to 1408. It has been observed that such a long stay in the Byzantine capital put Guarino in possession of a more thorough education in Greek than could have been acquired in Italy. He seems to have received a full training in rhetoric, which gave him a special skill in elaborately written descriptive passages. An account of lake Garda and a description of an ornamental inkstand can be cited as proofs.[18] But for the time being what had been achieved by those who learned their Greek at home was the ability to present Greek texts to Italians in a form that could really be understood. As Bruni remarked more than once, knowledge of the language had been restored after an interval of seven hundred years. The only surprising element in his boast is the underlying assumption that it had been widely known as late as *c.* 700, whereas he would hardly have been exaggerating if he had claimed that the interval was a millennium.[19]

There is a further hint of the impact made by Chrysoloras in Italy. His portrait exists in a well-known drawing in the Louvre.[20] The features of this portrait recur in a number of representations of Aristotle dating from the fifteenth century, and it is not unreasonably speculative to suppose that Chrysoloras was thought a worthy exemplar by artists who had to imagine the features of 'the master of those who know'.[21]

It comes as no surprise to learn that one of Guarino's last projects was an act of devotion towards his tutor. In 1452 – why the thought should have occurred so late remains unclear – he decided to put together a small collection of texts which would demonstrate the place that his master had occupied in the world of learning. It began with a funeral oration spoken by a Venetian nobleman, Andreas Iulianus; most of the remainder consisted of letters written by Guarino and his circle. The title was *Chrysolorina*, a word he invented on the analogy of the Latin adjectives *Manliana, Appiana, Decimiana* and *Luculliana*. These were the words used by the Romans to describe the fruits or trees introduced from the East by the famous epicure and others. Similarly Chrysoloras had introduced letters and the fine arts from Byzantium to Italy.[22]

3

Bruni and other early translators

The range of texts chosen by the early translators must be examined in order to see what light they cast on the reasons for studying Greek. A notable fact about the choice, particularly in view of Salutati's instructions about books to be obtained from Constantinople, is the absence of poetry. Of course Pilato's Homer was in circulation.[1] It is also true that various efforts were made to improve his raw Latin, the first being datable some time before 1398, and many further attempts were made in the course of the fifteenth century. For our present purpose the only one of interest is the short specimen prepared by Bruni himself in his later years, a prose rendering of *Iliad* 9.222-605.[2] This is the main part of a key episode in the poem, the attempt of the delegation sent by the Greeks to Achilles to persuade him to relent and return to the battle, and it is easy to see how it might present a challenge to students. But Homer is a special case because of his outstanding quality. If one is to analyse the motives leading to the revival and progress of literary studies and scholarship one must ask whether there is any other evidence in the activities of the generation inspired by Chrysoloras to lend support to the idea that poetry was of prime concern to these men. A survey of the attested translations strongly suggests that Bruni and his generation did not approach Greek literature with the same hopes and expectations as Petrarch and Boccaccio. During the first three decades of the century they do not appear to have taken an active interest in any other poetry, and though the linguistic difficulty of many Greek poets is considerable, it is hard to believe that in the presence of a talented teacher and translator they would have allowed themselves to be defeated by such an obstacle. Philosophy, oratory, and the essays and biographies of Plutarch, account for the majority of the titles selected. Science is barely represented at all, the only text being Ptolemy's *Geography*, begun by Chrysoloras himself and continued by Jacopo Angeli da Scarperia. Other types of literature are found in very limited quantity.

Let us now consider the selection in a little more detail, noting that most of these translations were completed by *c.* 1420. The only work which obviously falls within the range of subjects normally studied in the middle ages is Roberto Rossi's version of Aristotle's *Analytica Priora*.

Rossi's preface addresses itself to the question why he translates Aristotle when there is a version already available and why he does not choose Plato or Thucydides instead. He claims to have given a reply to the question elsewhere (whatever the work was it appears to be lost), but in the present preface he notes that the old word-for-word translation had a sterile harshness about it and therefore needed to be replaced. He also expresses the hope, given the necessary time, of going on to Plato and Thucydides, and appears to assert that he has already made some other translations.[3]

Just as traditional philosophical studies were of little concern, so too the quantity of theological reading matter was not much increased by the translators of the first two decades of the fifteenth century. Guarino's version of a Greek life of St Ambrose of Milan cannot be included here because it belongs to a later period of his career.[4] A very minor contribution was the version of the Letter of Aristeas, known to have been produced not later than 1403.[5] This text provided an explanation of the name Septuagint, since it gave an account of the preparation of the Greek version of the Old Testament by 70 or 72 translators working in Egypt under orders from king Ptolemy II in the third century BC.

Far more important was one of Bruni's earliest ventures in the field, a version of St Basil's essay on the value of Greek literature, the oldest extant copy of which bears the date 1403 (Laur. 25 sin. 9). Bruni's version enjoyed enormous popularity; over three hundred manuscript copies are extant, a figure which must prove that the work was accepted as a kind of charter for a liberal education.[6] St Basil had expressed a distinctly liberal opinion on the admissibility of pagan literature as part of a Christian's education, regarding it as a propaedeutic of some value if used with caution. Acceptance of his attitude by the church authorities, who did not necessarily have to rely on St Basil as their sole support for such a position, ensured that the classics continued to dominate Byzantine education, with the result that pupils in a typical school probably did not read much Christian literature apart from the Psalms and some orations by St Gregory of Nazianzus. This surprising imbalance between the pagan and Christian elements in education still existed at the very end of the Byzantine epoch, and it is essential to realise that it was taken for granted by the Greek refugees who came to teach in Italy. Whereas they were normally men of sincere religious belief, the curriculum they imported was easy to reconcile with the secular tendencies that existed in Italy. Although St Basil's brief protreptic to his nephews does not seem to have led to debate or discussion of educational theory in Byzantium, and has not always impressed modern critics, it proved invaluable in Bruni's day as a weapon in controversy with opponents brought up in a less liberal tradition. And there was controversy at the time, since Salutati had been engaged in debate with Giovanni da San Miniato of the Camaldulensian order. The argument

was still going on, and in 1405 the Dominican Giovanni Dominici in his
Lucula noctis denied the value of pagan literature. But in the meantime
Bruni had produced an answer to the critics which seems to have satisfied
his contemporaries and several subsequent generations both in Italy and
further afield. Since this is one of his most significant works and also falls
early in his career, it is worth pausing briefly to consider the quality of
the version and the evidence it provides of his linguistic competence at
this date.

The first impression is one that Bruni intended: we feel that we are
reading Latin of good quality which conveys a clear message. When we go
on to ask how accurate it is, the result of a test is reassuring, with the
qualification that some of the finer points of syntax and idiom seem to
have eluded him. In such passages, however, the result is not always
seriously misleading. From time to time there is a free rendering, which
may be in the interest of elegance. Occasionally the reader needs help, as
for instance when the Greek refers to the Presocratic philosopher
Prodicus as 'the sophist from Ceos'; Bruni sensibly gives his name,
omitting the description, which he could have retained. But one can sense
that in a few passages he was out of his depth. Near the beginning of
chapter 2 there is a sentence expressing the typically Christian
sentiment that the things of this world are of no value. In the list of such
things given by St Basil the first four items are 'distinguished ancestors,
physical strength, beauty, stature'. Bruni's list begins *non itaque
dignitatem, non amplitudinem maiorum, non corporis vires, non formam*.
The first of these concepts is his own addition, and though it is a notion
which might easily occur to someone familiar with Roman ideals, there is
a nuance here which is not in the Greek. This is a relatively minor point;
more serious is the omission of two clauses of the Greek which state 'we
do not even think these attributes desirable or look up to those who
possess them'. Although Bruni succeeds in conveying the basic meaning
of the passage, it is a pity that one forceful element in it has been lost, and
one would not expect him to have had any serious difficulty in
understanding the original. Another blemish of this kind occurs in
chapter 5, where St Basil asks 'what else are we to suppose Hesiod had in
mind when he composed those verses, which everyone quotes, except
encouragement of the young to virtuous action?' The reference is to some
famous lines of the *Works and Days* (287ff.) in which the difficulties of
following the path of virtue are outlined. In the Greek there is an unusual
mixed construction instead of regular syntax, and Bruni omits the last
phrase with its reference to the encouragement of the young, leaving us
with the impression that he was unable to cope with what should have
been a minor obstacle. Later in the same chapter the Greek word talent
becomes *talentum* which in classical Latin had been used only to refer to
the unit of currency or a weight, whereas here the other sense, 'scales for
weighing', is required. In chapter 8 a serious distortion occurs because of

a failure to understand adjectives referring to animals devoid of reason and ships without ballast; while the latter is a rare word, the former should not have been obscure in the context. But despite these blemishes Bruni would have been entitled to feel pleased with what he had done.

If we turn now to history, we find, contrary to what might seem a reasonable expectation, that the thirst for knowledge of this kind was not satisfied within a few years by the provision of complete versions of Herodotus or Thucydides or other leading historians. Guarino seems to have prepared a version of part of Book 1 of Herodotus (1-71) in *c.* 1415, but it looks as if he may not have possessed a full copy of the original text until 1427.[7] On the whole the history of the ancient world was made accessible through Plutarch's *Lives*, and to a much lesser extent his other essays.[8] Some twenty *Lives* were translated in the early period. The exploits of the great heroes of antiquity supplied examples of all the virtues and must have been attractive to a public brought up to think of Livy as the greatest historian. Dante after all had called him *Livio che non erra*. The preface to his Roman history made clear the intention of providing in his account a gallery of models to be followed or avoided. It would be interesting to know whether Plutarch provoked any deeper thought about human psychology. He had had to face the question whether the character of some of his subjects had changed or new patterns of behaviour were to be interpreted as the unmasking of a character previously hidden under a veil. Such thoughts occur in the biographies of Sertorius (ch. 10), Sulla (ch. 30) and Pericles (ch. 38.2).[9] *Sertorius* was translated by Bruni *c.* 1420, and it has to be admitted that his preface does not make any allusion to Plutarch's discussion of character, his main concern being to defend in rather general terms the superiority of the ancients against the attacks of those who thought that the moderns excelled them in most if not all respects.[10] An interest in ethical questions is clearly revealed by the versions of Plutarch's essays, especially *On the education of children*, and two treatises by Isocrates, *To Nicocles* and *To Demonicus*, which give advice on behaviour. These three texts were all put into Latin by Guarino, and were therefore soon available to teachers who felt it a duty to consider questions of principle.

It is less easy to understand what prompted Guarino to tackle another essay by Isocrates, the encomium of Helen. The letter of dedication to a Venetian nobleman (preserved in Oxford, Bywater 38) does not provide the answer. Isocrates' composition is intended as an exercise in rhetoric, but despite the title it has as much to say about the Athenian hero Theseus as it does about Helen, and it opens with a long polemic against Isocrates' rivals in the Athenian intellectual world. There is no immediately obvious reason why this rather untypical specimen of a rhetorical genre should have had an appeal in the early fifteenth century.

A more literary concern is demonstrated by translations of speeches by Demosthenes and his great rival Aeschines. Bruni himself tackled all three orations by Aeschines and several by his opponent, including the *De corona*. It is not hard to believe that oratory still had its uses in Florence. Bruni, who was to draw on Plutarch in order to write a fresh biography of Cicero, may have been aware that the greatest Roman orator had not been too proud to devote some time to making versions of the two most famous speeches of Demosthenes and Aeschines, in which they attacked each other's record during the years of Athens' struggle against the advance of Philip of Macedon. The *De corona* was Demosthenes' acknowledged masterpiece, the perfect test for an aspiring humanist who wished to demonstrate the merits of Latin as a medium of expression or display his own powers as a stylist. Bruni's version was followed by no less than five others in the course of the century.[11] The best known of the later versions is due to Valla, whose preface contains an interesting tribute to Bruni. Although Valla was not a man to avoid controversy or leave unexposed the faults of others, he allows that all Bruni's translations are good, and that in the *De corona* he excelled himself, reproducing the power and splendour of Demosthenes' style in such a way that one need not regret greatly the loss of Cicero's version of the same oration.

A small proportion of the energies of the translators was spent on belles lettres. The author who benefited most from these attentions was Lucian (*c.* 120–*c.* 180). The choice requires a word of explanation. In Byzantium he had been at all times one of the most popular classical authors, despite certain philosophical views which on one occasion led a pious reader to heap a large number of abusive epithets on him.[12] His saving grace was probably his satire on the deities of pagan religion, and it is the satirical element which perhaps appealed most to his new readers in Italy. In Byzantium, however, his popularity was due at least as much to his prose style, for though he was a late author of the Second Sophistic age his imitation of classical Greek was thought to be good enough to make him a model of style for the archaising mandarins who filled the ranks of the civil service. Refugee Greeks teaching their language in Italy no doubt still appreciated him for the same reason; the more intelligent of them may have realised that his language would not be difficult for beginners to master and that his rhetorical skill in handling even the most humdrum and unpromising subject matter would not be entirely lost when presented in Latin dress. Their hopes proved justified, and though by no means all the eighty-odd dialogues, essays and sketches appeared in Latin, Lucian soon became one of the most widely read authors, stimulating Alberti and others to try their hand at compositions in the same manner.[13]

The first Lucianic pieces to attract attention were the *Charon, Timon* and *Calumnia*. Of these versions one is an anonymous production, the second is by a certain Bertoldo, of whom nothing whatever is known, and the third is due to Guarino. In the first of them Charon obtains leave from his duties as the ferryman of the underworld and travels up to heaven, where he meets Hermes and asks him about human life. Charon remarks that, judging by his own recent observation, mortals seem to depart from the world with great regret. The dialogue is a facile essay on the theme of the vanity of human aspirations. Close study of the version shows that it was made from a copy of the Greek transcribed by an Italian (Urb. gr. 121) from the copy that belonged to Chrysoloras (Vat. gr. 87). The date must be *c.* 1400 (one of the copies of the Latin was written in 1403).[14] *Timon* is a dialogue between the notorious misanthropist of fifth-century Athens and Zeus, Hermes, Wealth, Poverty and other figures. Once again various forms of injustice in society are easy targets for attack.[15] The general tenor of both pieces is quite consistent with views commonly expounded by preachers. There is also a serious air about the third essay, the full title of which means 'On not crediting slander readily'. It begins with the story of the painter Apelles, who had a narrow escape when king Ptolemy gave credence to the slanderous assertions of a rival painter and was on the point of punishing him for complicity in a plot to cause a rebellion at Tyre. The essay had had the odd distinction of being translated into Syriac in the sixth century; its power to influence was now revealed in a very different way, since Guarino's version allowed it to be taken up by contemporary painters, the most famous result being the picture by Botticelli now in the Uffizi.[16]

Among the texts offered to the Italian public at this date much the strangest is a short piece in praise of the god Dionysus by Aelius Aristides. Once again we have to do with a writer of the Second Sophistic epoch, who enjoyed much the same degree of favour with Byzantine writers as Lucian, but not for exactly the same reason. While not having satirical gifts he was thought equal to Lucian as a stylist, a verdict which modern scholars would hardly endorse, and he was valued partly for his polemical essays which replied to Plato's charges against rhetoricians, partly for his encomium of the Roman empire and some works giving a picture of classical Athens. The middle ages largely neglected his *Sacred Discourses*, a fascinating autobiographical account of psychosomatic illness, and in 1416 the educated public was not ready for that.[17] Instead it was offered a very short epideictic piece that is not important and could not be expected to have wide appeal. The translator was Cencio de' Rustici, the occasion a visit to Constance during the church council in the company of Chrysoloras. A preface in which he mentions Chrysoloras' views on the inadequacy of literal translations goes on to explain the reason for his choice. 'Nothing seems better suited to this place, where everyone behaves with bacchic frenzy in almost barbarian fashion, than to give an account of Bacchus in Latin.'[18] It is much more likely that he had been driven by boredom to borrow his master's bedtime reading, and chose from a series of unpromising rhetorical compositions the only one which struck a chord at the time.

The mention of Aristides requires a brief digression, which will give an idea of the importance occasionally assumed by a Greek author even if the text in question was not a classic of first-class quality and was not made available in any translation. Although very few contemporary Hellenists can have known anything of Aristides unless by some chance Chrysoloras had recommended him strongly, Bruni obviously knew the *Panathenaicus* and used it as a source of inspiration for his *Laudatio Florentinae urbis*. The sophist's encomium of Athens as the focal point of Greek culture and of the organised resistance to the threat of invasion by a foreign tyrant gave Bruni two themes well suited to the political circumstances of *c.* 1403, when Florence had stood up against the ambitions of Milan.[19]

Finally we come to philosophical texts. Bruni did a good deal to ensure wider circulation and better understanding of Aristotle. While his version of the *Politics* is dated 1438 and is therefore one of his latest works, in the period which concerns us at the moment he produced the *Nicomachean Ethics* by 1416 and the spurious *Oeconomica* in 1420-1. A survey of the surviving manuscript copies of the latter has shown that 223 can be traced, and although this figure is substantially less than that quoted for the version of St Basil, it nevertheless proves that these Aristotelian versions could reach a wide public.[20]

We have other indications of how Bruni thought of Aristotle. He found the *Politics* a wonderfully rich source of historical examples, sufficient to create the impression that the philosopher was omniscient in such matters. This high praise dates from the end of his career, but there is another document from his mature years which throws light on his judgment and opinions, a short life of the philosopher composed in 1429.[21] This makes it quite clear that he had the highest regard for Aristotle as a repository of well-organised knowledge. Plato, though agreeing with Aristotle in all essentials, seemed less systematic but possessed of an eloquence beyond the normal human range. Aristotle could serve as a source of instruction for men of all ages, whereas Plato's less rigorous expositions made him better suited to mature adults. Bruni says of Aristotle as a writer that he filled his style with every kind of figure and ornament. He admits that many scholars have doubted the accuracy of this assertion, and he tries to refute them by saying that they are used to encountering Aristotle in poor translations. He asserts that Aristotle is a most polished writer and adduces Cicero as an authority for this opinion, citing a large number of passages in various works. Bruni is to a large extent mistaken here, since he does not realise that the praise heaped on Aristotle by Cicero was intended for the popular works in general circulation in Hellenistic times, whereas all subsequent ages have read the less elegant compositions aimed at a narrower circle of experts, and although these do contain passages which rise to a higher level of style, it is curious that Bruni, being aware as he was of the charm of Plato's writing, should not have seen how different most of Aristotle's surviving work is.[22]

The essay on Aristotle shows that Bruni cannot be regarded as iconoclastic in his philosophical tastes. Nevertheless he did at least prepare the ground for one of the fundamental philosophical debates of the Renaissance by giving prominence to Plato. The middle ages had known the *Timaeus* in the fourth-century version by Chalcidius and the *Phaedo* and *Meno* from Henricus Aristippus' version made *c*. 1160. Bruni first turned his attention to the *Phaedo c*. 1403, presumably intending to replace what he regarded as an unsatisfactory medieval rendering.[23] He later produced the *Gorgias* (1409) and *Crito* (before 1423), the latter revised within a few years. Four more works were added later. It is worth noting that a search for manuscript copies of the two versions of the *Crito* has brought to light about fifteen of the earlier and about thirty of the later.[24] If such figures could be proved to be typical of all the translations of Plato made at this time, they would show that the revival of Platonism, though significant, fell far short of ousting Aristotle from his position of dominance.

The preface to the *Phaedo*[25] is addressed to Pope Innocent VII and contains assurances that both on the immortality of the soul and on other questions Plato is in full agreement with Christian doctrine. The claim is incorrect and one wonders if the Pope can have been unaware that a leaning towards Platonic doctrines had caused the early church father Origen to be declared a heretic. Sympathy with Platonic teaching had also led Byzantine scholars of the eleventh century into desperate difficulties and the church authorities had formally placed an anathema on those who believed in the Platonic theory of forms; but it is very unlikely that Bruni or anyone else in Italy at the time was aware of the episode. Bruni makes another claim on behalf of Plato, namely that he is the most acute and wise of all the ancients. He says that he has no difficulty in understanding why Plato was thought to have learned from Jeremiah during a visit to Egypt or to have had access to the Septuagint. He correctly notes that the second of these notions is impossible for chronological reasons. Both had been a regular feature of early Christian apologetics, and Bruni had come across such ideas in the essay by St Basil mentioned above.

To these indications of a revival of interest in Plato must be added one other important fact. The *Republic* exists in a Latin translation that goes under the names of Chrysoloras and Uberto Decembrio, the division of labour apparently being that the tutor stated the literal meaning of the words so that his pupil could convert it into something more idiomatic. Chrysoloras himself perhaps did not have the command of Latin that would have enabled him to produce a version of the quality he aspired to, and there is no convincing evidence that his pupil had mastered the language fully; indeed, if we were to believe Guarino, who is probably not a reliable source on such matters, he knew no more Greek than the letters and the diacritical signs, so that his part in the enterprise would have been limited to lending his services as copyist while his master dictated. But this extreme account is no doubt to be rejected. The work was done in 1400-03 while Chrysoloras was living in Milan and Pavia.[26] One may guess that he had already spoken to his Florentine audience of the importance of Plato, and his willingness to make the *Republic* available may suggest that he was less anxious than many Byzantines about the consequences of reading Plato for the purpose of mastering the contents as opposed to enjoying the literary quality. Strictly orthodox intellectuals felt obliged to follow the guidance of the Greek church and limit themselves to an appreciation of the elegance of Platonic prose style.[27] But it may be that the political doctrines of the *Republic* were the reason for Italian curiosity; Uberto's prologue suggests that Plato's authority could be cited against republican liberty.

This was not how Bruni saw the matter. Some years later he received a letter from a correspondent who had come across what seemed to him a bad version of the *Republic* and asked whether Bruni would consider producing one himself. The reply was that he would have done so long ago if the text had given him any pleasure. But it contained many ideas abhorrent to modern thinking, and so he felt it better for Plato's good name not to reveal them to the public.[28] The same reservations about some Platonic doctrines emerge in his biography of Aristotle. In addition to the question of the pre-existence of the human soul he mentions the principles of communism applied to property and wives.[29]

As a pendant to this account of Bruni's work as a translator one should note a clear implication from his essay on the art of translating. It is that the stylistic qualities of an original text can be conveyed well enough to allow the reader of the version to form a proper idea of them. Bruni cites passages from his own rendering of Plato's *Phaedrus* in order to demonstrate the beauties of Platonic prose. He notes in particular the use of metaphor and antithesis, the balance of important ideas within a sentence, and contrast of long and short sentences. The unprejudiced reader will readily admit that there is something in his claim. It wears a trifle thin when he passes on to make an equally enthusiastic claim for Aristotle, backed by quotations from the *Nicomachean Ethics* and the *Politics*. His praises are less specific but not less lavish: of one passage he remarks 'Not even Demosthenes or Cicero could have done better'. This is the celebrated description of the highest form of happiness (*EN* X 8.7-8, = 1178b3-32), and it is indeed well expressed in the Greek, so that Bruni was right to draw attention to it. What is less correct is the implication that such a passage is typical of the stylistic level of Aristotle, and we have already noted his extravagant admiration. This does not, however, detract from the interest of his notion that the merits of a writer's style may survive a transfer from one language to another.[30]

Although Bruni set a standard for translation that was clearly higher than the level achieved by any of his medieval predecessors, it did not follow that he was immune from criticism. In particular his rendering of the Greek abstract expression *to agathon*, a neuter adjective with the definite article (literally 'the good'), provoked discussion. The absence of a definite article in Latin had long been a source of difficulty to translators, and Bruni's solution in this case was to use the expression *summum bonum*, 'the highest good'. This did not escape the attention of critics, who could reasonably argue that in certain contexts it would be misleading.[31] Later in the century various other solutions are on record. According to cardinal Bessarion *bonum ipsum*, 'the good itself', was proposed by John Argyropoulos, the Byzantine refugee who held a chair in Florence.[32] A more intelligent approach is recorded of Donato Acciaiuoli, a pupil of the Florentine scholar Manetti. Writing *c.* 1472-4 on Aristotle's *Politics* he claimed that the Greek phrase should sometimes be translated as *summum bonum*, sometimes simply as *bonum*.[33] The problem is also encountered in Filelfo's correspondence. His contribution is less positive.[34] Whatever the critics might say, however, Bruni's failure to give satisfaction in the rendering of this central concept could not seriously mar his achievement.[35]

4

Consolidation

(i) A first glance at Venice

It might have been expected that when Chrysoloras moved to Pavia scholarship would flourish there, creating a centre to rival Florence. But although he stayed in Lombardy as long as he had in Tuscany, it appears that he had to divide his time between teaching and diplomatic business, and no doubt that is the reason why he did not make his mark so effectively in his new home. One may note in passing that his later visit to Rome in 1411-13 also failed to have any very noticeable effect, presumably for the same reason.[1] In order to trace the progress of Greek studies we must turn our attention instead to Venice. This was the port where travellers from Constantinople normally arrived, and although commercial considerations generally took precedence over cultural interests in the city itself, the university of Padua, which had been absorbed into the Venetian republic in 1405, was one of the most vigorous in Italy. Although the so-called prehumanists of Padua had not succeeded in making Greek a regular subject of study, and Petrarch's wish to found a public library in Venice had come to nothing, there are signs of an interest in Greek in the first two decades of the fifteenth century, perhaps in part a by-product of the republic's network of trading stations in the eastern Mediterranean. At this stage the main figures in the story are Guarino, who had moved from Florence in 1414 and came to Venice for five years, and Francesco Barbaro (1390-1454), who learned Greek from him. The tutor had the advantage of having spent four years in Constantinople, during which time he devoted part of his energies to serving as secretary to the governor of the Venetian trading station, and the rest to learning Greek with Chrysoloras and his nephew. He acquired sufficient knowledge of the language to begin his long career as a translator with Plutarch's *Alexander* and two essays by Lucian. A volume containing his tutor's *Erotemata* and the three plays of Aristophanes normally read in schools, which he bought in 1406, still survives (Pal. gr. 116), but it is not clear whether he built up a large private library. On his return to Venice he may have begun teaching at once. A spell of four years in Florence followed and then he returned to Venice for the years

1414-19, during which time he achieved satisfying results, despite the existence of some hostility to non-vocational studies. Only a small number of intellectuals in the Venetian aristocracy were sympathetic.[2]

His most notable pupil in these years was Barbaro. He too translated Plutarch, producing versions of the *Aristeides* and *Cato* in 1416, while a fellow pupil, Leonardo Giustinian, undertook another pair of biographies, the *Cimon* and *Lucullus*. While these versions may not meet modern requirements, they served their purpose, being in good Latin and satisfying Guarino's expectations.[3] The spirit in which the task was undertaken is made clear by a passage in a recently published letter of Barbaro, dated November 1416. Speaking of his friend Giustinian he remarks: 'So as not to fail in the duty of the good citizen, he was anxious even in his leisure moments to be of some benefit to our city, which he will be serving as its employee. While staying at Chioggia for reasons of health he translated the biographies of Cimon and Lucullus, men of great eminence, from the Greek of Plutarch into a Latin of such dignity that I cannot decide whether the variety and importance of the subject matter gives more pleasure or the solemn character of the style lends it more weight. For this activity he will earn the warmest thanks not only of those who are distant from literary studies but also from our fellow citizens, if they treat him as they should. His honourable labours have ensured that the lives of Cimon and Lucullus, distinguished men, are before the public like living images, to be imitated. And if they observe the features attentively, like careful painters, they will transfer them exactly to their own characters, and they will readily admit, if they wish to reproduce these literary models, that they can easily live in magnificent and noble style and perform noble services to the state.'[4]

This whole paragraph invites the reflection that civic humanism was not a monopoly of the Florentines. The value attached to Plutarch's biographies is the same for Barbaro as for Bruni. One slight difference from Bruni's approach to the Greek legacy can perhaps be detected. In a letter of 1418 addressed to Camillo da Ferrara, apparently to be identified with the first teacher at the Rialto school from 1408 to 1414, Barbaro writes: 'If you could get some Greek book for me, I would have payment sent to the person you nominate. I especially want sacred texts.'[5]

Although Barbaro's private library cannot be reconstructed in detail, and there is not yet any evidence that the Greek section of it was large, it is worth noting, even if the fact is pure coincidence, that he was the owner of two manuscripts of considerable importance to modern editors, a Plato now in Vienna (supp. gr. 39)[6] and a Lucian now in Rome (Pal. gr. 273), the latter given to him by John Symeonakis of Candia, which is a useful reminder of the value of Crete to the Venetians in more than merely commercial matters.[7]

Barbaro also made efforts to employ Greeks as copyists of texts. We know that he was in touch with George Trapezuntius *c.* 1416 when he arrived in Venice as a young man,[8] and that a copy of Plato (Laur. 85.7) made in 1420 by another of the early refugees, Girard of Patras, was transcribed from the exemplar in Barbaro's possession.[9] Neither George nor Girard stayed long in Venice. Was Barbaro a difficult employer, or was there not enough work to keep them alive? Venice for them, as it was later for others, served as a staging post on the way to better openings.

What is more remarkable about Barbaro, however, is his attempt in 1416 to consult the Florentine Pandects for the passages of Greek that they contain. He was unsuccessful, because even Niccolò Niccoli could not overcome the superstitious reluctance of the Florentines to let their relic be seen.[10] It is important not to lose sight of this episode when discussing the motives of scholars and the range of their interests. Unfortunately Barbaro's later career was devoted mainly to serving Venice as diplomat and governor of various cities in its sphere of influence, leaving no time for his scholarship to mature.

It is convenient to mention at this point in the account another member of the Barbaro family, Francesco's nephew Ermolao (1410-1471) who became bishop of Verona in 1453. He is presumably to be identified with the scribe who in 1430 signed and dated a copy of the first three essays in the Isocratean corpus (Casanatense 483), describing himself as deacon and protonotary of Venice. One would like to believe that he is the man shown in an early Italian portrait of a man holding a book in his hands with an inscription that turns out to be the incipit of one of the three essays.[11] But if this hypothesis is incorrect, the manuscript and the portrait become two separate indications of the influence exercised in the Renaissance by an author who has since lost his popularity.

(ii) The significance of the year 1423: Aurispa

The year 1423 deserves to be treated as a critical point in the development of Greek studies. An event with important consequences was the appointment of Vittorino da Feltre at Mantua, where his school soon achieved fame, inducing even other humanists to send their sons to him to be educated. Although it may be doubted whether scholarship of a really advanced level took place under his aegis, the influence of the school was lasting. Thanks to the descriptions of the school given in various more or less contemporary sources and to the identification of a number of books written by the professional copyists employed there, it is possible to form a reasonably accurate impression of the curriculum. Vittorino will be the subject of the next chapter.

Another important event of 1423 was the return of the Sicilian humanist Giovanni Aurispa (1376-1459) from his second journey to Greece. He brought back with him an enormous collection of manuscripts. The figure 238 which is usually quoted refers to the volumes containing pagan texts, and while these were probably his main interest he is known to have collected some patristic literature, so that the sum total of his acquisitions was even larger than is generally realised.[12] No doubt there were duplicates in plenty, but his collection is remarkable, since the number of Greek manuscripts which can be identified as having belonged to Italian scholars before 1423 is not very large. Some texts must have been in short supply, and it is noteworthy that even Guarino after four years of residence in the Byzantine capital owned no more than a handful of Greek books.[13] When he took up his position in Florence *c.* 1410 he will no doubt have been relieved to find that Antonio Corbinelli (1376-1425), the minor government official who arranged his appointment and acted for a while as his host, was a keen book-collector. The Greek section of his library eventually reached the very large figure of 79 volumes, and no less than 65 of them contained texts by pagan authors. In due course these passed into the possession of the Badia in Florence; it is a pity that we cannot trace the growth of the collection in detail, for it would appear to have been the best of its kind in the first quarter of the century.[14] Yet with Aurispa's additions to the available stock the supply of texts must have been greatly improved.

It is an odd fact, but a fact none the less, that acquisitions had almost invariably to be made in Greece, even though there were many Greek monasteries, some of them equipped with libraries, in those parts of Italy and Sicily which had been bilingual during the middle ages. Among educated Italians in the north there must have been some awareness of this cultural diversity, and in fact they had earlier appointed a teacher from Calabria. Perhaps the experience was a deterrent to further experiments of the same kind. For whatever reason the large libraries of the so-called Basilian monasteries (they were not strictly speaking members of an order) remained unexploited until about the middle of the century. It is true that most of them would have furnished no texts other than biblical and patristic writings, but there were exceptions, and cardinal Bessarion is believed to have acquired a variety of books from St Nicholas of Casole at Otranto. The nearest of all the Greek monasteries was at Grottaferrata, little more than ten miles from Rome, and in 1426 Francesco Barbaro took the opportunity to make a visit in the company of Leonardo Bruni. Their experience is briefly reported in a letter from Barbaro to Guarino.[15] They found 'Greek manuscripts notable for their number and quality, all theological in content, and written so elegantly that they deserve to be shelved in the library of a Varro or a Ptolemy rather than in that cupboard'. Had Traversari been with them he might have insisted that the absence of secular material in the library should not cause it to be written off as of little account. But Barbaro, despite an expression of regret at the neglected state of the library, does not seem to have made any purchases from it. The supply of classical texts in the north could not have been improved in any case.

Since books changed hands frequently in the Renaissance, quite often losing an ex-libris in the process, and owners did not usually make their own inventory, it is not possible to reconstruct Aurispa's collection.[16] But he can hardly be denied the credit for discovering and bringing to Italy some of the most important manuscripts of the leading authors. One or two striking claims that he himself made need to be examined. One of these concerns a pair of volumes containing 'Aristarchus on the *Iliad*'. It is as certain as anything can be that the work of the greatest Hellenistic critic of Homer was not transmitted through the Byzantine age, and Aurispa is probably making a pardonable error. He could have been misled by references to Aristarchus in the marginal scholia of two important manuscripts which later belonged to cardinal Bessarion and are now in the Marciana Library in Venice (Marc. gr. 453 and 454). Alternatively he might have been unduly impressed by the magnificent parchment volumes now in Florence which contain the commentary on the *Iliad* compiled by the twelfth-century archbishop of Thessalonica Eustathius and are indeed his autograph master copy (Laur. 59.2 & 3).[17] A more dubious boast, which is also more difficult to explain, relates to the poem called *Katharmoi* by the Presocratic philosopher Empedocles. While it is scarcely possible to believe that he possessed a copy, there is no obvious explanation for the mistake, nor a motive for a mendacious claim.[18]

Aurispa's success as a collector may have helped him to obtain the chair of Greek at Florence, which he held for a brief period (1425-7). One may note in passing that a few years before he had taught Lorenzo Valla the elements of Greek. At first sight this must seem to be a great feather in his cap, but a less enthusiastic assessment is probably called for, as will become clear from the examination of Valla's knowledge in a later chapter. In general Aurispa was not successful as a teacher, and does not appear to have been a gifted scholar. He took part in the fashionable activity of translating Lucian, choosing the *Toxaris* and the twelfth *Dialogue of the Dead*. At the end of the latter he made an alteration to the text. In the original there is a comparison of Alexander, Hannibal and Scipio. Minos as judge of the underworld gives pride of place to Alexander. Aurispa altered this, and in his version Scipio is awarded the palm. Although he claims that the change is no more than an emendation made by the fourth-century sophist Libanius, who taught for most of his career in Antioch, it is clear that he cannot be telling the truth, since Libanius was fanatical in his support of Greek culture against the ever-growing threat posed by Rome. While the reason for the change is not certain, its effect can be traced within a few years, when Poggio Bracciolini, involved in controversy with Guarino, cited the false version and was corrected by his opponent. The argument concerned the relative merits of Scipio and Caesar, who represented the best of republican and monarchical ideals and were therefore not irrelevant to current political concerns in Italy.[19]

To return to the year 1423, we may note another reason for treating it as a significant point. It so happens that one of Bruni's most important translations, that of Plato's *Crito*, exists in both an early and a revised version, of which the first cannot be later than 1423, while the revision belongs to the years 1423-7. This short dialogue was important to the humanists because of its portrayal of Socrates thinking about the obligations of the citizen. Bruni did not normally issue his work in revised form, and it is reasonable to suppose that the improvements imply a feeling of greater confidence in handling the original language.

This is worth investigating in a little more detail. As a whole the second redaction reads better than the first. One small yet revealing indication of the character of the earlier version is that three Greek words were transliterated instead of being translated (they are *dogma, politia* and *coribantes*). At a pinch all three might have been understood by an Italian reader well-versed in the Latin classics, but there is no doubt that Bruni did well to eliminate them. Another difficulty which he resolved in revision was the idiomatic meaning of a verb which normally means 'to value' but in a judicial context refers to a seemingly quixotic Athenian legal provision whereby the defendant proposed the penalty which he thought appropriate to the case (*timasthai*). An interesting question arises at a point where both versions fail to do full justice to the meaning of the original. Reference is made (51 d 3) to the Athenian custom of *dokimasia*, which was a formal procedure before the admission of a young man to full citizen rights. Bruni omits the Greek verb used, and the same is true of the much more famous later translation made by Marsilio Ficino, which borrows details from Bruni. Evidently this Athenian practice remained a mystery for a long time; later in the century cardinal Bessarion, who might have been expected to know about such things, tried to solve the puzzle by altering the text. The episode demonstrates an important truth about fifteenth-century scholarship: even the greatest scholars could be led astray in matters that are now thought quite simple, because there were not yet any reference books to provide general information about the classical world. On the other hand, to balance the negative impression created by this failure, one should note that Bruni was capable of making improvements to the text as it stood in the copies available to him: he is to be credited with a minor but necessary change adopted by modern editors and wrongly attributed to the nineteenth-century scholar Buttman.[20]

The short preface to the second version is valuable for a revealing passage about the reasons for reading the dialogue. It is said of Socrates:.

sed praesertim in ea parte admirabilis est, in qua de officio civis erga patriam disserit. ibi enim tamquam ex intimo philosophiae sacrario pretiosissima quaedam promuntur ad cognitionem disciplinamque nostram.

(But he is admirable most of all in the part of the dialogue in which he speaks about the duty of the citizen towards his country. For there some most valuable ideas are produced as it were from the inner sanctum of philosophy for our information and instruction.)

This might be taken as the motto of civic humanism.

(iii) The second half of Bruni's career

A brief résumé of Bruni's activity as a Hellenist after the year 1423 is necessary here. In 1427 he achieved the same distinction as Salutati by being nominated chancellor of Florence, but the appointment seems to have had little or no effect on his literary energy. His later works include the revision of his translation of Plato's *Apology*, a version of part of the *Phaedrus* (he accepted the tradition that it is the earliest of the dialogues),[21] of part of the *Symposium* and the *Letters*, not all of which seemed genuine to him. The *Phaedrus* was addressed to Antonio Loschi, prominent both as a poet and as an administrator, and Bruni chose the part of the dialogue in which Plato speaks of the nature of poetry.

In his dedication of the *Letters* to Cosimo de' Medici Bruni reveals his attitude towards these problematic texts. He thinks that the first and fifth of them are not by Plato, but should be attributed to Dion, the tyrant of Syracuse who succeeded Dionysius I and failed to govern the city on Platonic principles. Bruni also rejected the thirteenth letter on stylistic grounds. Other humanists went further in their scepticism and Pier Candido Decembrio seems to have regarded the whole collection as spurious. Bruni declares that he has enjoyed them more than Plato's other works, because he felt that he was having a conversation with the author in person, whereas in the dialogues the reader is presented with imaginary conversations between speakers who do not simply reflect the author's views, and there is irony and fiction on the part of speakers who are actors. The *Letters* have the advantage of showing directly the author's virtues, which Bruni lists at some length in justification of his view that Plato is a person whom one would wish to take as a model of behaviour. He even goes so far as to say that he has learned more from the letters than from several other volumes.[22]

One may also mention here the *Commentaria rerum graecarum*, a study of Greek history of the classical period, designed to provide material for statesmen to meditate on. His biography of Aristotle has already been referred to, and in the late 1430s he performed his last service to the Stagirite by producing a version of the *Politics*. In this there are a few passages where he appears to have made an improvement to the Greek text as it is transmitted in the manuscripts.[23] The task was originally undertaken at the request of Duke Humfrey of Gloucester, who had been impressed by the quality of the version of the *Ethics* and went so far as to invite Bruni to England. It would have been naive to entertain any serious hope that a man of Bruni's standing and responsibilities could accept such an invitation, but the episode reveals how his influence reached the fringe of the civilised world. The translation was ready in 1437 and after some delay a presentation copy was sent to the Duke in the following year. But this was not the only copy prepared at Bruni's request; another was made at the same time and sent with a covering letter to the eminent antiquarian Flavio Biondo with the request that it be offered to Pope Eugenius IV.[24]

Bruni reiterates his opinion that Aristotle's style is polished and elegant. He states that the *Politics* is to be valued for its doctrine and its incredible wealth of information. He was no doubt referring to the many interesting but often tantalisingly incomplete allusions to the history of Greek city-states, which even modern scholars are not generally able to exploit to the full despite the increase in the amount of historical information available to them. So it is hard to take seriously this part of Bruni's claim. One might with more reason try to identify notions of Aristotelian political theory which appealed to the Florentine translator. The dislike of the allegedly extreme constitutions in which power belongs either to a single ruler or to the whole of the citizen body may well have seemed attractive. But one of Aristotle's fundamental views will have commended him strongly to intellectuals. He favoured a city-state with a limited number of full citizens, all of whom needed to have leisure in order to be able to devote time to thinking about the needs of the community.

One venture into unfamiliar territory should be recorded at this point. Although Greek drama does not seem to have stimulated any interest in Florence at this time, there is a version of about a quarter of Aristophanes' *Plutus*. The first lines of it are perhaps due to Giovanni Tortelli rather than Bruni. The date of this exercise is unknown; it may have been undertaken *c*. 1439, as one of the manuscript copies in which it is found contains mainly works relating in some way to the Council of Florence (Ferrara, Antonelli 545). It is not clear what motive induced the two humanists to turn their attention to drama and choose a specimen of comedy rather than tragedy. The *Plutus* was the first play in the selection of Aristophanes read in Byzantine schools and linguistically it may well be the easiest. These two facts will probably have been known to Bruni and Tortelli and have governed their choice. But they seem to have been easily discouraged, and the little that they produced is by no means free from error. It is not perhaps surprising that the sexual practices referred to in lines 152ff. induced the translator to expurgate them, and the removal of line 171 deletes a reference to a meeting of the Athenian assembly which might not have had much point for a Florentine reader. But these are blemishes, and there are other faults, some of them serious. Bruni was defeated by the alternative meanings of two common words where the variation is indicated by a change of accentuation, one being an adverb which instead of meaning 'unskilfully' becomes 'simply, in fact', the other an adjective that normally means 'wicked' but with a change of accent becomes 'wretched'. It is also disquieting to see that he failed to recognise the future of a fairly common verb meaning 'weep', perhaps because he was misled by the use of the middle voice for this tense, although the phenomenon is not rare among the Greek verbs. Still worse is that he took a future optative to be a past tense.[25] We are forced to the conclusion that Greek verse was still for the most part beyond the reach of competent scholars.[26]

There is another late product of Bruni's pen which reveals an unexpected application of his Greek scholarship. In 1441 he composed a history of the Gothic War, a grim period in the middle of the sixth century when Italy was reduced to a desperate condition by the invasion of the Goths and the efforts of the Byzantines to recover lost territory. The population of Rome is said to have been reduced at one moment to less than a thousand. Bruni remarks that he would much rather have written about happier times, but he feels that knowledge of the period is desirable, since any serious citizen wishes to know about the origin and progress of his country. He adds that Italy is now a flourishing land, exercising great influence abroad, besides being cultivated, civilised and the home of the arts, in which as originator and pupil it has no equal. For his history Bruni had no Latin sources and used the Byzantine historians Procopius and Agathias. Both were contemporaries of the events they narrated and Procopius had taken an active part in some of the campaigns. Bruni had recognised and exploited good material, and the quality of the resulting narrative seems to have led to charges that he was passing off a translation as his own work. Naturally he had no choice but to follow his sources closely, but the unfairness of the criticism later stimulated the Roman humanist Cristoforo Persona to produce versions of both texts.[27]

Yet some time was to pass before Byzantium came to be recognised as a civilisation worthy of the same kind of study as classical Greece. More typical of the immediate response to Procopius' narrative was Bruni's own delight and surprise when in 1442 king Alfonso of Aragon succeeded in capturing Naples by the same stratagem that Procopius reports of Belisarius, who found a hidden way into the city through the sewers.[28] Though history repeated itself, one may suspect that parallels from the strictly classical period would have been more welcome.

(iv) Traversari

The figure of Bruni and the concept of civic humanism occupy a prominent position in accounts of Florentine culture. As a result it is easy and tempting to underrate another important personality of rather different cultural formation, Ambrogio Traversari (1386-1439).[29] A monk who had become general of his order in 1431, Traversari might have been expected to have serious doubts about classical studies, and it is certainly true that he devoted his energies mainly to the translation of Greek patristic literature. The list of his works amounts to some fifteen items, a few of them undertaken before the year 1423 which I have identified as a critical point in the history of scholarship. Almost all of these versions await a detailed study. The earliest substantial results of his labours were issued in 1417 and 1419. These were a treatise by St John Chrysostom (*c.* 350-407), the most prolific and probably the most popular patristic writer in Byzantium, directed against critics of the monastic vocation, and the *Ladder of Paradise*, an ascetic treatise by the seventh-century writer John Climax ('the ladder'), a hermit of Mount Sinai who became abbot of St Catherine's monastery. This too was an extremely popular text in Byzantium. The significance of both these works for the translator needs no comment. How influential his various versions were is not clear in every case. But one that is believed to have circulated widely is his last venture, the writings of pseudo-Dionysius the Areopagite, begun in 1430-1. These essays in mystical theology ascribed to St Paul's Athenian disciple were one of the most audacious and successful forgeries ever made. They had been translated in very incompetent fashion twice during the ninth century as a result of the gift of a copy of the text from the Byzantine emperor to king Louis the Pious of France. Traversari's version will have brought them to the notice of the educated public once again in a much more intelligible form. It was not long before Lorenzo Valla challenged their authenticity.

Traversari's patristic studies had practical applications. He could use passages from the Greek fathers to make a point in argument, as he did at the Council of Basle in 1434, where we find him citing the cases of Athanasius and Chrysostom to show that it had been the custom in the early church to appeal to Rome for support in controversy with heretics or other opponents.[30] At the Council of Florence he played an important part, and one of his letters tells us that he had to do all the translating required, a very demanding and responsible task. The most important text in the debate between the two parties was the treatise by St Basil *Against Eunomius*, which contained statements acceptable to the Roman church on the question of the *Filioque* clause. There was also a passage in the less well known and less respected writer Epiphanius. Apart from mastering these texts Traversari eventually had to prepare a draft in Greek of the decree announcing the union of the two churches.[31]

Traversari was not just a prominent ecclesiastical figure. He was well read in the classics, and the work by which he is best known is his version of Diogenes Laertius, *The Lives of the Philosophers*. A presentation copy was made for Cosimo de' Medici in 1433 (Laur. 65.21), and many other famous men owned copies. Even cardinal Bessarion had one (Marc. lat.

246); why he should have needed it is not at all clear. Diogenes' work is an unimpressive compilation, and Traversari could see its weaknesses. He also had doubts as to whether such work on pagan philosophers was consistent with his vocation.[32] But there is a vast amount of information in Diogenes, and Traversari persisted with his task. It cost him enormous effort, and for the Epicurean philosophy in Book 10 he was obliged to turn for help to Carlo Marsuppini, a humanist who occupied himself in 1429 with a version of the curious pseudo-Homeric jeu d'esprit *Batracho-myomachia*, and from 1431 held a chair in the university of Florence. Traversari had two manuscripts of the Greek text, and wrote to a friend to ask for a third in the hope that it would be less damaged and corrupt.[33] The account of Epicureanism, given with long direct quotations from letters of Epicurus, is perhaps the most valuable feature of Diogenes' book, not only for modern students, but also because it gave the Quattrocento humanists a fresh and reliable body of information about a philosophical school which Cicero had ridiculed and misunderstood in *De finibus* 1-2. It must have been of interest to a man like Lorenzo Valla, who had just published in 1431 his *De voluptate*.

Traversari also had some pupils. He seems to have organised a course in Greek in his monastery in Florence in 1425. He asked Francesco Barbaro for a Greek Psalter to help the pupils, a fact which recalls his statement about his own method of learning the language.[34] But his relations with Bruni were bad. There was heated controversy between them, and Traversari did not have much respect for his rival's translations. A typical comment relates to the partial version of Plato's *Phaedrus*, which he described as 'Phaedri deforme fragmentum'.[35]

5

Vittorino da Feltre

The school established by the ruler of Mantua and directed by Vittorino da Feltre (1378-1446) has for long been recognised as one of the milestones in the history of education. It came to have at least forty pupils; one of our sources puts the figure as high as seventy.[1] Not all came from the families of the rich; some were subsidised by Vittorino himself. The school combined a good academic education with instruction in fine arts such as music, singing and drawing, and with physical training every day. While it may be true to say that Vittorino retained to a large extent the traditional concepts of the trivium and quadrivium – such at any rate is the inference to be drawn from the account by Sassolo da Prato – the results of the curriculum were anything but medieval. Although the head of the school himself left no account of his views, a good deal can be reconstructed from comments by pupils and from books which survive from the school library. Our picture is improved still further by the recent discovery of a list of books sent by Vittorino in 1445 to his pupil Gian Pietro da Lucca in Verona; the Greek texts are not less than twenty-five in number.[2]

Classical literature was predominant. Although Pisanello in his portrait medallion of Vittorino chose to describe him as 'mathematicus et omnis humanitatis pater' there is no sign of any special concern with mathematics in the school, let alone other branches of natural science, and the first half of the inscription may be an allusion to his feat of mastering Euclid unaided after being refused instruction by the leading contemporary authority Biagio Pelacani. This knowledge Vittorino did put to use, and we are told that during a winter he once read Euclid after dinner with a pupil; evidently this was a special case rather than regular practice. It is also reported that Gianlucido, son of the marquis, made a great impression on Traversari in 1435 by demonstrating with figures two propositions arising from Euclid. But the evidence does not indicate an emphasis on mathematics in the school. If we can trust the report of Sassolo, himself a product of the school, Vittorino made it his policy to devote particular attention to Vergil, Homer, Cicero and Demosthenes.[3] Master and pupils alike would surely have been gratified if they had been able to foresee that this practice would still be exercising its influence in

34

one of the great seats of classical learning after half a millennium. Up to the beginning of the Second World War the four authors named were a major element of the syllabus in the first part of the Oxford classics course. The members of the school at Mantua would perhaps have been less delighted to learn that in student slang these authors were referred to as 'the four beasts'.

The distinctive feature of the school is the place accorded to the study of Greek authors in the original language. Vittorino had not learned Greek as a young man; he had to wait until Guarino moved from Florence to Venice in 1414. We are told explicitly that he taught both the classical languages, believing that the knowledge of each complements the other.[4] But it is possible that he may not have felt confident enough of his command of Greek to deal with advanced topics. Aurispa described his knowledge as 'moderate', but that may be untrue or unfair.[5] At all events his school normally had native Greeks to teach the language. According to one report there were sometimes three or four of them.[6] They served also as copyists, and in return were taught Latin. Two who transcribed a large number of manuscripts can be identified; they were Peter the Cretan and Girard of Patras. Some more famous figures passed through the school. In 1431 George Trapezuntius was there, and later Vittorino had the good fortune to engage Theodore Gaza, who soon after arrival in Italy went briefly to Pavia and then moved to Mantua, where he was to be found in 1444 and where he may have stayed until Vittorino's death.[7] Most of the translations which made him a figure of note date from later in his career, but one was published at this stage, a version of the handbook of rhetoric attributed to Dionysius of Halicarnassus. Although this was hardly a significant work, one may imagine that Gaza used his time in Mantua to prepare the grammatical textbook which is his other main claim to fame.

A valuable eye-witness account of the school and the Greek holdings of its library is given by Ambrogio Traversari, who visited it in 1433.[8] He found that some of the pupils were far enough advanced with their Greek to be engaged in translating Plutarch's life of Camillus, the fables of Aesop and some writings of St John Chrysostom. His account of the Greek volumes from the library begins with Augustine on the Trinity, Plato's *Laws, Letters* and *Republic*, and Chrysostom. The first of these will have been the Greek version made by the distinguished late Byzantine scholar Maximus Planudes *c.* 1300, and it is hard to see what interest the average western reader would have found in it. Vittorino perhaps acquired it more by accident than design. But Traversari was primarily concerned with theological and patristic studies, and to him the translation may have provided a welcome proof that the Greek church could not plead ignorance of the writings of the great Latin fathers of the church. With talk of union between the Greek and Roman churches in the air, Traversari may well have been alert to such considerations. He tells us that he saw about thirty volumes, mainly of common texts, but with a few rarities. He then mentions some titles. Ancient writers on musical theory were well represented in one volume, which contained Ptolemy, Aristides Quintilianus and Bacchius.[9] Traversari looked at the second of these writers and found that he was a good stylist. Then there was a manuscript with four of the orations of the emperor Julian. The pious Traversari might have been expected to condemn the oeuvre of the notorious apostate, but he confines himself to remarking that the essays seemed prolix. The same manuscript contained a life of Homer allegedly written by Herodotus; Traversari, naturally enough not questioning that attribution, took it away with him and read it. Then he found a book by John the consul on various questions; what he means is far from clear, as there is no text obviously corresponding to the description. He continues his account by noting that there were many texts of Aristotle, all available already in Florence, an assertion which will need to be examined in a moment. Apart from them he recorded seeing lexica, grammar books, Herodotus, Thucydides,[10] Arrian, a good many poets and Plutarch's lives. He obtained leave from Vittorino to have copies made for Niccolò Niccoli of Julian, the life of Homer and Bacchius.

The insistence on Greek sets Vittorino apart from most of the other educators of the Renaissance. The contrast between his practice and the theoretical treatises of the time is very noticeable in this respect. Neither Vergerio nor Bruni make any specific reference to Greek in their handbooks, and Aeneas Sylvius mentions it only in order to express his regret that there is no opportunity for studying it in Germany or Hungary.[11] The remark is less odd than it may seem, since he was addressing Ladislas, the king of Bohemia and Hungary. Yet evidently there was a general assumption that Greek texts would be read in translation. But in Mantua things were different. There is just one piece of conflicting evidence, a statement that Paolo da Sarzana left the school in order to study the subject with Filelfo in Florence,[12] which makes one wonder if for a time there was a lack of a suitable teacher beyond an elementary level. But usually the subject was prominent and we have some information about the selection of authors read. Homer was far from being the only poet, if Platina's account is to be trusted. He tells us that Hesiod was thought of as offering useful precepts, which suggests a rather literal approach to the didactic element in the *Works and Days*. Theocritus was seen as an admirable example of his genre, and it should not be a cause for surprise that the model for Vergil's *Eclogues* found favour. It will not have been an easy text, and the same applies to Pindar, who is also mentioned in the same context. If Vittorino read them both, perhaps his pupils did not. Then comes a reference to Greek drama. Aristophanes was regarded highly for the purity of his diction and was believed to offer material useful in forming the character of the reader because of the criticisms of moral failings made in his comedies. Vittorino is said to have omitted or toned down any passages that struck him as obscene or distasteful.[13] All three tragedians are listed. Aeschylus will certainly have been very difficult, with the possible exception of the *Prometheus Vinctus*, but if the syllabus suggested by the refugee Greeks corresponded to the practice of the schools they had known in Crete or Constantinople, that will have been the first and perhaps the only play attempted, and in the light of this consideration the report is perhaps to be accepted. There is however very little evidence for the reading of tragedy at this date in Italy, since most of the plays will have been beyond the linguistic capacity of even gifted pupils, and it must be added that while many manuscripts written by the Greek scribes resident in Mantua can now be identified, with one dubious exception copies of tragedy are not to be found among them.[14]

More convincing than the argument from silence is the clear implication of a recent discovery. We now know that Giovanni Tortelli, author of a treatise on orthography, was at one time a student in Mantua.[15] Then he went to Constantinople and took lessons there in the years 1435-7. It is to this period that he refers in the entry about Sophocles in his *De orthographia*, which reveals his study of this text under the guidance of Isidore, the Greek later appointed cardinal of Russia. Tortelli's notes, mainly elementary explanations of Sophocles' *Ajax* and *Electra*, accompanied by others on Aristophanes' *Plutus* and *Clouds* – in each case he was reading the first two works prescribed by custom in Byzantine schools – can be taken as further proof that not every pupil at Mantua was initiated into Greek drama.[16] Tortelli's wording even seems to imply that he had not read any Greek poetry in Mantua, which is very unlikely unless he had been forced to leave the school much earlier than intended; but perhaps his Latin can be interpreted as meaning that Sophocles was first among the poets in quality, not the first that he made the acquaintance of.[17]

The copy of Hesiod used in the school may be the one written by Peter the Cretan and now in Florence (Laur. Acquisti 60).[18] Possibly it was one of the books seen by Traversari in 1433. Had his account been more precise it would have been of even greater value. As it is one has to be cautious in assigning all Peter's products to the school library, and the same applies to Girard. Among other texts transcribed by Peter are the post-classical didactic poets Dionysius Periegetes (Ambr. M 85 sup.), Nicander (Marc. gr. 477) and Oppian (Vienna, phil. gr. 135). Although Dionysius had probably served as a means of imparting some knowledge of geography to Byzantine schoolchildren, and the other two authors had not been entirely neglected in Byzantium, they all seem too obscure to be likely components of any reading programme in the school at Mantua. Of Oppian's two productions, on hunting and fishing, the former might have been of some interest to members of a fifteenth-century court. Nicander would have been much too difficult. Less open to such objections was one of the other texts he copied, the *Argonautica* of Apollonius Rhodius (Wolfenbüttel 10.2 Aug. 4°). Prose texts from his pen include a Julian now in Paris (gr. 3020), presumably the one seen by Traversari. It contains the orations, which would have been much more objectionable to orthodox sentiment than his correspondence, which was often read in Byzantium and apparently did not provoke outbursts of pious indignation. Peter's transcript of Xenophon was given to Sassolo by Vittorino as a leaving present (Laur. 55.21).[19] With the exception of the *Hellenica* it is an almost complete collection of Xenophon's writings. One would not expect the head of the school to part with it unless it was a duplicate, and there is reason to think that it was, because there is a similar collection of Xenophon's writings among the manuscripts copied by Peter's partner Girard (Perugia B 34).

Peter's remaining work includes Aesop (Ambr. A. 59 sup.), Aristotle's *De interpretatione* (Barocci 216) and the volume of essays on the theory of music already mentioned (Naples III C 1).[20] The last item attests the school's concern for that element in the quadrivium. Finally come two books of more practical character. One is the reference book known as Suidas or the *Suda*, a Byzantine amalgam of dictionary and encyclopaedia which despite its bulk was often recopied because of its proven value to students of the classics (Laur. 55.1).[21] The other is a collection of texts by Byzantine grammarians useful for linguistic instruction, the main item being the *Erotemata* by Manuel Moschopoulos, another influential scholar of the late Byzantine period (Canon. gr. 14).[22]

The other Greek scribe whose activity is associated with the school, Girard of Patras, can be traced in Italy from 1420 onwards. How long he spent in Mantua between that date and 1443, when we last hear of him, is not known. At first, as we have seen, he worked for Francesco Barbaro. Later he appears to have performed a small commission for Lorenzo Valla, since a copy of Aristotle's *Poetics* accompanied by the short text known as the Greek Donatus (Vat. gr. 1388, folios 51-93), is enclosed in what looks like a wrapper with his name on the outside. He is also possibly to be connected with Guarino, since there is a reference to 'Gerardus librarius tuus' in a long polemical pamphlet written by George Trapezuntius against Guarino. As the date of the quarrel is 1437, Girard (as he always spells his name) will have moved by then if the hypothesis is correct.[23] It looks as if his contacts were wide enough to enforce the conclusion that we should not assign work to his Mantuan period unless there is positive evidence. The necessity for such caution is regrettable, since his pen was fluent and there are more than twenty known products.[24]

One that was certainly made for the school, because the colophon mentions Mantua, is Plutarch's *Lives* (Laur. 69.1, dated *c.* 1430). Many of the others could have been produced for Vittorino, since they agree with what we know of his interests, and it is noteworthy that few biblical or theological texts are found among them. There are two copies of Homer (Holkham gr. 116 and Perugia E 48), one of Isocrates, an author mentioned in Platina's life and in the list of 1445 (Canon. gr. 87), one of Herodotus (Ambr. A 253 inf.) and one of a grammar by Manuel Moschopoulos (Vienna, phil. gr. 263).

No less than eight volumes contain works by Aristotle.[25] These reflect an interest of Vittorino's that was already known from other evidence: a letter of Filelfo dated 1430 records a loan to him of Aristotle's 'dialectical' works,[26] and a copy of the *Rhetoric* (Paris supp. gr. 1285) which had been in Filelfo's possession has Vittorino's ex-libris (it later came into the hands of Francesco Barbaro). Among the copies produced by Girard there are three which surprisingly include the *Poetics*. It is generally held that this text did not circulate in Italy until much later in the century.[27] One wonders whether any of the three were among the books seen by Traversari, who claimed that the library at Mantua added nothing to his knowledge of Aristotle. Girard's transcripts, assuming that they were made in Italy, are a much better proof of interest in the text than the presence of the text in a batch of manuscripts brought back by Aurispa or another collector from Greece. There is now some evidence to suggest that it could have begun to exert influence in the second quarter of the century; but owing to the difficulty of interpreting Aristotle's concise and elliptical style and the slender evidence for the study of tragedy at this date, again because of its linguistic difficulty, one should be cautious in asserting without qualification that such influence began at once. Nevertheless it is worth mentioning that a recent writer has detected echoes of the *Poetics* in Leon Battista Alberti's essay *De pictura*, composed in 1435.[28]

Another book which may be mentioned here probably takes us outside the cultural horizon of Mantua. It is a miscellany now preserved in Leiden (Vulcanianus 93). Although it includes Aesop's fables, which were often used in schools, the same cannot be said of the other contents. Of these the best known is the Alexander Romance of pseudo-Callisthenes, very widely diffused in many languages. The others are less known. The so-called *Stephanites and Ichnelates* was a translation, made in the eleventh century from the Arabic, of a fable about jackals who intrigued against a lion. The *Iliad* of Constantine Hermoniakos is a late Byzantine production of *c*. 1330 which presents the Trojan saga in octosyllabic verse and simple language. Among the known or potential patrons of Girard in Italy there is no one who seems likely to have commissioned such a strange medley of texts and one wonders if it goes back to his years in Greece.

The list of 1445 enables us to add to the picture of this well-stocked library in a few respects. Among the poets, not specified by Traversari and not fully indicated by the other sources, we find two Hellenistic writers, both characteristic of the Byzantine intellectual world: Aratus,

whose didactic poem on astronomy had been used for many generations
to teach the elements of the subject, and Lycophron, whose *Alexandra*
was little more than a series of riddles and must quite certainly have
been unintelligible to any Italian of the time. Among the other prose
writers it is not surprising to find Aeschines, the great rival of
Demosthenes, in view of the emphasis given to the latter by Vittorino.
There were also some Atticist writers of the Roman empire, generally
popular in Byzantium; in this category come Aristides, the Platonist
Maximus of Tyre and the Christian Neoplatonist Synesius of Cyrene.
Two items in the inventory are surprising or obscure: they are 'Polybius
on barbarism and solecism', a very rare text on grammatical matters
which is known from two copies, neither of which can have belonged to
the school in Mantua, and 'some letters of Dionysius'. Science is
represented by Ptolemy's *Geography*: we cannot tell whether this was the
original or the version by Jacopo Angeli da Scarperia.

Although the school's library was impressive, one should not assume
that it included all the leading authors or could easily fill any gaps in the
collection. There is a revealing letter of Gian Francesco Gonzaga written
in 1444.[29] Addressing himself to Guarino the duke says that he has long
wanted a copy in Greek of Josephus' *Jewish Antiquities, Jewish War* and
various polemical writings against the detractors of the Jews. He adds
that he has a friend who is about to leave for Constantinople, and he has
asked this friend to look out for a copy. Such were the difficulties
experienced by one of the most privileged men in the whole of Italy.

What should our final judgment on the school be? On the negative side
we are obliged to record that it did not produce any theoretical statement
of educational principles or significant works of scholarship. The writings
of Theodore Gaza dating to his Mantuan period cannot constitute an
exception. It is also necessary to note that the school did not continue for
more than a year or two after Vittorino's death, still less lead to the
foundation of a learned society, whether an academy or a university. One
is bound to ask why the marquis did not persist in an effort to maintain a
deservedly famous institution, which added to his prestige. The simple
answer is to suggest that the personality of the teacher was so
outstanding that no successor could hope to step into his place and seem
worthy of it. A third and related consideration arises from the saying
'Imitation is the sincerest form of flattery'. That highest of compliments
the school at Mantua did not receive, a fact which must reflect to some
extent if not on the values, at least on the resources, of Renaissance
rulers.

The positive achievement of the school is clear. It taught a generation
of intellectuals and rulers who were thereby equipped to hold their own
with the intellectuals. Did Vittorino have visions of bringing about Plato's
dream of a society where kings study philosophy and philosophers
become kings? To cite his pupil Federico da Montefeltro as a case in point

would be an example of the fallacy *post hoc ergo propter hoc*. The list of the school's pupils should be examined afresh. Our supposedly most reliable source says that Valla was among them, an idea which conflicts with the usual account of his early years. As he had reached the age of sixteen by the time the school was set up it is legitimate to doubt the accuracy of the source.[30] But there is no need to cast doubt on the success of the school in turning out highly competent humanists such as Niccolò Perotti.

The other important achievement was to bring Greek into the curriculum of a secondary school. It was inevitable, given the need to import Greek teachers, that the influence of Byzantine practice in methods of learning and choice of texts would be very strong. To what extent did the Greek element alter the character of the education offered? In one important respect it did not need to alter the general aim of the school, since the arts of the trivium and quadrivium were just as much a feature of Byzantine as of western education. But Vittorino must have read Plutarch's treatise on education; although we cannot trace his copy of the Greek text, he may equally well have known it in the version prepared by Guarino in 1411. And reading Plutarch could have led him to put into practice classical customs which the Byzantines for all their imitation of antiquity never seem to have taken seriously. So the study of music could become the practical study of the art and cease to be based on theory, even if texts expounding the theory had found a place in the library, whether by accident or out of deference to Byzantine notions. And the concern to provide for physical education was the realisation of ancient Athenian practice. Platina records that the Athenians were Vittorino's masters in this matter as in all others.[31] He saw how to use the material that the Byzantines made available to him without accepting their limited vision of what classical Greece had to offer. Byzantine education had laid great emphasis on the study of ancient texts as a means to acquire the bizarre skill of writing in the same style as the authors of antiquity. Italians saw better reasons, philosophical, theological and scientific, for learning Greek. The majority of Byzantine and Italian intellectuals accepted the principle that literary study served as a propaedeutic. The seven liberal arts led to higher things. Vittorino decided to apply the principle to both the classical languages. And he went one stage further than other teachers by pondering on the Greeks' own view of education and putting it into practice.

6

Guarino

Guarino (1374-1460) had a great reputation as a teacher during his long career, the last thirty years of which were spent in Ferrara.[1] He was an elder contemporary of Vittorino and the two men were on excellent terms. Their outlook had much in common, particularly in two essentials, a belief in the need for good relations with pupils and in the importance of learning Greek. In addition Guarino is reported to have had some interest in the fine arts and physical education. As the senior man he may have been the source of all these ideas, and it is worth recalling that his version of the allegedly Plutarchan treatise on education may have served as an inspiration to his younger colleague. On the other hand Guarino is thought to have developed some of his views on education only at a late stage in his career, and he may have been less wholehearted in his application of the Greek legacy. With the benefit of hindsight it can perhaps be said that despite his reputation he had fewer really important pupils in his mature years and achieved less for the promotion of Greek studies. If such a judgment is fair to him, the justification for it may be sought in the fact that he had more distractions than Vittorino, being sometimes occupied with diplomatic business or administrative burdens, frequently suffering interruption of his teaching because of outbreaks of plague, and having to contend with the responsibilities of a very large family. None the less he is a figure of real stature. He was the first humanist to spend some time in the Byzantine capital learning the contemporary spoken language really well. His early appointments in Venice (1408-9, 1414-19) and Florence (1410-14) prove his reputation, and he was invited in 1422 to move from Verona to Mantua. By declining he left the way open for Vittorino. His efficacy as a teacher is probably indicated by the good reception given to his revision of the *Erotemata* of his tutor Chrysoloras. He would be entitled to still greater credit on this score if it were certain that he compiled a Greek lexicon in 1440, since the lack of such basic aids must have been keenly felt, and the lexica formerly used by the Byzantines were an inevitable but not wholly satisfactory substitute.[2]

There is not much material to throw light on his classes; he must have commented on texts he read with his pupils, and a certain amount of his work on Latin authors has come down to us. It would almost certainly repay further study by throwing light on his command of both the classical languages.[3]

Guarino had a considerable reputation outside Italy, and talented men came from as far away as England to sit at his feet. Three examples may be cited:[4] William Grey, bishop of Ely, who was in Ferrara in 1445-6 but does not appear to have learned any Greek; Robert Flemmyng, nephew of the founder of Lincoln College, Oxford and himself dean of Lincoln from 1452 onwards, who was in Ferrara some time between 1446 and 1451 and did learn some Greek; and John Free, who also learned Greek in 1455-8 and spent the remainder of his short career in Italy. A notebook survives to give us some idea of the lecture courses he attended. It is in Free's hand and seems to be a record of classes on Vergil, Horace and Terence. Greek words are quoted quite often.

Guarino's command of the language which he so strongly recommended others to study receives some rather uncertain illumination from the notes made of his lectures on Vergil's *Georgics*. In the course of some comments on 1.43-4 he gives an etymology for the Greek name of the north wind Boreas; his explanation is in Greek, μετὰ βοῆς ῥέει which he renders as 'it comes with force'. The noun in fact means 'shout, commotion' and Guarino appears to be confusing it with βία. *Humanum est errare*, and this may just be an oversight, but it creates a bad impression and is not a lapse to be readily credited to Guarino if there is any other way of explaining the evidence. Although the notes are in Free's hand it is not stated explicitly that he was attending Guarino's lectures, and though the school is obviously the place where he is likely to have made such notes, it does not follow that the only teacher was Guarino himself. In fact it is known that in his last years his sons and other teachers took over some tasks in the school, and one would rather ascribe such an error to one of them.[5]

It is instructive to see how uncertain command of the language combined with inability to assess the reliability of sources could lead to dubious interpretation and distortion of a Greek concept. On 5 November 1447 Guarino wrote to Leonello d'Este about his plan to commission a set of paintings depicting the Muses. He explains that they are to be understood as concepts of the various types of intelligence which lead to advances in arts and skills. He cites the rare Greek word μῶσθαι with the meaning *to seek* and treats the word Muse as a derivative of it meaning *seeker*. One can hardly blame him for a false etymology when sound principles of linguistics had still to be evolved, and in any case he was probably doing no more than repeat a notion put forward by Plato in the *Cratylus* (406a); but his account of some of the Muses is very strange. While it may not be extravagant to see Erato as the patron of marriage, one asks how Thalia can be said to have invented agriculture and why Polyhymnia is described in almost identical terms. This eccentric view of

Thalia is found in the ancient commentator's note on Apollonius Rhodius, *Argonautica* 3.1, but the only text which can have served as a source for the remark about both Thalia and Polyhymnia is Byzantine and dates from the twelfth century. John Tzetzes (*c.* 1110 – *c.* 1180), a verbose and notoriously inaccurate student of the ancient classics, gives such a description of them in his notes to the first line of Hesiod's *Works and Days*. It is not difficult to imagine that when reading Hesiod Guarino had had a copy which contained the commentary by Tzetzes in the margins. Whether he should have accepted as true all the information it offered is a moot point; an acute critic might have been put on his guard by the Byzantine's manner, and it is perhaps only fair to Guarino to note that at the end of his letter he admits that others may wish to assign to the Muses different spheres of influence.[6]

Another work which no doubt could be made to yield valuable information is the *Commentarioli*, a collection of short notes, each consisting of a single paragraph ranging from a few lines to a page in length on a wide variety of topics. It first came to light in a version containing 27 items (Bologna, Bibl. Comunale 16.b.III.3), but a much extended version with 84 items has been known for sixty years and has received no attention.[7]

It raises the question whether Guarino in some sense anticipates Politian's *Miscellanea*, but a cursory inspection suggests that this would hardly be a correct description, and the contents are more like a scrap-book anthology, in which a good many items are probably derived from the writer's acquaintance with Plutarch (the sources are not usually named). The incipit of one is of immediate interest; it reads 'legebam Sophoclis tragoediam quae de Aiace furente composita *Aias mastigophoros* inscribitur'. The proof of Guarino's knowledge of the *Ajax*, which came first in the Byzantine syllabus, is welcome in itself, since there is not much evidence of Italians reading such difficult texts until quite late in the fifteenth century. Guarino takes as his starting point Ajax's stern injunction to Tecmessa 'Silence is an ornament for women', remarking that it is one of many valuable precepts in the play, and gives what is in effect a little sermon on the virtues of silence, the last part of which cites the probably apocryphal anecdote of Leaena, the friend of the legendary Athenian tyrannicides Harmodius and Aristogeiton. The story went that under torture she bit off her tongue in order not to be able to reveal any information and the Athenians commemorated her by a statue of a tongueless lioness (that being the meaning of her name). The tale is recorded by many classical authors and it is therefore quite uncertain whether this is yet another piece of information that Guarino owed to his reading of Plutarch, but it is important to note that if he derived any enjoyment of drama or poetry from the Sophoclean text, he keeps it to himself.

His ability to restore Greek passages in Latin authors, such as Aulus

Gellius or the commentary by Servius on Vergil, must have been widely appreciated. The extent of his contribution to the restoration of Greek authors is much harder to estimate. One reason is that very few Greek books from his library can be identified. The Aristophanes acquired during his early stay in Greece has already been mentioned (Pal. gr. 116). There is an Aristotle containing a wide selection of works, including the *Physics* and *De anima*, which has been liberally annotated by Guarino in the margin; it was copied in 1445 and so was not one of his early acquisitions (Vienna, phil. gr. 75). His reading of Greek poetry other than Homer and Sophocles is proved by his ownership of a Hesiod and the late poem on geography by Dionysius Periegetes (Paris gr. 2772). Another copy of Hesiod's *Works and Days* with his notes is known (Vat. gr. 1507). He appears to have had two or three copies of Xenophon, not quite identical in their contents (Wolfenbüttel 71.19 Aug.2° and 56.22 Aug.8°).[8] His Lucian is also extant (Wolfenbüttel, 86.7 Aug.2°). But this list is probably no more than a fraction of the library he eventually built up, and we should assume that he had copies of all the standard texts needed for a curriculum based on Byzantine precedents.

He seems to have been influenced by the Greek authors he read, and a practical result was the adoption in various speeches of the rules given in the treatise on rhetoric ascribed to Dionysius of Halicarnassus (it had been translated by Gaza during his time in Mantua, and Gaza joined Guarino in Ferrara in 1446-9). Further evidence of dependence on classical models is seen in a piece on historiography which owes much to Lucian's humorous attack on some bad historians of the Parthian wars in his *De historia conscribenda*.

There is also an essay on Plato, which is very heavily dependent on the ancient biography by Diogenes Laertius. But Guarino does not have much claim to be regarded as a serious student of Plato. Although he owned and annotated a copy of the current version of the *Republic* (Reg. lat. 1131), it looks as if his reading was confined to Books 2-5, so avoiding some of the most interesting discussions of moral and metaphysical questions, and in any case his notes do not suggest that he had a highly developed philosophical approach to Plato. The hypothesis has been put forward that he only tackled this text in order to give help to his friend Francesco Barbaro, who was composing an essay *De re uxoria*. If true this is most paradoxical, since Plato's views on marriage and the position of women will have seemed nothing less than bizarre to fifteenth-century thinkers.[9]

If we dare trust an assertion made in the course of a disagreeable controversy that he had with his former pupil George Trapezuntius, Guarino may claim the distinction of being one of the earliest humanists to read Pindar. Trapezuntius, writing in 1437, asserts that when they knew each other in Venice in 1417-18 Guarino was reading Pindar (the word he uses could mean 'conducting a class') and asked him for his opinion of the poet and an explanation of his metres. Trapezuntius says that within two days he gave his tutor an account of all kinds of metre. An attempt to master the Theban author's victory odes would have been a bold venture at that date, and few pupils would have volunteered for the experience. Whether Guarino was unique at this date, assuming the story to be true, is uncertain, since it appears that Antonio Corbinelli had this author in his library, where it may nevertheless have remained unread.[10]

Guarino's best efforts were devoted to translation, and he was no doubt right to regard this as the best way to bring Greek thought to the notice of the public, however much he advocated study in the original language. Several pieces go back to his years in Constantinople; Plutarch's *Alexander* and Lucian's *Calumnia* and *Musca*, the last of these being a short piece of a type much favoured by ancient rhetoricians, the praise of something that is normally thought of as wholly bad, an exercise aimed at testing the ingenuity of pupils in school. Guarino's range was wide, and he not only produced versions of Aesop, some Herodotus, some passages of Homer, but also a few patristic texts. But most of his energy was spent on Plutarch and by the end of his career he had translated at least thirteen of the biographies and a few of the *Moralia*, including the important treatise on education which is now reckoned to be spurious but was highly influential. The biographies of Sulla and Lysander were presented to Leonello d'Este, his pupil and future ruler of Ferrara, as a wedding gift in 1435. Four years earlier Guarino had read with the same pupil Isocrates' *Ad Nicoclem*, one of a pair of treatises which served as primers on relations between a ruler and his subjects, and therefore well chosen (both were available in translation about this time, the *Nicocles* in a version by Guarino himself, but the view that both were translated by Guarino has had to be abandoned).[11]

A recently discovered letter of Guarino, dating from 1458 or 1459, seems to indicate that his translations of Plutarch were even more numerous than has been supposed. In response to a request from Piero de' Medici he mentions the *Lives* of Agesilaus, Alcibiades and Demetrius. The first of these is referred to in a way that suggests that the version is his own work, and for the second and the third the implication of the context is identical. Yet the letter reveals a fact which can only be described as very odd. Guarino has no copy in his possession in Ferrara and has to send to Verona for the *Agesilaus*. Brought face to face with this remarkable confession the interpreter is bound to look afresh at the evidence and see whether it is capable of bearing any other meaning. The three *Lives* mentioned were in the end included in the copy destined for the Medici library (Laur. 65.26 and 27), but the versions were not from Guarino's pen; they were new renderings by Donato Acciaiuoli and Alamanno Rinuccini. And we should note Guarino's statement 'cum reposci mea videatur opera'. Since the noun is feminine singular rather than neuter plural the meaning is 'activity' and not 'writings', and one may suggest that what is being requested of him is his help in putting together the best available collection of such translations; he was the doyen of translators and had himself done much of the work required; on being asked to add still further to his output he may have demurred on grounds of age or other commitments.[12]

Towards the end of his life Guarino had begun work on a difficult task rather different from the others he had attempted, the translation of Strabo's *Geography*. This was a commission from Pope Nicholas V, begun in 1453; when the Pope died two years later Guarino had reached Book 10, and he continued work while looking for a new patron, who was eventually found in the person of an eminent Venetian, Jacopo Antonio Marcello. The text of Strabo had lacunae and the task was far from easy. Guarino's autograph happens to be preserved (Canonici class. lat. 301), and one can see from it that he sometimes was unable at first to find an equivalent for a Greek word, leaving it in Greek letters initially until he solved the puzzle. There are some marginalia of interest. Where Strabo makes a brief mention of the translator's birth-place Verona, local pride was not satisfied with such treatment and a long note on the city was added in the margin, with an instruction to future copyists not to include this matter in the text proper. Another type of annotation deserves mention. Guarino remarked on the passages where Strabo states that the earth is a sphere (folios 12r, 27v, 42r, referring to 1.1.20, 1.4.1 and 2.5.2) and that there had been a circumnavigation of Africa (folio 38v, on 2.3.4) (there was of course a less scientific report of this in Herodotus 4.42 which might have sparked his curiosity), while near the beginning of Book 3 he was prompted to write *circumnavigari terram ab ortu et ab occasu*.[13]

7

Filelfo

Another figure of some note whose career as a teacher began more than a decade before the Council of Florence and continued until well into the second half of the century was Francesco Filelfo (1398-1481). He spent the best part of seven years in Constantinople (1420-7) and married a member of the Chrysoloras family. His command of everyday Greek must have matched or surpassed that of any of his contemporaries; it does not necessarily follow that his understanding of the classical language was beyond criticism. In his very large correspondence there are 110 letters written in Greek,[1] and his other writings include a number of compositions in Greek verse. In this latter category we find addresses to many eminent contemporaries, either in elegiac couplets or in the much less usual metre of the Sapphic stanza. Among the recipients of these productions were Theodore Gaza, John Argyropoulos, Andronicus Callistus, cardinal Bessarion and Sultan Mehmet the Conqueror. Other humanists of his generation could not compete in this unusual skill, and the next Italian to do so was Politian, who composed epigrams in the style of the *Greek Anthology*.

Filelfo's letters do not give an entirely flattering picture of him. One that is well known reports his son's failure to learn anything useful in Constantinople. After observing that the idea of sending him there had been a mistake Filelfo looks back to his own experience of the Byzantine capital. He claims to have made great efforts to acquire copies of the writings of the ancient grammarians Apollonius Dyscolus and Herodian, but never had a whiff of success. One can perhaps give him credit for wishing to read the best work that antiquity had to offer on the subject and one may note with regret rather than surprise the failure of the local libraries to satisfy his needs. His letter continues with a condemnation of all the instruction that was available in the schools as worthless. Although the verdict is harsh, it is perhaps not grossly unjust, since it would be difficult to claim that cultural life was flourishing in Byzantium at the time. Filelfo adds the particular complaint that he had been unable to obtain any clear and reliable guidance on matters of syntax, prosody and accentuation. Even allowing for the modest level of competence achieved by such teachers as George Chrysococces, in whose school he studied alongside the young Bessarion, his negative judgment seems exaggerated, and our suspicions are aroused by the next remark, which may be translated as follows: 'The Aeolic language, which both Homer and Callimachus employed for the most part in their works, is completely unknown there.' Filelfo is guilty here of a gross error: Aeolic is not the language of Homer or Callimachus, and it is difficult to see how anyone who had received even elementary instruction from a Byzantine master could have acquired this misconception. As a result one is bound to hesitate before taking at its face value any statement on a scholarly matter made by Filelfo.[2]

The major part of his career was spent in Milan; it has been noted that extremely little written work apart from a boring introduction to Aristotle's *Politics* survives from this period.[3] Before that he had held posts in Bologna (1428), Florence (1429-33), Siena (1434-8) and again in Bologna (1439); after his long spell in Milan he moved to Rome for a few years from 1474 onwards. His peripatetic existence was partly due to his awkward character which led him into frequent feuds.[4] In Florence he was attacked and stabbed by a person whom he imagined to be acting under orders from the Medici.

Of his teaching in Florence it is known that in 1429 he offered to give courses on the *Iliad*, Thucydides and Xenophon. We have evidence that on arrival he read the *Iliad* and two years later Aristotle's *Nicomachean Ethics*. Both these texts were obviously central; the same cannot be said of Aeschines, the great rival of Demosthenes, on whom he lectured in 1431-2, but the mere fact of that rivalry was enough to create interest, and Bruni had already made a translation.[5] In a letter to Aurispa he claimed to have an audience each day of some 400 or perhaps even more, the majority of them men of standing or aristocrats, including the future Pope Pius II, Niccolò Niccoli and Carlo Marsuppini.

His first essay in translation dates from his return journey to Italy. He claims to have felt the need to recover fluency in his native tongue after almost seven years absence abroad during which he had neither read nor spoken it; one senses, as often with Filelfo, some exaggeration. Reading a letter from Bruni to Salutati which he had in his luggage he noted a remark that poets invent names and facts, which set him wondering how many stories in ancient authors are fictions or distortions. It occurred to him that Herodotus reported having heard from Egyptian priests a quite different account of the Trojan War from that given by Homer, and though Herodotus was sometimes accused of invention the general view was to treat him as the father of history. Moreover, in the present case the poet Stesichorus also was known to have contradicted Homer. Puzzling over the conflict of evidence Filelfo recalled that Dio Chrysostom (*c.* 40 – after 112) had written on the subject. As one of the leading writers of the Second Sophistic Dio had continued to enjoy a certain popularity in Byzantine literary circles but will have been known to few if any Italians in 1427. Filelfo read the text of the *Trojan Oration* (it is not implausible that he should have been travelling with a fairly well stocked library), enjoyed it and decided to make a translation. This text, which has been characterised as the most sophistic of all Dio's numerous writings, pursues still further the idea that Homer's account is not be to taken as historical fact and maintains that the city was never captured by the Greeks. Such a vision of the past may have been designed to flatter nostalgic notions entertained by the inhabitants of the Roman city on the site. But if that was the historical context of Dio's composition, Filelfo is unaware of it and treats the epideictic tour de force as mere ammunition against the view of Homer as a historical source.[6]

When he arrived in Bologna to take up his first appointment he found the members of his class keen on rhetoric and he was asked to make available in Latin the supposedly Aristotelian *Rhetorica ad Alexandrum*. In the preface to his version[7] he observes: 'we are not all so enthusiastic about Greek because we need it for use in Athens or Byzantium but because we hope it will improve our command of Latin as readers or writers' (the phrasing is rather vague, but I suppose this is the right way to take the words *Latinam litteraturam atque eloquentiam*). There is further evidence here of the limitations imposed by the difficulty of the language. Filelfo admits that one does not appreciate the full beauty and charm of Greek orators, poets or philosophers without long and hard study. Hence the demand for translations. But he adds that it would be better to immerse oneself in the language, and at first he was not too keen to agree to the request, which presented him with a difficult task.

In a long consolatory address to a member of the Venetian Marcello family on the death of a son Filelfo took the opportunity to insert a number of translations of short passages from the Greek classics which seemed relevant to his theme. Among examples of pagan authors who believe in the immortality of the soul he cites Euripides, offering a translation of the opening speech of the *Hecuba*, in which the ghost of the murdered Polydorus introduces the plot. Filelfo does his best to render the Greek iambic lines by their closest equivalent in Latin, a metre found in Roman comedy and tragedy. His metrical knowledge is not by any means perfect, but his contemporaries were in no position to criticise him on that score. The rendering must be accounted fairly accurate, and since he was operating under the constraints of metre his skill is creditable. There is just one point where he seems to change the sense without need. At line 9 the Thracians among whom Polydorus had lived as a refugee are described as 'lovers of horses', which Filelfo converts into the uncomplimentary epithet 'fierce' (*ferocem*).[8]

His other translations included two medical treatises by Hippocrates, Plutarch's *Lycurgus*, *Numa*, *Galba* and *Otho* and the two collections of his *Apophthegmata*; some of Lysias and Xenophon, in particular the *Cyropaedia*, completed in 1467. It is accompanied by a fulsome letter of dedication to Pope Paul II, in which much emphasis is laid on the merits of monarchical government, a subject not unrelated to the education of a prince as described by Xenophon. While not being aware of Valla's partial anticipation of his work, which was presumably not in circulation, Filelfo is critical of a version by Poggio which he claims is an abridgement, reducing to six books the original eight and failing to do justice to the content or the stylistic beauty of the Greek. On both counts Filelfo accepts the usual estimate of an author whose stock has subsequently fallen a little.[9]

Whether Filelfo has a claim to be ranked among the most distinguished scholars of the Quattrocento must remain doubtful. If the references to Greek authors which abound in his letters could be taken at face value, one would be obliged to conclude that he was exceptionally well read. But a great many of the supposed quotations and allusions are specious. They refer to authors who are not extant. This is second-hand learning, and Filelfo is doing little more than drop names. It may be said that few ordinary mortals resist the temptation to indulge in this form of vanity; be that as it may, Filelfo has to answer the more serious charge that he did not read all the important authors that he undoubtedly had in his personal library. Certainly he had read Plutarch, and he used the *Suda* lexicon as a source of information as well as a dictionary; in addition it is clear that he exploited the *Lexicon* of Harpocration, a guide to technical terms of Athenian law and constitutional practice used in the Attic orators, which may not have been known to all the humanists. But there are grounds for suspecting that he had not read Aeschylus, Apollonius Rhodius and the *Hymns* of Callimachus. There is also reason to believe that he knew nothing of Euripides beyond the *Hecuba* and *Phoenissae*, small portions of which he translated. This is an astonishingly disappointing performance for a man who had spent so long in the Byzantine capital, and it is not much improved if we allow that in addition to those plays, which were the first and the third in the Byzantine curriculum, he also knew the *Orestes* which was the second.[10]

The failure to read widely undermines the merit attributed to him even by his critics, that he was tireless in his search for copies of unknown texts. There is little to show that he read each new text he acquired, and though he did bring a number of manuscripts back from Greece his services in this respect did not match those of Aurispa or the agents of cardinal Bessarion.

Nevertheless he deserves some credit for his effort to obtain more correct texts when possible. We find him sending his son to Bessarion to ask for the loan of a copy of Sextus Empiricus, an abstruse and fairly rare philosophical author from whom Filelfo translated three short passages. He intends to compare Bessarion's copy with his own, which has lacunae (it has been identified as Laur. 85.19), and if his hope of obtaining a more intelligible text is disappointed, then at least there will be the consolation of offering some improvements to Bessarion for his copy (no doubt Marc.

gr. 262).[11] A similar problem arose when he found that his copy of a text by Plutarch was defective.[12]

Various pronouncements on questions of Platonic and Aristotelian philosophy can be found in the writings of Filelfo. They do not necessarily indicate a long-standing and deep interest in these topics. Like any other scholar he will have realised that the differences between the two systems were frequently a source of controversy and it would have been unwise not to accept the fact that changing fashions might lead to material changes in the patronage offered to humanists who committed themselves to particular views. Whether for this reason or because of intellectual uncertainty he is found sitting on the fence in 1464.[13] His prudence, if that is what it was, does not appear to have prevented a breach with Bessarion in 1469.[14] Although it may be noted in his favour that in his opening lecture on Aristotle's *Nicomachean Ethics* he modestly disclaims expert knowledge of philosophy, in a letter of 1439 addressed to the future patriarch George Scholarios he commits himself to the view that the defence of Aristotle's doctrines is tantamount to the defence of truth.[15] His translation of the *Rhetorica ad Alexandrum*, dating from 1428, is of course a contribution to the study of rhetoric rather than philosophy, but we may also note that he translated Plato's *Euthyphro* and three of his *Letters*. And in a pair of letters addressed to Andronicus Callistus in 1464 we find him asking about the precise wording of a passage in pseudo-Plutarch *De philosophorum placitis* in order to discover Aristotle's definition of the important term *idea*.[16] This will have been a key point in any discussion or comparison of Plato and Aristotle.

Filelfo's intellectual and moral flexibility was well displayed in 1473, when he made overtures to Florence in the hope of obtaining an appointment there again. Almost forty years had passed since his departure under a cloud, but he was not happy in Milan and had been trying for some time to find another post. His method of currying favour in Florence was to send Lorenzo de' Medici an essay on a fundamental concept of Platonism, entitled *De ideis*, which elicited a favourable response from Ficino. Although the essay seems not to have survived there are ways of inferring the gist of it, since two other preserved writings deal with the same subject. It would appear that there was a learned discussion based on a number of sources. But in one respect it was paradoxical: direct use of Plato's dialogues cannot be traced, although Filelfo had translated the *Euthyphro* and three *Letters* and can hardly have failed to read some of the other works. The most prominent source is St Augustine, and Filelfo accepts his view that Ideas are the eternal archetypes in the mind of God. Another feature of the essay which seems at first sight very strange is that Plato is not credited with the invention of the term Idea. This view results from accepting as genuine the treatise *De mundi anima* which circulated under the name of Timaeus of Locri, the main speaker in Plato's *Timaeus*. Filelfo, like any other scholar of his day, may be pardoned for thinking that Plato was not the first to use the term.[17]

An episode which demonstrates his antiquarian interests has recently been brought to light. In his correspondence he twice refers to Greek script as Attic letters, a phrase which he could have found in a number of ancient sources where the meaning is clear. It designates the local Athenian alphabet in contrast to the slightly different version used in Ionia until the Athenians adopted Ionian practice at the end of the fifth century BC. This however is not the meaning intended by Filelfo, who seems to have had in mind the capital letters seen in ancient inscriptions. His correspondent, the epigraphist Ciriaco d'Ancona, wrote out specimen alphabets of this kind more than once, and one of the specimens is in a book that found its way into Filelfo's hands. Filelfo would have liked to own books in this script, and it has been suggested that the copy of the *Iliad* and *Batrachomyomachia* written for him by Theodore Gaza (Laur. 32.1) may be an attempt to satisfy his desire. The hand is very large, and although epigraphic would not be the right adjective to describe it, there are enough capital letters in it to suggest that the scribe may have been doing his best to satisfy a most unusual and difficult request.[18]

Filelfo cannot be ranked with the greatest figures of the Quattrocento. As a translator he was not as productive as Bruni or Guarino. As a teacher he did not have a comparable following of pupils and admirers. His writings do not include a substantial monument of scholarship or a popular new grammar.[19] It is alleged that one of the manuscripts written in his hand is a Greek-Latin dictionary, which if true might represent a considerable service to students; but in fact it turns out that the only part of the manuscript which is autograph is a fly-leaf with an insignificant letter by Filelfo, and at most one may suppose that he is giving the dictionary to a friend without having had any hand in its composition.[20]

On the other hand it must be admitted that he was capable of displaying knowledge and ingenuity. He knew Greek well enough to rebut Cicero's well known special pleading that in some respects Latin had a richer vocabulary, and makes plausible suggestions to fill the gaps alleged by Cicero.[21] Moreover he was able to adduce a story in Herodotus (1.82) to help with the explanation of a passage in Ovid's *Fasti* (2.663ff.). But his insistence on the relevance of the parallel led him to adjust the text of the Greek author in order to explain a difficult phrase in the Latin, and he fell into the temptation of suggesting that there are manuscripts of Herodotus which present the text with the wording that he recommended. So far as is known this is not the case, and modern scholars solve the difficulty by making a very slight adjustment to the Latin. Filelfo's procedure, leaving aside the dubious implication about the evidence furnished by the manuscript tradition, can at least be said to exhibit the facility of recall that a scholar needs and some understanding of the way that texts must on occasion be corrected.[22]

8

Greek prelates in Italy

(i) The Council of Florence (1439) and its consequences

Critics of the modern academic world have been heard to say that
conferences are a waste of time. A more charitable view is that they are
valuable not for their formal agenda but for the other activities that go on
when scholars gather. It is tempting to make the same comment about
the church councils of the Renaissance. What Poggio discovered between
the sessions of the Council of Constance does not deserve to be thought
less important than the decisions of that assembly. If the same notion is
applied to the Council of Florence, the specious union of the Greek and
Roman churches which it achieved has to be weighed against the
extraordinary consequences which have been attributed with some
plausibility to the presence of one member of the Greek delegation. I do
not refer to Bessarion, remarkable though his part in the debates of the
Council had been, but to his elderly friend and former tutor George
Gemistos Plethon, for whom two claims have been made, neither based
on incontrovertible evidence.

The first relates to the notion of an academy. Such bodies, which were
often nothing more than a private group of like-minded friends, seem to
have been one of the important inventions of fifteenth-century Italy.
While Greek and Latin were taught in schools and universities,
academies could also further the study of the ancient world. Their history
has never been fully investigated, but it looks as if the name may have
been used for the first time in Florence. A learned group had been
meeting there in the monastery of Santo Spirito as early as 1421; but
probably the first group to use the name of Academy was Alamanno
Rinuccini's of 1454; the most famous was at Cosimo de' Medici's house at
Careggi where Ficino translated Plato. Ficino himself tells us at the
beginning of his preface to Plotinus that the idea was implanted in
Cosimo's mind when he attended lectures given by Plethon during the
Council of Florence.[1] It is odd that the plan was not put into effect for a
long time, and it is also worth noting that Cosimo had had the chance to
make himself familiar with Platonic thought with the help of versions by
Bruni and others. Apparently the idea had not occurred to him before and
took a long time to mature. Although one is inclined to be sceptical about

Ficino's statement,[2] it is not difficult to believe that there was something special about Plethon, which caused him to make a great impression in Florence. And it is certainly worth while to explore the hypothesis that the application of the name Academy owes something to Byzantine precedent.[3] Although Ficino's words do not allow any such inference, a sixteenth-century humanist, Scipione Bargagli, gives the impression that he thought the concept of an academy had been imported from Byzantium. Is it possible that he was right? Plethon was the leading member of an intellectual circle at Mistra. Its precise nature is a matter of dispute; he is usually thought of as a secret upholder of paganism and therefore a leader of a potentially dangerous group opposed to Christianity. A solution of that difficult problem lies outside the scope of the present discussion. For our purposes it is enough to say that the pupils of a Byzantine teacher might have been referred to collectively as a *thiasos*, a word which originally designated a guild of worshippers of a pagan deity and was then extended to other groups. It is also highly probable that a combination of cultural antiquarianism and loyalty to a gifted teacher whose principal interest was in Platonism would have caused his school to be referred to as an academy. The suggestion of Byzantine influence is therefore plausible enough. One should only enter the caveat that when Plethon or his admirers used the term there is no proof that they thought of a society with its own set of rules and a formal commitment to a programme of advanced study. This idea may have evolved gradually in the various Florentine circles of the fifteenth century and if so it represents an important step forward in the progression towards the modern concept of such a body. Another step is perhaps to be seen in the Neakademia formed by Aldus Manutius at the end of the century. It ensured through the firm's publications a far wider diffusion of most of the leading classical authors and some others of less importance.

Another fascinating hypothesis which would confirm the critics' view of conferences and similar gatherings has been put forward in connection with the Council of Florence. Again it concerns Plethon. It can be summed up as follows. First of all it was he who recommended the study of Strabo as a supplement to the geographical knowledge already available from Ptolemy. Secondly, and this seems very likely, he met in Florence Paolo Dal Pozzo Toscanelli (1397-1482), who later communicated, perhaps indirectly, with Christopher Columbus. Thirdly Columbus, as is attested in the biography by his son, was decisively influenced by two passages of Strabo. Supporting evidence can be found in the undeniable fact that Plethon made some excerpts of Strabo and wrote a short essay on errors he had detected in him. Although copies of Strabo had been brought to Italy by Aurispa and Filelfo, there is no sign of the *Geography* exercising any influence before the date of the Council of Florence, whereas it was later made generally available by Guarino's Latin version, completed in

1458. Plethon would therefore share with Guarino the credit for providing Columbus with the information essential to his enterprise.[4]

Of the two passages of Strabo in question the first occurs in a criticism of Eratosthenes' calculations of the dimensions of the earth (1.4.6). He is quoted as having said: 'If the immensity of the Atlantic did not prevent us, we could sail from Iberia to India along the same parallel.' The second is part of a critique of Posidonius, who had claimed (2.3.6): 'If you sail from the west using the east wind you will reach India at a distance of 70,000 stades.'

This attractive theory is in need of modification. Plethon's excerpts seem to be a work of his extreme old age, in 1447-8, when Ciriaco d'Ancona was staying in Mistra and visiting him. One copy they used (Eton College 141 + Laur. 28.15) was a book obtained recently by Ciriaco from Constantinople. Plethon seems to have had another which has not been identified. These facts do not preclude the possibility that in 1439 he already knew of Strabo and recommended him enthusiastically to his new Italian acquaintances. A copy was brought to Italy in 1438 or soon afterwards (Marc. gr. XI.6), but Plethon was not its owner.[5]

So instead of the hypothesis outlined above one may suggest some alternatives. If the text of Strabo was available in Florence in 1439, it may have been brought by Bessarion rather than Plethon. If Bessarion was the person who urged its importance as an additional source of geographical information, he may equally well have done so later when he became a permanent resident in Italy. And if Paolo Toscanelli was a vital link in the transmission of the information, although he knew Greek he probably did not exploit his knowledge until the Latin version by Guarino made the text generally accessible. The occasion when Strabo was strongly recommended to the Italians and the identity of the person who made the recommendation have not yet been demonstrated with certainty.

One other anecdote about Plethon's behaviour at the Council of Florence may be added here, even though it cannot be shown to have a direct bearing on our main theme. In 1458 George Trapezuntius published a comparison of Plato and Aristotle, in which he remarked in passing that he had met Plethon at the Council and had a conversation with him. Plethon asserted that the whole world would soon adopt a single religion. When asked whether it would be Christian or Mohammedan he replied: 'Neither; it will not be different from paganism.' George's comment is that ever since he has always hated and feared Plethon as he would a poisonous snake. Modern work on George has made all too clear the extent of his prejudices and the weakness of his judgment, so that scepticism is in order; but it does seem clear that the two men might have met if George stopped in Florence at the time of the Council.[6] On the other hand it has to be said that there does not appear to be any other sign of pagan doctrines gaining currency at this time, and despite the condemnation of Plethon some years later by the Greek patriarch George Scholarios it is very notable that cardinal Bessarion's loyalty to his old teacher does not seem to have been shaken.

(ii) The Greek cardinal

Plethon returned to Greece after the Council and ended his days there; Bessarion went with the rest of the party, but did not stay long. His contributions to the debates in Florence had been the decisive factor leading to the union between the Greek and Roman churches proclaimed on 6 July 1439 by cardinal Cesarini and Bessarion himself, and the pope's appreciation of his services to Christian unity was shown in the immediate offer of a pension, which would be payable at a higher rate if he chose to become a member of the Roman curia. A few months after returning to Constantinople he was made a cardinal and at the end of 1440 he was back in Florence. From now on he remained in Italy and from 1443 he took up residence in Rome, except for a period as governor of Bologna in 1450-5 and some time spent travelling on diplomatic missions to northern Europe. His main energies were devoted to two causes that failed, the union of the churches being rendered largely ineffective by the resistance of the majority of the population in what remained of the Byzantine empire, while the intimately related question of raising military support in western Europe to help defend Byzantium against the Turks, an uphill task in any circumstances, faltered all the more as the Greeks' attitude became clear. But dedication to church affairs and international politics did not take up all his time. He gave further proofs of his great ability as a scholar and after settling in Rome did much to help both compatriots and Italians. The group which gathered round him is another of the bodies commonly referred to as an academy. He mastered Latin to a higher degree than any previous Byzantine intellectual open-minded enough to take an interest in western thought and literature. Lorenzo Valla was quite right to pay tribute to his mastery of the two cultures by calling him *inter Graecos latinissimus, inter Latinos graecissimus*.[7]

The ability to translate into a language which is not one's mother tongue is a great test of linguistic skill, and Bessarion found time for some work of this kind. St Basil's sermon on the nativity of Christ is a short piece of no special significance which he offered to pope Eugenius IV. To cardinal Cesarini he dedicated a version of the *Memorabilia* of Xenophon. One would like to know what attraction these rather unsophisticated sketches of Socrates can have had for leading churchmen; Bessarion seems to claim that what Socrates says on many moral questions should encourage the average person to feel that virtuous actions are within his power.

Rather more significant was the translation of Aristotle's *Metaphysics*

accompanied by the brief essay of Theophrastus which goes under the
same title. It appears that in this case Bessarion took the existing
medieval version by William of Moerbeke as a starting-point and made
improvements to it. In this way an important part of Greek philosophical
thinking became available in a form that could be understood more easily
than before. Finally we may note an application of classical oratory to
contemporary problems. At the end of his life, while attempting to raise
support for a crusade against the Turks, he made a version of
Demosthenes' *First Olynthiac*. The Athenian statesman's call to his
fellow-countrymen to face up to their responsibilities and recognise the
gravity of the threat from Philip of Macedon had an unambiguous
message for any leader capable of looking beyond short-term and
sectional interests. Bessarion appended his version to some speeches of
his own addressed to a wide public, including the princes of Italy. He
notes the extraordinary similarity of the circumstances facing the ancient
Athenians and the contemporary Christian community of nations, and he
expresses the hope that the reader will be swayed by the voice of an
ancient authority, whom he describes as an unrivalled orator and
excellent philosopher. A quotation from another passage of Demosthenes
is added: 'God can not be asked, nor indeed can a friend, to help those who
are sleepy or lazy.' Bessarion presumably knew enough ancient history to
be aware that Demosthenes' efforts were ultimately unsuccessful. He
foresaw that failure in his own day would lead to consequences for Italy
which he could not bring himself to spell out in full; one wonders if in his
heart of hearts he was hopeful that the union of western powers capable
of checking the Turks would come about.[8]

Bessarion's years of study with Plethon in Mistra had given him a
better than average understanding of Platonism, and as a result he was
able to demonstrate knowledge as well as loyalty to his master when he
took part in the philosophical discussion and polemic arising from
Plethon's unconventional standpoint. To follow the controversy in detail
by giving an account of each contribution to the debate would take us
outside the scope of this history, but one substantial work by Bessarion
must be mentioned. In 1458 his unreliable protégé George Trapezuntius
published *Comparationes Aristotelis et Platonis*. This was not the first
essay of its kind, since Plethon had written about the difference between
the two philosophies during his stay in Florence. But his work was in
Greek and remained untranslated for the time being. Trapezuntius by
writing in Latin could reach the whole of the educated public and his
essay was an extreme attack on Platonism, suggesting that it led to
heresy and immorality. Bessarion was not prepared to tolerate these
accusations, and he replied with what became his best known book, *In
calumniatorem Platonis*. It went through various drafts and was
published in both Greek and Latin, the latter version even appearing in
print during his lifetime in an edition of one thousand copies. A

wide-ranging discussion of Plato divided into four parts was accompanied by two appendixes, one of which criticised Trapezuntius for the incompetence he had displayed in his version of Plato's *Laws*, issued a few years earlier.

Although Bessarion's intention was to refute the claims of his opponent, he arranged his material in such a way as to avoid the impression of indulging in mere polemic. There is a reasonably full exposition of the main features of Platonic thought, which was welcomed by readers. There had not previously been any general introduction to the subject, and so Bessarion must be credited with an important achievement of popularisation. There was probably not much exaggeration in the claim (2.3.2) that Plato's opinions were unknown to almost all the Latins, partly through lack of translations, partly because such translations as existed were faulty. It looks as if we have to accept the implication that Bruni and others had not succeeded in reaching a wide public.

Bessarion's view of Plato is somewhat coloured by Neoplatonism, and he quotes from Plotinus and other later authors of that school. He accepts the traditional view that Plato had learned something from Moses by visiting Egypt. He also accepts a notion which we shall find in a slightly different form in Ficino, that Plato was influenced by Orpheus and the Pythagoreans. Inevitably he is much concerned with the similarities and differences between Platonism and Christianity. At some points he quotes from the writings of Dionysius the Areopagite, explicitly calling him the oldest and best of the fathers of the church (2.4.2). One of the most important passages concerns the notion of the Trinity (2.5.3). Bessarion is quite clear that neither Plato nor Aristotle, nor indeed any of the pagans, spoke of the Trinity in the way that Christians are able to, thanks to the divine revelation of the Scriptures. Purely human reason cannot attain to such truth; it is acquired by faith, not reason, and no one should praise Plato or Aristotle for having discussed the Trinity. In Plato he is willing to allow that there are some key concepts which can be thought of as constituting a trinity, but it is quite different from the Christian understanding of that term. Nevertheless, Bessarion hopes to show that Plato's doctrines are closer to Christianity than those of Aristotle (2.1). In stating this aim he makes it clear that he has no intention of trying to prove that Plato was a Christian. He was far too intelligent to wish to maintain that Plato's teaching on all subjects was correct, and he cites as features of Platonism which he cannot accept the pre-existence of the soul, the multiplicity of gods and the notion that the heavens and the heavenly bodies are possessed of souls (2.3.3). These are pagan doctrines which the church has condemned. The whole of his Book 4 is occupied by a rebuttal of charges made against Plato on moral grounds, such as that he practised or recommended homosexuality, and that in the *Republic* he put forward strange and unacceptable proposals about marriage. Some of these charges are difficult to dismiss, and it will be recalled that Bruni had been very shocked by the *Republic*. Bessarion argues that Plato has to be judged by the standards of his own time, when the advantages of certain Christian doctrines had not been tested by experience (4.3.1), and he also notes that the adventurous suggestions of the *Republic* are countermanded by the teachings of the *Laws* (4.3.9). Whether he was well advised to use this argument may be questioned, since he also has to answer the charge that Plato sympathised with tyranny, and on that matter some special pleading has to be employed if the evidence of the *Laws* is to be discounted. But George Trapezuntius did not have the skill to press that charge, which in modern times has assumed great importance.[9] Bessarion was able to argue that Plato was emphasising the advantages which can result from the government of an enlightened monarch (4.10). A curious minor feature of the defence of Plato's character is Bessarion's assertion that he was rarely seen to smile and never laughed (4.1.16). This is advanced as a proof of his modest and upright nature. The idea has precedents both in patristic and in pagan thought. The Greek and Latin fathers of the church had little use for laughter, Jerome being especially severe.[10] A pagan parallel can be found in Porphyry's portrayal of Pythagoras.[11] There were Christians who believed the same to be true of Jesus. St John Chrysostom in one of his homilies on Matthew asserts that Jesus never laughed or smiled, giving as his reason the fact that none of the evangelists ever says that he did.[12]

Although Bessarion's appendix is a devastating catalogue of the hundreds of errors committed by Trapezuntius in his version of the *Laws*, there is one other feature of his work which must be recorded. In a dedication to the Republic of Venice and in correspondence with the leading Venetian humanist Francesco Barbaro, Trapezuntius put forward the astonishing hypothesis that the founding fathers of Venice had used the *Laws* to good advantage, producing a mixed constitution with elements of monarchy, aristocracy and democracy. George may have known of such political concepts in other ancient writers; in the *Laws* he could have been struck by a passage in which Sparta is discussed in such terms (712de). Not unnaturally the Venetians were flattered by such thoughts, which were developed into a political dogma. It did not occur to anyone that there could not be the slightest foundation for George's assertion that at the time of the foundation of Venice there had been no lack of Italians able to read Greek.[13] Although Bessarion had ended Book 4 of his treatise with an attack on George's behaviour towards the Venetians (4.17.3-6), he was not concerned with the historical implausibility of the claim and limited himself to emphasising the inconsistency of George's attempt to use Plato to bolster the patriotic pride of Venetian intellectuals while at the same time composing a fierce attack on most of his doctrines.

We must now turn to consider other evidence of Bessarion's scholarly capacities. They were put to a severe test at the Council of Florence when he found himself dealing with dishonest colleagues. The pamphlet he wrote shortly after in justification of his position is a famous landmark in the development of scholarly method. At the Council there had been six copies of St Basil's treatise *Against Eunomius* in the possession of various members of the Greek delegation. Bessarion's position in the negotiations depended on one key passage, which turned out to be missing in one copy, that belonging to the patriarch, because, as Bessarion says, someone had mutilated the text, adding some words and removing others. On his return to Constantinople shortly after the Council he searched for other copies of the treatise and found that all those of recent date had been tampered with. He permits himself an exclamation of amazement and regret that men should falsify the truth. Two of the manuscripts that he came across during his search were in the library of the Soter Pantepoptes monastery, 'one on parchment and very old to judge from its appearance, but of what date I do not know because the year was not written in it', the other on paper and three hundred years old, as was easy to calculate from the colophon. In the parchment copy someone had erased the vital passage, but not completely, so that it was still half legible. In the paper copy ink had been poured over it, but later Cydones had restored the passage by writing the text afresh in the margin with an angry comment aimed at the forger. Bessarion remarks that no westerner could have concocted a passage of such excellent Greek; so there could be no question of trying to claim that it had been introduced by an upholder of the Roman church's doctrine.[14] This episode scarcely entitles us to claim Bessarion as the first palaeographer, but he is admirable for his common sense and devotion to the truth.

A more elaborate demonstration of scholarly principles in the service of truth is provided by another famous pamphlet, which arose out of a reading of St John's Gospel in his house in Rome. At 21:22 there was a dispute as to the correct reading; was the Vulgate right to give *sic eum volo manere*? The Greek had ἐάν, implying that *si* should have been Jerome's rendering. The question generated a great deal of heat, and Bessarion's essay is a reply to one by George Trapezuntius.[15] One infers that according to the conservative critics of the time it was not legitimate to alter as much as an iota or an accent in any text of scripture. In such circles it was held that *sic* was the reading of Jerome, Augustine and other early church fathers, and that the Greek conjunction was used in assertions as well as in conditional clauses. Bessarion gives a convincing refutation of these views. His view is that Jerome made no mistake, but that the text was corrupted by sleepy copyists – the epithet is employed more than once – and that many mistakes involving a single letter can easily be made. He emphasises that Jerome himself found a variety of readings in the manuscripts that he had before him and so was forced to make a choice between readings. He is able to cite an interesting parallel from the middle ages, the work of Nicholas Maniacutia, who was alert to the existence of the Hebrew of the Old Testament and had complained of the same kind of variety among the manuscripts as Jerome.[16] Then Augustine is quoted for the view that one must go back to the original source and if there is doubt the Greek is to be preferred to the Latin text. A number of other instances of error in the Vulgate are cited; Bessarion had clearly looked into the matter in some detail, and one is left in no doubt that he could have written the same kind of work on the subject as Valla. He notes that the Greek conjunction ἐάν is proved to be the ancient reading by the exegesis of the passage given in the commentaries of such early fathers as Origen, Chrysostom and Cyril. One's only regret in reading Bessarion is that he lacked the inclination or perhaps the time to write a large systematic account of such problems.[17]

Bessarion's most famous monument is his library, which as far as Greek books were concerned had no rival during his lifetime except the papal collection. The explanation of its size is not that he suffered from bibliomania. It is rather that, as he tells us in a letter written after the fall of Constantinople, he was struck by the need to form as complete a collection of Greek literature as possible. This may have been intended to match Nicholas V's project for a Latin library. Venice was chosen to be its permanent home, logically enough, since this was the focal point of communications with the territories of the former Byzantine empire and had a Greek community. In 1468 the cardinal handed over the main part of his collection. The inventory lists 482 Greek volumes. Although there are naturally many duplicates it is a remarkable collection, containing a fair number of the most important manuscripts of classical authors. It was most unfortunate that the Venetian authorities failed for about half a century to honour their obligation to house the books in such a way as to permit easy consultation. Despite the efforts of his agents Bessarion did not succeed in finding many rare texts, and in general very little is known about the provenance of individual manuscripts. One report is that he acquired a good number of books from the monastery of San Nicola di Casole, just outside Otranto, which was later destroyed by the Turks during their brief invasion in 1480. The report may be true, but it has to be noted that the ex-libris of the monastery is not now visible in any of his manuscripts. There is also a story, depending partly on an autograph note by Constantine Lascaris, who taught in Messina, that Bessarion recovered from Otranto the text of two late Greek epic poems by Quintus Smyrnaeus and Colluthus. Again the story is likely enough, but one wonders why the Otranto codex did not find its way into Bessarion's collection. These texts were not a great addition to the stock of Greek literature.[18]

Whereas some of Bessarion's books are in mint condition, in others he made annotations, which have not all been examined closely by modern scholars. They may yet prove to contain valuable and interesting material, but it is perhaps significant that such material has not yet been brought to light, and at least provisionally a negative conclusion follows. Support for this point of view can be derived from the case of Simplicius' commentary on the Aristotelian *De caelo*. Bessarion's copy (Marc. gr. 491) provided a text full of errors and lacunae. He went through it painstakingly, using as a guide the medieval Latin version. Where there was a gap in the Greek he concocted his own reconstruction on the basis of the Latin. But it is evident that he did not always understand it correctly, and where he attempts to correct passages of the original Greek the results tend to be poor. The overall verdict on his perusal of the text cannot be flattering.[19]

It would be a lengthy and perhaps rewarding task to seek further evidence of Bessarion's scholarship by going through all his books and examining the notes and corrections he made. I will mention a few that may serve as evidence of his capacity.

In 1445 and the following year Bessarion made notes on the flyleaf of his copy of Theophrastus' botanical works (Marc. gr. 274). It appears that the exemplar from which it had been prepared lacked a title, so that proof of Theophrastus' authorship was desirable, given the existence of the pseudo-Aristotelian treatise on the same subject. Bessarion records that he found the necessary proof in Galen, who cited a passage from *Historia plantarum* 8.9.2. Galen gave a reference to Book 7 rather than Book 8, and Bessarion noted this fact, explaining that there must have been a faulty division of the text. His success in resolving this confusion implies either that he had a splendid memory, able to recall almost everything that he had read, or that, having once found the error in the reference, he exercised great patience in going through a large amount of the text until he found what he was looking for.[20]

The next instance is less flattering. It relates to the text of the *Crito*. The passage which caused difficulty to Bruni and later to Ficino (51d3-4) was not resolved by Bessarion. He did not know about the Athenian review of youths being admitted to the privileges of citizenship and tried to put the text right by changing δοκιμασθῇ to δοκιμάσῃ.[21] He read the *Republic* with some care and made adjustments to his copy (Marc. gr. 187) with varying success; there are half a dozen plausible suggestions and a fair number of others which seem less attractive.[22]

When reading the historians Herodotus, Thucydides and Xenophon (all in Marc. gr. 365) Bessarion did little more than add in the margins a word or phrase indicating the content of a passage. In Thucydides he counted the number of speeches in each book. When he came to Book 5 he included, rather oddly to our way of thinking, the statements made by the parties in the Melian Dialogue, and at the end of Book 8, again rather oddly, he fails to note the absence of speeches. The rhetorical aspect of Thucydides was clearly important to him, as to other Byzantine scholars. On the much quoted antithesis (2.40.3) 'ignorance brings

confidence, rational calculation leads to hesitation' he airs his unusual
learning by remarking that this is the source of the same remark in
Sallust.

In reading the biographies of the ancient philosophers by Diogenes
Laertius (Marc. gr. 394) his marginalia give the same general impression.
There is one small difference. In three passages where there appeared to
be difficulty in the text he made his own suggestion, prefaced with the
word 'perhaps'. In one passage (1.113) he was in fact misled by an
unfamiliar Doric dialect form and need not have attempted to make a
change. On the second occasion he proposed a perfectly reasonable
correction of some incoherent numerals (6.87). The third case was a faulty
syllogism (7.80), where he made a good attempt, not knowing that there
was a deeper fault in the context.

Bessarion possessed Eustathius' commentary on both the Homeric
poems. In his copy of the *Odyssey* commentary (Marc. gr. 460) he recorded
his opinion that it is Eustathius' autograph. While his view is shared by
modern scholars it is a pity that he did not expound his reasons. The
usual clue in such cases, if there is no signature, is the presence of
numerous alterations in the wording, of a kind which cannot be expected
from a copyist but appear typical of an author making improvements in
what he has written. The autograph of the *Iliad* commentary has
survived and can be recognised as autograph in this way, but it was not in
Bessarion's collection and is now in Florence (Laur. 59.2 & 3). The puzzle
still awaits a final explanation. Perhaps the Venice manuscript had a
signature on the original first leaf, one of a few now missing; if badly
damaged they might have been discarded. Perhaps there are (or were) a
few author's alterations in it which Bessarion spotted but which have not
been brought to light by modern scholarship. It is more hazardous to
suppose that Bessarion had seen the autographs now in Florence,
recognised them as such and observed the identity of the script in his own
book. Still greater credulity is required to accept the hypothesis that it
was known to have been bought in Salonica, where Eustathius had been
the archbishop, and was in addition known to have been not merely part
of his personal library but a transcript made for his own use.[23] With
regard to the *Iliad* Bessarion had to content himself with a fresh copy of
the archbishop's work, prepared by contemporary calligraphers. As the
text is much longer it filled two volumes (Marc. gr. 461 and 462), in the
first of which he noted that it contained an excellent exegesis of the first
nine books of the epic. It is perhaps a trifle surprising that he does not
comment on the inordinate length of the commentary, but the material is
without doubt valuable.

In contrast to the manuscripts that we have been considering some
others look as if they were never read. There is for instance a beautiful
copy, written on fine parchment by one of the most active of contemporary
copyists, George Tribizias. It contains Sophocles, the three plays of

Aeschylus read in the Byzantine curriculum, and several plays of Euripides (Marc. gr. 470). This luxury article gives the impression of never having been consulted by its owner or his wide circle of friends.[24] It follows that one should be cautious in making inferences about the significance of the library. Its excellence and range may tempt us to suppose that all potential applications of Greek studies were being followed up, if not by Bessarion personally, at least by learned men meeting in Rome under his aegis. Palaeographers are accustomed to assert that manuscripts are documents to be exploited as primary sources for the history of culture irrespective of the quality of the texts that they contain. The generalisation is true but should not be pressed too hard. It is not safe to infer from Bessarion's ownership of any given text that it must have been the subject of close study in his circle. A reference collection of this kind is bound to contain a number of works for future rather than immediate use. As examples one might cite various mathematical and scientific texts. It cannot be assumed that anyone in Bessarion's circle could use them in such a way as to advance significantly beyond the stage reached by the ancient authorities. Though the range of Greek texts being studied at the time of Bessarion's death was probably wider than it had been at the time of his arrival in Italy, several decades were to elapse before all branches of ancient knowledge could be exploited. When Theodore Gaza presented to the Pope his versions of works on botany and zoology he did so in such a way as to imply that this moment had not yet arrived.

Bessarion's wonderful collection is worth comparing with the curious library list put together by G. Zacchi (1425-1484), bishop of Osimo from 1460, who was a friend of Bessarion and had been his secretary. His inventory amounts to 570 items, of which nearly all are Greek, only those numbered from 527 onwards being Latin. There are many lost texts in the list, including such remarkable phenomena as 72 plays of Aeschylus, 53 of Sophocles, 60 of Euripides and 65 of Menander. If these entries are meant to represent single volumes they are absurd, as no ordinary codex could contain so many texts. One section of the inventory begins with an allegedly complete Polybius. That is one of the least incredible entries relating to lost texts. Items 278-302 are simply taken from the index of sources given by Pliny in Book 7 of his *Natural History*.

The whole inventory might be taken to be a forgery, but no obvious motive or likely victim of the deception can be suggested and the bishop was not a dealer. A curious fact is that a number of the books are described with a little detail such as being bound in the Greek style or having illuminations, the latter being implausibly suggested for the comedies of Aristophanes. The right explanation of the inventory is almost certainly that it is a joke, rather than that it represents some kind of ideal library.

But one can go further towards explaining it than its editor has done.

There is a note after item 252 indicating that some of the books are to be left in the bishop's residence, while the volumes of Chrysostom are to be sent with the remainder of the collection except for those volumes which are in the possession of Bessarion. Though the wording of the note is not entirely clear, it is probably intended as a humorous suggestion that certain volumes could only exist in a library such as that of the cardinal, if at all. And at two points in the document there are dates, 13 and 16 February 1468. The choice of year is not random. It was on 23 March 1468 that the Venetian senate was informed of the successful negotiations between Paolo Morosini and Bessarion for the acquisition of the latter's library. The bishop of Osimo knew what was going on and indulged in some good-humoured fun about the riches of his former patron's library, which was valued at about 15,000 ducats.[25]

The cardinal's influence was far-reaching. During his years in Bologna he intervened in the affairs of the university. The young humanist Niccolò Perotti was appointed at his suggestion. It can hardly be a coincidence that in the fifties we find in Bologna Andronicus Callistus, an intelligent man who can be identified as the copyist of numerous surviving manuscripts and of whom there will be more to say later.

In 1464 the university of Padua decided for the first time to appoint a professor of Greek, and it chose one of Bessarion's protégés, Demetrius Chalcondyles. His inaugural lecture acknowledges a debt of gratitude to his patron. In the same year we find the German mathematician Regiomontanus lecturing in Padua, and he tells us that Bessarion had sent him there.[26] Bessarion might easily have become instrumental in facilitating important new developments in astronomy and mathematics. He had invited Regiomontanus to Italy in 1461, wishing to obtain expert comment on Ptolemy's *Almagest*. Some of his notes on this text are preserved in one of Bessarion's manuscripts (Marc. gr. 526), and he advertised that he was seeking the advice of Theodore Gaza and Paolo Toscanelli in an attempt to eradicate the errors made by Trapezuntius in dealing with this admittedly difficult text.[27] In 1462 Regiomontanus made for his patron an astrolabe which is still preserved, and he dedicated to him an important work on trigonometry. He has some claim to be thought of as the founder of modern astronomy; he later established in Nürnberg an observatory, a printing-press and a workshop for scientific instruments. But for some reason he left Italy after only five years.[28]

Bessarion's influence was most powerfully felt in Rome. There he appears to have been the moving spirit of a circle which one of its members described as 'the Academy of Bessarion'. The remark came from Niccolò Perotti, by now bishop of Siponto, writing *c*. 1470-2, and it is not clear how long this description had been current. Among the names he lists are those of Theodore Gaza and Andronicus Callistus. Whether this society had meetings at regular intervals or a formal constitution may be a matter for doubt; but there is no need to be sceptical about the beneficial effects of the cardinal's company or the loss to intellectual and literary life on his death in 1472.[29]

9

Valla

The most important member of Bessarion's circle in Rome, though his membership of it was limited to two brief periods, was Lorenzo Valla (1407-1457). He was a prolific author of historical, philosophical and philological works, and is probably best known for his remarkable essay on the so-called Donation of Constantine, in which he unmasked as a forgery the text used to justify the Papacy's claims to temporal power. Not surprisingly there was some difficulty in arranging for him to return from Naples to Rome in 1448. The sceptical intelligence and historical understanding exhibited in the famous essay are visible in some of his other writings.

Since the early part of his career is not well documented his progress as a Greek scholar cannot be followed in detail. His master, Rinuccio da Castiglione, was not first-rate, and in later life, when confronted with the problems of understanding Thucydides, Valla made it clear that there would be little point in turning to him for help.[1] Yet in 1436 Valla was thought of as an expert in Greek, if we may trust the description of him in a letter by another humanist, Lapo da Castiglionchio. Already in 1434-5 when he was in Florence he had begun a translation of Demosthenes' speech *On the crown*, which he later revised. Since this speech had already been made available to the Italian public by Leonardo Bruni, Valla must have thought hard before duplicating the work of so distinguished a predecessor. In a preface which is extremely polite towards Bruni he explains that he wanted to give himself a really good test; he goes so far as to say that any other text would be child's play, an opinion which later experience forced him to revise. Translation as such seemed to hold out little promise of fame; all the credit rests with the original author. But he wanted to compete with Demosthenes, Cicero and Bruni, and he accepted the challenge of a literary exercise as Cicero had done. The Greek could not always be followed very closely, but the differences of Latin idiom had an advantage: they allowed some hope of improving on the original. In this respect Valla's outlook is analogous to that of a classical author contemplating the possibilities within his chosen genre. He observed that his own style differed from Bruni's; the terms he used mean literally 'military' and 'civilian', and perhaps he implies by this that Bruni seemed to be content with a faithful representation of the Greek, while his own aspirations were directed to showing what the Latin language could achieve.[2]

It may be that Valla's work on a version of the *Iliad* reaches back to the same period; according to an obviously malicious suggestion of his enemy Facius he set eyes on Niccoli's copy of the early version by Leonzio Pilato, made a few adjustments to it and passed it off as his own;[3] but even the slightest acquaintance with Pilato's work enables one to say that no minor revision would have made it fit for the refined literary sense of Valla, whose *Elegantiae* remained for decades the repertoire of good Latin. Valla himself reports that his *Iliad* had progressed as far as Book 4 by 1439 and Book 10 in 1441. In that year king Alfonso of Naples saw the first ten books, was much impressed, and urged Valla to continue. Valla replied that he needed a Greek dictionary, not so much in order to increase his pace of work but to allow him to polish and improve what he had written. The king wrote twice to Messina, where Valla told him there should be a suitable manuscript in the library of the monastery of the Santissimo Salvatore, asking that it be sent.[4] It is not known what the result of the request was, but Valla reached Book 16 in 1443, after which he appears to have given up a task which he found much more difficult than his version of Demosthenes.

Two more products of this kind belong to the year 1438. In the booty taken from a ship there turned out to be a text of 33 fables of Aesop, and Valla spent two days making a version of them. This information comes from his preface, which is brief and fails to explain why he undertook the task. One may speculate that as the fables had sometimes been used as a text in the Byzantine school curriculum and Latin versions had long played a similar role in western education, Valla's aim was to produce an improved version. It was not the first attempt to translate this collection; in 1422 the twelve-year-old Ermolao Barbaro, under the guidance of Guarino, had already anticipated Valla. But there was no reason for him to know that. The second product of 1438 is a version of Xenophon's *Cyropaedia* 1.1-4.15 (it is uncertain whether Valla ever took it any further). The subject matter being the education of a prince, Xenophon's book had an obvious relevance in the world of Renaissance politics, and the motive for Valla's version was to provide some advice on moral questions for the young prince Ferrante of Naples.[5]

In the middle period of his career we find Valla working under difficulties. A complaint of the lack of books in the kingdom of Naples occurs more than once, and on one occasion it is specifically Greek that he refers to,[6] presumably alluding to the absence of reference books rather than primary texts, although one cannot be sure. Sometimes he worked very fast; a version of St Basil's 19th Homily, *On the forty martyrs*, which occupies the equivalent of about ten modern printed pages in Migne's *Patrologia graeca*, was completed in a single evening. But speed did not always imply great confidence and at the end of 1443, speaking of his *Collatio Novi Testamenti*, he described his knowledge of Greek as modest. Diffidence was justified, as may be seen from his handling of a Greek inscription in Naples.[7] It is a dedication of a temple to the Dioscuri by Tiberius Julius Tarsus in conjunction with Pelagon, who is described as a freedman of Augustus. Valla's interpretation of the text is marred by two errors, one serious, the other less so, but nevertheless of interest for our purpose. He treats the dedication as the work of one man, Pelagon, whom he supposes to have been born in Tarsus, become a slave of Tiberius and then released. This howler is perhaps provoked by his second error, which is to render the Greek word meaning 'having contributed'[8] as *cum consummasset*, i.e. 'when he had made up the necessary sum', an intelligent but incorrect guess. However, it must be said that the Greek term in question is not a notably rare or difficult word and one is a little surprised to see Valla stumble here.[9]

A reconstruction of Valla's library of Greek texts is not possible. But one may note that he seems to have possessed part of a copy of the grammar book supposedly translated and adapted by Maximus Planudes from Donatus (Vat. gr. 1388, folios 80-93). It would make good sense for the author of the *Elegantiae* to own such a text, and probably any work associated with the name of a famous grammarian was eagerly examined at the time owing to the lack of good reference books.

In the same manuscript the adjacent text is Aristotle's *Poetics*, transcribed in the same hand, which happens to be that of Girard of Patras, the copyist resident at Mantua. It would be fascinating if one could infer that Valla also read the *Poetics*, since he gives the impression of quoting one of its famous remarks about the difference between history and poetry in the proem to his *Gesta Ferdinandi Regis*, and the source of his quotation would then be explained. In 1445 when he wrote his history the number of Italians who could read the *Poetics* was very limited indeed. But the mystery cannot be entirely clarified, since the proof that he owned one part of MS Vat. gr. 1388 consists of what appears to be the wrapping enclosing folios 80-93 with his name on the outside (now folio 79 recto), and as the manuscript is bound at present (with the other half of the wrapping now forming folio 94) there is no sign that any other part of it originally belonged together. The alternative is to suppose that he had hit upon a copy of the medieval version by William of Moerbeke; but that is not likely, since it seems to have been a very rare text, there being only two surviving copies.[10]

Yet another indication of the limitations to his knowledge comes from a letter of 1447,[11] of which the autograph is preserved. He was unable to spell correctly the Greek title of Terence's play *Heautontimoroumenos*, making two mistakes, of which one is venial, the other much less so. He evidently had difficulty with the common verb that forms the second element in the title and wrote Ἑαυτοντημερούμενος. Verification of the original shows that there can be no doubt about these two lapses, puzzling though they are.

In the light of these proofs that there were weak points in his command of Greek one is entitled to take seriously his own admission that in dealing with the speeches in Thucydides he needed help. A modern scholar, if he is candid, will make the same admission. We have already noted that he did not think his old tutor very likely to give him the required assistance, and in the same letter he rules out George Trapezuntius on the ground that he would probably be unwilling for reasons of personal animosity. That leaves no alternative but Bessarion, an interesting indication of the state of Greek studies in 1448. An undisputed case of beneficial contact with Bessarion is Valla's note on St John's Gospel 21:22 in his *Collatio Novi Testamenti* (846b), for we know from *Antidotum* 4 that Bessarion drew his attention to the textual problem, which he had not noticed himself. Bessarion, as has been mentioned already, wrote a pamphlet on the subject, which had arisen in the course of a discussion in Rome in 1448 or 1449. Whether in fact Bessarion gave any help with Thucydides remains dubious, for a reason which will shortly become clear.

Nicholas V's commission to translate Thucydides was an extremely severe test of Valla's abilities, as he himself confesses in a brief preface.[12] While the speeches were the hardest part of the task, the difficulties were not confined to them. All hope of producing a really good version disappeared when Bessarion left Rome to serve as papal legate in Bologna. Valla adds that he believed Bessarion responsible for suggesting his name to the pope. The impression left by the preface is that Valla wishes he had never been given this task.

With these facts in mind we may turn to the fascinating question of the merits of Valla's version, which editors of Thucydides are glad to acknowledge as the source of a number of readings either evidently correct or at least worthy of consideration. There appear to be 123 passages where Valla anticipates an emendation by a modern scholar. Was Valla relying on his own native wit to restore the text, or did he have the good fortune to possess an excellent manuscript that has since been lost? The question has been much debated, and the latest contributions appear to give an answer which is all but certain. Valla worked with a lost manuscript (known to editors by the symbol of the Greek letter xi), some readings of which passed into an extant manuscript (known as H, Paris gr. 1734). The evidence which tips the balance in favour of this conclusion comes from a small part of Book 5 chapter 47, where Thucydides gives us the text of the treaty between Athens and Argos, Mantinea and Elis in 420 BC. By a lucky chance an official copy of the treaty was discovered by archaeologists in Athens in 1876 near the theatre of Dionysus. In some details the text inscribed on the stone differs from that given by the manuscripts of Thucydides. Valla's version in several places follows the text of the inscription, not that of the manuscripts. Neither he nor any other Renaissance scholar can have had any knowledge of the inscription, and it is in the highest degree implausible to imagine that one of the other copies of the treaty at Argos or Olympia or Mantinea had been transcribed by an early traveller such as Ciriaco of Ancona and made available by *c.* 1450. That would be too much of a coincidence, even if one allows that Ciriaco saw inscriptions which are now lost and that not all his work has been published. The conclusion is inescapable. Valla's divergent text depends on his manuscript source unless it can be shown that specific difficulties in the context would have stimulated an intelligent reader to make changes. In 5.47.6 his two changes are both anticipations of proposals by Kirchhoff, and a reflective translator might have made them on his own initiative. But the same is not true of the two passages in the following section, where the text presented by all manuscripts known to us can be translated easily enough. One cannot believe that Valla would have felt impelled to make the two small alterations if they had not been in the copy he read. This in turn leads to the conclusion that all other readings peculiar to his version may derive from that same copy.[13]

Valla also translated Herodotus. Once again the commission came from Nicolas V, at the beginning of 1453. Modern editors have varied in their estimates of the importance of this work, but none has put it alongside his Thucydides. The only serious recent study of it comes to the conclusion that a number of passages once alleged to prove its derivation from an excellent lost manuscript demonstrate nothing of the kind. They are the result of the translator allowing himself a little freedom. His work is not free from errors. There are a few improvements of the text, none of them very notable and all easily attributable to the intelligent scholar that Valla undoubtedly was.[14] It is a pity to have to reject an attractive suggestion made recently about the Delphic oracle cited by Herodotus at 1.47.3. The hypothesis has been put forward that one feature of Valla's rendering implies that he knew of a variant reading in the text of the oracle, which could have been communicated to him by Ciriaco of Ancona. It seems much more likely, however, that Valla was trying to do justice to a very rare word found in all the manuscripts.[15]

Before making his translations of the Greek historians Valla had begun to use his knowledge to test the accuracy of the Vulgate version of the New Testament. Over a long period he made notes on individual passages, revising his remarks as his knowledge increased, so that there is a considerable difference between the two recensions that have been printed. Perhaps the most important feature is common to both, namely his use of the phrase *graeca veritas*, the implication of which was not lost on Erasmus, who used it in the title of his edition of the New Testament.[16] His discovery of the later redaction of the *Annotationes* in the abbey of Parc near Louvain led to its being printed in 1505. The enthusiastic preface will have done more to guarantee a wide circulation than the mere fact of printing what was probably an almost unknown book.[17]

It was an easy game to find fault with the Latin Bible, but Valla's notes display a depth of historical understanding that entitles him to be treated as a major figure in the development of textual scholarship. He visualised the hazards to which the text had been exposed. First the Greek had had to be translated, and some mistakes are identified as being due to that process. For instance on Matthew 20:15 (817ab), without being able to reconstruct the text exactly as it stands in modern editions, Valla makes the sound observation that the translator may have been misled by the similarity of some Greek letters, which creates the possibility of confusion between the equivalents of the Latin *si, an* and *aut*. After the translator had done his work the scribes played their part in preserving the text, not always well, and at Matthew 23:3 (818b) Valla explains an error which is now termed haplography as due to scribal carelessness. He is also capable of leaving open the question whether the translator or a later copyist is to blame (on Matthew 28:8) (823a). A further refinement is the distinction between a copyist and an interpolator, made in the note on John 10:29 (843b). The most famous of the notes is perhaps the one referred to earlier on John 21:22 (846b), where the mistaken *sic* for *si* is refuted by reference to the Greek ἐάν, and the value of Augustine as an authority, however great it admittedly might be in other matters, is contrasted unfavourably with that of the *graeca veritas*. As we have seen already, Bessarion had been able to use Augustine's authority to better effect, and it is strange that Valla does not follow him, especially as he elsewhere acknowledges that it was the cardinal who first urged him to take note of John 21:22.[18]

Another paragraph might have caused its author some notoriety if widely circulated. On Acts 17:34 (852b) he devoted some space to the identity of Dionysius the Areopagite and came to a sceptical conclusion about the authorship of the books which circulated under that name. The key point in his note is worth citing. 'Finally it is uncertain whether this Dionysius, whom neither the Latins nor the Greeks refer to, wrote anything. And not even Gregory indicates that the author of the books which circulate was an Areopagite. Some of the most learned Greeks of the present day reckon that the author of them was Apollinaris.' Gregory is Pope Gregory the Great, and the mention of him is elucidated by a remark in the encomium on Aquinas which he gave in 1457. Valla there says that he has not found the Areopagite quoted by anyone earlier than Gregory.[19] The reference to Apollinaris, a church father of the fourth century, allows us to infer that someone in his circle had looked at the commentaries on the Dionysian corpus and found a note suggesting that Apollinaris was the author. We cannot identify with certainty the learned reader who hit upon the note; but it will be seen later that there is a good chance it was Theodore Gaza. The note itself merely alludes to the idea in passing, dismissing it instantly as nonsense. Valla's source, whoever he was, was evidently provoked to reflect at more length on the subject.[20] Valla's own conclusion was that there must be more than one Dionysius in question. This logical and intelligent point of view was unfortunately not accepted, even in the best circles. We have already noted that Bessarion persisted in treating Dionysius as a genuine author, and we shall find that Pope Nicholas V wished to do the same. It is hardly surprising that others continued to follow suit. One of the leading figures of the early sixteenth century, Giles of Viterbo, could still describe Dionysius as the greatest luminary of Greek theology.[21]

It is worth mentioning one very curious omission in Valla's work on the New Testament. He appears not to have commented on I John 5:7-8, the so-called *comma Johanneum* which later involved Erasmus in a tiresome controversy. The Vulgate has an additional passage which was used in the Middle Ages as the best support in Scripture for the doctrine of the Trinity. Valla has nothing to say about it, and yet is is very difficult to imagine that he did not notice its absence from the Greek manuscripts he had at his disposal (there are in fact only four Greek manuscripts now extant in which the words in question are found, and it is virtually certain that when Valla wrote there were none). Can he have been inhibited on this one occasion from raising a question about one of the most fundamental doctrines of the church?[22]

Valla's command of Greek certainly allowed and perhaps encouraged him to be critical of previous exegetes who had been less well equipped than himself from a linguistic point of view. He saw that St Augustine could flounder for this reason and he was critical of Thomas Aquinas.[23] The criticism of Thomas occurs in the *Annotationes* on I Corinthians 9; it is not found in the earlier *Collatio*, and naturally enough it is not allowed to surface in the encomium of Aquinas pronounced by Valla in the Dominican church of Santa Maria sopra Minerva a few months before his death in 1457, even if one senses from some remarks about the Greek and Latin traditions in theology that it may have been in the back of his mind. Although Valla was not temperamentally much inclined to admire the middle ages, he might have been impressed by the work of two men if he had come across it, Nicholas of Lyra (d. 1349), who used Hebrew sources to good effect in interpreting the Old Testament, and Nicholas Maniacutia (d. *c*. 1150). The latter, a deacon of San Lorenzo in Damaso, took advice from a learned Jew and shows that he had a considerable grasp of the scholarly techniques required of an interpreter. We have no proof that Valla was acquainted with his writings, but it is curious that some of them are preserved in the same codex as Valla's own *Annotationes* (Brussels 4031-3), and while that may be coincidence pure and simple, it is possible to imagine Valla making up a volume containing some works of his predecessor together with a master copy of his own studies. And it is clear that Bessarion knew and appreciated the work of

Maniacutia, since there are two favourable references to him in the pamphlet on John 21:22, in one of which he invites the interested reader to consult Maniacutia's book for more details.[24] Valla does not appear to acknowledge any debt to his Roman predecessor, and no doubt it is legitimate to point out in his defence that by the time Maniacutia's work was drawn to his attention he had developed independently his own critical procedures.[25] And when all due allowance is made for what he may have learned from Maniacutia, Valla's display of technique and historical understanding in manipulating the concepts of translator, scribe and interpolator in the transmission of the biblical text is to be seen as a landmark in intellectual history.[26]

One cannot claim that the task of translating Thucydides sharpened Valla's sense of historical accuracy and led him to make his brilliant observations about the Donation of Constantine. This pleasing sequence of cause and effect is excluded by chronological facts.[27] Nor can it safely be maintained that Valla's entry into the field of biblical criticism was due to the influence of Greek intellectuals living in Italy. Here it is not simply a question of chronology, for the Byzantines, despite the example of Photius, had not had a tradition of textual criticism of the New Testament. Valla's interest arose from his concern with the niceties of Latin idiom, the results of which he codified in the *Elegantiae*, a reference book of astonishing popularity (it was printed 59 times between 1471 and 1536). On the other hand it would be wrong to deny that in the later stages of his career his membership of Bessarion's circle bore fruit.[28]

10

Rome under Nicholas V and his successors

The presence of Bessarion and Valla in Rome created a centre for intellectual life. Yet it would be wrong to give them all the credit. They owed much to the cultivated humanist Tommaso Parentucelli, who became Pope Nicholas V in 1448 and was a patron of scholars. One of his ambitions was to set up a library with a complete collection of works in Latin. He intended that it should include a large number of Greek texts in translation. Theodore Gaza, who gives us this information in the dedication of his version of Theophrastus' botanical works, says that one may hope for almost all Greek literature to be available in this form before long. Though his words may be coloured by optimism or flattery they are another good indication of the rarity of a working knowledge of the Greek language. Nicholas can certainly take credit for having achieved a good deal by commissions to Gaza and other humanists. It was also extremely fortunate that one of his successors, Pius II, who held office from 1458 to 1464, had similar interests at heart. Although not all the pontiffs were equally enthusiastic, a certain tradition of Greek learning can be traced in Rome during the second half of the fifteenth century.

In Nicholas' reign the chief Hellenists apart from Valla and Bessarion, who was away for much of the time in Bologna, were George Trapezuntius and Theodore Gaza. Trapezuntius is a cantankerous and unattractive figure, who had a notorious brush with the most famous member of the Curia, Poggio Bracciolini, in which they came to blows. He gradually alienated his patrons and protectors. Both he and Gaza had long careers, which took them to many Italian cities. Their paths crossed in Rome when each was at an important stage in his career.[1]

Trapezuntius was a prolific author of translations and had taught in Venice, Vicenza and Mantua before entering the papal bureaucracy under Eugenius IV. Under Nicholas V he was teaching in Rome. His strongly held and often incorrect beliefs about historical facts and points of scholarship do not create a favourable impression. The description of Valla as a thoroughly ignorant man (*hominem penitus indoctum*) immediately alienates sympathy.[2] And it was stupid of him to claim, contrary to existing tradition, that Ptolemy the astronomer and other bearers of the name were descendants of the Alexandrian royal house.[3] His translation of the *Almagest* soon came under heavy fire from Jacopo Cassiano of Cremona, who had made a version of Archimedes for Nicholas V. His command of Roman history was no better. He supposed that Pliny the Younger's famous letter about the Christians was written from Spain to the emperor Vespasian, whereas it must have been common knowledge that it was sent to Trajan from Bithynia.[4] We have already seen that he had odd views about the persistence of a knowledge of his native language in Italy after the fall of the Roman Empire.[5] On the other hand some of his opinions on rhetorical questions are less objectionable. He recommends the writer of Latin prose to observe the rules governing the rhythm of clausulae, that is to say to follow certain metrical patterns in the final syllables of clauses and periods; but it has to be admitted that his description of them leaves one with the impression that he did not have the slightest idea of what the correct patterns were.[6] He also implies that he could detect clausulae or rhythm in prose (his meaning is not entirely clear) in Greek writers such as Plato, Isocrates and Aristotle.[7] When making his own version of Demosthenes' *De corona* he went so far as to claim that he followed the original in its clausulae, rhythm and structure, a bold and doubtless much exaggerated claim.[8] But one must note with approval a rare demonstration of common sense in one of his remarks about the art of rhetoric: he felt that it was more a matter of practice than a subject capable of being codified.[9] Much time and effort would have been saved if more people had agreed with him. And in matters of Greek he was not wholly out of his depth. It was reasonable to note that Albertus Magnus and Thomas Aquinas might have written better if they had had more elegant versions of Aristotle to work from.[10] An episode from his controversy with Guarino raises a point which is of interest even if his position was coloured by prejudice. He alleges that Guarino thought Greek poets used great poetic licence, altering any word in order to suit the metre they were writing in. George replied that licences were the legitimate result of having more than one dialect available for use in literary composition, which is indeed partially correct. Equally one has to be sympathetic to the predicament of any humanist trying to cope with the scansion of a Homeric hexameter.[11]

When it came to the rendering of philosophical texts Trapezuntius was heavily criticised by Bessarion as we have seen,[12] and Gaza took an equally unflattering view of his efforts. But it is worth noting that so acute a judge as Politian gives a much less damning verdict. He found that though Gaza had been very hard on his rival he had not scrupled to make extensive use of his work, while Erasmus, writing about two generations later, was aware that Gaza made adjustments to his own versions in response to adverse comment from Trapezuntius. Modern scholars have uncovered a small amount of additional evidence which suggests that whatever the faults of Trapezuntius' versions he occasionally had some bright ideas.[13]

After Gaza's arrival in Rome in 1449 the two men were soon on bad terms, and Trapezuntius reports an occasion when Gaza attended one of his lectures and created a scene by interrupting. An academic quarrel followed, with Valla joining in on Gaza's side, and Trapezuntius was gradually excluded from intellectual circles.

Gaza has already been mentioned in connection with Vittorino's school. He spent the years 1442-6 in Mantua, where he evidently learned Latin to a very high standard. Then he moved to Ferrara for a few years, and received the honour of being nominated rector of the university. The authors he lectured on included Demosthenes.[14] Some of his addresses from that period are extant.[15] One, on the merits of Greek as an academic subject, shows that he felt the need to reply to the criticism that it is extremely difficult. He makes a complimentary reference to Vittorino, Aurispa and Guarino for their services to the cause. His main claim in favour of the subject seems to be that Greek helps in an understanding of Latin literature, and he emphasises that the ancient Romans took pains to be well versed in Greek. But it is not without significance that he urges upon his audience the advantages of reading Aristotle in the original, since the text is then freed from obscurity and asperity of style.

It was probably in Rome that Gaza did his best work. In general he has enjoyed a good reputation, subject to occasional expressions of dissent. Although it is quite often necessary when writing the history of scholarship to mention the deficiencies of even the most gifted men of past periods, one can at least note with pleasure that Gaza has recently been cited for having understood better than one of his modern counterparts an idiom which he met in Aristotle's *Problems* and which he had no doubt seen quite frequently in other Hellenistic or later writers.[16] Another modern investigation has revealed that when he came to transcribe the minor works of Theophrastus (Ottob. gr. 153) he was able to make several corrections anticipating the good work of the later French scholar Turnebus.[17] It may in addition be worth noting one other work, which dates from 1470, an essay on the calendar of ancient Athens.[18] The names of the months, their length, and the Athenian method of indicating dates, are topics which certainly need an explanation, particularly if a student wishes to examine historical texts in any detail. Gaza put together useful information derived from a variety of sources. He is quite emphatic about the matters which can easily cause confusion for those used to the Roman or modern calendars: the Athenian year began with the month of Hecatombaion at the time of the summer solstice, and each day was regarded as beginning at sunset, not midnight.

The letter which Gaza wrote to Nicholas V to accompany his version of the zoological treatises is revealing. Though he does not complain, one can see that he had not found his work easy. It had been necessary to read many Latin authors in order to find all the necessary technical terms.[19]

The Greek text itself was not in good order, partly through the fault of the scribes who did not understand what they were transcribing, partly because of the history of the text reported by the geographer Strabo. Here Gaza alludes to a famous story, according to which the Aristotelian writings intended for the philosopher's own pupils, as opposed to those aimed at a wider public, had been out of circulation for a long time, stored in a cellar, and when they were recovered the text was no longer in perfect condition.[20] As a consequence the translator found himself obliged to make corrections to the text. If he simply made a version of what he had in front of him, there would be many unsatisfactory passages and he would be blamed as if he had made the mistakes himself. One major change that Gaza made was to transpose Book 9 so that it became Book 7. Then, in accordance with Aristotle's stated programme, the account of human reproduction would follow immediately on that describing other animals. On this point Gaza has been followed by subsequent students of the problem.

Another interesting aspect of his remarks is the series of reasons which he offers for reading this part of the Aristotelian corpus. Great emphasis is laid on the moral virtues which can be exemplified from the behaviour of various members of the animal kingdom. The reader will also be led to admire the workings of nature and its creator. The philosopher will gain a better understanding of the working of the various types of causation. Those who have to speak in public can benefit by exploiting amusing facts or analogies taken from the animal world. But one proposition which a modern reader might reasonably expect to find in a writer of this date is missing. It is not suggested that Aristotle should serve as a stimulus to further research of the same kind.

The preface to Gaza's Theophrastus is similar. While claiming to be very happy to serve the Pope in any way possible he makes it clear that he felt out of his depth. It was very difficult to find the right vocabulary in Latin for the wide range of botanical terms needed. His task was made still harder by the condition of the only manuscript he could find. The text was so disfigured by scribal error and other damage that in some passages he was forced to abbreviate. Yet elsewhere he managed to introduce some improvements; it is uncertain whether these are due to his own skill in conjecture or to a lost manuscript of superior quality. His handling of other works by Theophrastus already mentioned does not rule out the first explanation.[21] He says that he has done his best to produce a version in tolerable Latin, adding that he does not want to sink to the level of his medieval predecessor William of Moerbeke. But the most striking feature of the preface consists of an omission: he makes no mention whatever of any reason why one should wish to read Theophrastus. An explanation is not hard to find. Whereas doctors would have welcomed a pharmacological collection such as that of Dioscorides, Gaza was offering the public a scientific text, and one may suspect that there were few if any scientists ready to exploit it.

His remark about stylistic levels raises a question, since it left him open to the charge made by Trapezuntius, that he was making the style of technical matters too elegant and so distorting the meaning of the original. The complaint was made about his handling of Aristotle.[22] It is not easily reconciled with Politian's observation that Gaza was critical of his predecessor despite following him closely.

Another commission was for the Aristotelian *Problems*, followed a year later by a request for the similar work that was ascribed to the commentator Alexander of Aphrodisias. Gaza respected Alexander as a serious scholar and did not think the text was of the standard to be expected from him. The point is not of much importance in itself, but it is worth pausing for a moment to look at the way he introduces the topic. The dedication begins:

Num aegre interim feras, pater sanctissime, si ego falsam deprehendam libri descriptionem, an libros tantum illos de hierarchia auctoris esse Dionysii Atheniensis viri doctissimi velis, nequid religioni derogetur, cetera autem sint necne quorum volumina esse inscribuntur, parum referre censeas, modo fructus ex his aliquis capiatur; equidem ita censere te arbitror.

You are not likely to feel occasional annoyance, Holy Father, if I discover that a book is falsely ascribed. You would only insist, in the interests of the faith, that those famous books on hierarchy are by Dionysius the Athenian, a man of great learning, whereas with all other works you think it of little importance whether or not they are by the authors named in the title, provided that there is some benefit to be had from them. Such at any rate is my understanding of your view.

From this we may infer that the Pope had had his attention drawn to the question of the authenticity of the Dionysian corpus and had decided that the usual view must be maintained for the reason indicated. It does not follow that Gaza himself initiated the sceptical discussions, though it is possible.[23]

Nicholas' concern for what he believed to be the correct evaluation of a Greek patristic text serves to remind us that for all his humanistic interests both he and his successors up to and including Sixtus IV (1471-84) attached importance to this part of the Greek heritage.[24] For many years Nicholas had been aware of the issues raised by the negotiations with the Greek church. He had attended the Council of Florence and had given encouragement to Traversari's studies of Dionysius.[25] His patronage continued. He sent to Constantinople for a copy of Origen's defence of Christianity, *Against Celsus*, intending that Gaza should make a version of it, but the task was not undertaken for more than a decade. Gaza was too busy and merely wrote a preface for the version when it was eventually produced by Cristoforo Persona. On the other hand Trapezuntius made a number of versions of patristic texts, concentrating on the Cappadocian fathers of the fourth century and John Chrysostom, but including also some works by Cyril of Alexandria and Eusebius, whose *Praeparatio Evangelica* contained much material for anyone willing to think about the similarities and differences between Greek philosophy and the Christian faith. That such comparisons were in the air at the time is clear enough, and one result was that the young Niccolò Perotti, who enjoyed the patronage of the Pope and of Bessarion, made a version of Plutarch's essay on envy together with one on the same subject by St Basil. It is a pity that the brief letters of dedication to Nicholas do not reveal any profound thoughts on the value of studying pagan moralists.[26] A number of other scholars working under Nicholas V and his successors are known to have translated patristic texts. By no means all the versions have been examined closely, and it would be rash to pass judgment on the competence of their authors, but they no doubt served their purpose fairly well. Although literature of this kind must have been appreciated chiefly for its spiritual guidance and in some cases for its philosophical implications, from time to time its influence extended to more practical matters. At St John 21:15 Jesus says to Peter: 'Be the shepherd of my flock.' In the exegesis of the Greek fathers this instruction was understood as a command to Peter alone, and defenders of the temporal power of the church were not slow to realise that the text could be used to justify Peter's successors in their claims to authority. John Chrysostom and Cyril of Alexandria were cited for this purpose.[27] The Jewish author Philo was useful in a rather different way. The powers claimed for the papacy were found to have a convenient precedent in one of his essays, in which Moses was described as combining the functions of ruler, priest and lawgiver. This was treated as a prefiguration of the position of the Pope.[28]

Since the Greek fathers now attracted their fair share of attention, it is natural to ask whether thoughtful members of the church saw it as a logical consequence that they should acquaint themselves with the original text of the fundamental document of their creed. Even if Valla did not succeed in publicising his work on the New Testament, and perhaps had not made great efforts to do so, the mere fact that disputed passages could be discussed in Bessarion's circle and lead to an excellent treatment by him means that there must have been some appreciation of the value of consulting primary sources. But such awareness was very limited and there is only one tangible proof of it. For a short time Valla had as a colleague in the curia a remarkable Florentine, Giannozzo Manetti (1396-1459), a merchant who at the age of twenty-five began to take a strong interest in scholarly matters and in middle age became an important member of his country's ruling elite. He is also the prototype of the later ideal of the *homo trilinguis*, the man competent both in the

languages of pagan antiquity and in Hebrew. Manetti himself may well
have taken St Jerome as his model, since he speaks of him as a man of
great learning and highly skilled in the three most important
languages.[29]

As a Florentine he came under the influence of Bruni and Traversari.
His remarks on the art of translation prove that he had read Bruni's
essay on the subject, and he refers to Traversari and Bessarion as experts
in the art. Having become estranged from the Medici, Manetti spent the
years 1453-5 in Rome and there he made a new version of the Psalter
from the Hebrew. Within a year he found himself under attack, and we
have the defence he wrote, a good deal of which consists of a list of textual
variants somewhat in the style of Valla's observations on the New
Testament. He also gives an account of the origin of the Septuagint,
quoting at length from Eusebius, *Praeparatio Evangelica* Book 8. He
questions the accuracy of the story given there, referring to Jerome and
Augustine as better informants. Rather oddly he thinks that Eusebius
derived his notions from a tradition that was current about the text of the
Homeric poems, which were supposedly put together under the auspices
of the Athenian tyrant Pisistratus in the sixth century BC.[30]

On the death of Nicholas V he moved to Naples and worked on a fresh
Latin version of the New Testament, which is extant in two copies (Pal.
lat. 45 and Urb. lat. 6). It is extraordinary to have to report that even now
this work remains largely unknown.[31]

Several of the scholars resident in Rome at this time devoted their
energies both to classical and to patristic texts. Argyropoulos, who spent
most of his career in Florence as an Aristotelian scholar, came to Rome in
1471 for six years and returned in 1481 to finish his life there. While in
Rome he made a version of St Basil's *Commentary on the Hexaemeron*.
Curiously enough this work had been turned into Latin in late antiquity,
and one wonders why it should have figured high on any list of
desiderata. But the contents were of some importance, as Basil provided a
lengthy discussion of the biblical account of creation and rejected pagan
views about the origin of the universe. Persona, the translator of Origen,
who was appointed prefect of the Vatican Library in 1484, produced
versions of some other patristic writings, but did not confine himself to
this class of literature. He also found time to make versions of the two
most important early Byzantine historians, Procopius and Agathias.
Both authors are valuable, since they give a contemporary and in part
eye-witness account of Justinian's recovery of Italy from the Goths in the
middle of the sixth century. The exploits of Belisarius and Narses were
not entirely unknown to the educated public, since Bruni had
paraphrased Procopius when writing about early Italian history, but
Persona's version allowed readers to study the primary sources in more
detail.[32]

Yet another versatile scholar employed in the papal administration was Niccolò Perotti, who has already been mentioned briefly.[33] He had been a pupil both of Vittorino in Mantua and of Guarino in Ferrara before moving to Rome. There he was soon in touch with Bessarion, who installed him in a post in the university of Bologna. His principal claim to a place in the history of scholarship derives from his work as a Latinist, and in particular from his discovery of some otherwise unknown Latin fables. In Greek his main work was a version of another of the major sources used by Bruni for his history of Italy, the first five books of the Hellenistic historian Polybius, which deal with the First Punic War and much of the Second. The Perotti version seems to have been found useful, since it was printed fourteen times before being superseded by Casaubon's in 1609. The full list of his works as a translator amounts to ten items. They include a famous text of Stoic philosophy, Epictetus' *Enchiridion*, soon to be translated again by no less a figure than Politian. Perotti sometimes records his feelings about a text, as in the case of Plutarch's essay *De fortuna Romanorum*, which he translated for Nicholas V. He almost failed to complete this task, being much provoked by Plutarch's unexpected prejudice against the Romans, whose success is ascribed to fortune rather than to their solid merits. He came to the conclusion, after consulting Bessarion, that Plutarch must have left the essay unfinished, and modern scholars concur in recognising that the essay as we have it is a sophistical exercise in which only one side of an argument is put forward. Perotti was quite justified in thinking that the fair and balanced views which he expected of Plutarch required a statement of the other side of the case, namely that the achievements of the Romans were due to the practice of virtues commonly associated with them.[34]

Two other items in the list are much further from the beaten track. They are both monodies, laments in prose by prolific literati of the later Roman empire. One is by Aristides, and deals with the fate of the city of Smyrna when it was struck by an earthquake, the other is Libanius' composition on the death of the emperor Julian. The first of these events was not of outstanding importance, and though the figure of the apostate has been capable of stimulating curiosity in many different ages, Perotti's choice may still be thought to require some explanation. Fortunately he provides it for us in a letter to another member of the staff of the Curia.[35] Evidently he had been given the run of Bessarion's library and in it he found a volume containing some of his patron's own writings (Marc. gr. 533). Among them was an exercise in the genre in question, composed for the death of the emperor Manuel Palaeologus in 1425. Perotti read it and was impressed by the genre and the quality of this specimen. He looked for other examples and found them in the oeuvre of post-classical writers. He professes – and here one does not know how much allowance to make for flattery or the enthusiasm of personal friendship – to prefer Bessarion's work to the other two. Despite this verdict he made a version of all three, and he tells us that it took him four days.

The same letter is valuable for other information that it offers about Bessarion. It can be dated to the last year of his life, and reveals that he was still extremely active. He was giving help to scholars in other cities in Italy; Perugia, Siena, Florence and Bologna are named, but the individual beneficiaries are not. In Rome itself his circle of acquaintances is described as a workshop of philosophy (*philosophiae officina*); it will be recalled that elsewhere Perotti dignifies it with the title of academy. And the wide influence exercised by the cardinal is suggested by the fact here reported about the print-run of his *In calumniatorem Platonis*: it is said to have been published in an edition of one thousand copies, a figure that allows favourable comparison with many specialised monographs published in modern times.

A few other facts may be added in order to fill out the picture of Greek studies in Rome. During his two spells away from Florence Argyropoulos seems to have inspired interest in some prose texts that fall outside his usual range of philosophy and theology. He lectured on Thucydides, and though one is tempted to assume that this author must have been one of the most closely and frequently studied despite his awkward style, it is legitimate to ask whether Valla's version may not have been vastly more popular and accessible than the original. Argyropoulos' audience included the German Reuchlin, and we find another German studying with him. Jacob Questenberg of Freiburg, who in 1490 was a papal official, made two transcripts of Athenaeus' *Deipnosophistae* in the epitome version, and it can be shown that one of the two was made for Reuchlin, who originally intended to give it to the bishop of Worms but retained it in his own library (Würzburg, Univ. M. p. gr. f. 1). The *Deipnosophistae* is a strange compilation of mainly antiquarian interest, which modern scholars find of great value for its numerous quotations, mostly all too brief, from lost authors of ancient comedy which inter alia throw a good deal of light on food and drink in ancient Greece. But scholarship had not yet reached the point where it was seen to be useful to collect the fragments of such lost authors. What a papal official, even one serving at the notoriously hedonistic court of the Borgia Pope Alexander VI, can have found to exploit in the abbreviated form of this often obscure text must remain a difficult question; one presumes that the second copy (Laur. 60.2) was also destined for a learned patron.[36]

Enthusiasm for Greek culture in the establishments of prelates and dignitaries of the time can be traced in contemporary sources. One of the cardinals nominated by Pope Paul II (1464-71) was reputed to maintain such an extraordinarily literate household that even the kitchen staff were given lectures on Aristotle's *Ethics*.[37] Less bizarre is the story of a feast given by the Venetian envoy Francesco Diedo on the day of Epiphany 1482. During dinner and after there were rhetorical displays in which speakers took it in turn to praise various arts such as music, oratory, poetry and skill in military affairs. Some recitations were given in Greek, and there were plays modelled so closely on classical drama that they seemed hardly different from the originals. At first sight it might appear that our source is referring to a performance of a Greek drama, but a close look at his account leads me to think that the dramatic productions are to be taken as a separate element in the list of entertainments, and a performance of a Greek play would have been an event of such rarity that one would expect it to be singled out for greater emphasis than it actually receives. So the Greek element in the entertainment was in all likelihood no more than a series of readings.[38]

11

Florence in the second half of the century

(i) Argyropoulos

From the mid-fifties the Florentine chair was held once again by a Byzantine scholar. Since the departure of Filelfo there had been a hiatus in the formal provision for the subject. In 1440-2 it was partly filled by the hiring of George Trapezuntius to teach *poesia*.[1] After the death of Bruni, Marsuppini was given the post of chancellor and did not have any formal teaching duties again until 1451, when he was appointed to a chair of Latin and Greek; but he survived only two years. In 1456 the situation changed with the appointment of John Argyropoulos, a refugee then aged at least forty.[2] He had first come to Italy for the Council of Florence and returned shortly after for a second visit, spending the years 1441-4 in Padua. There he was supported by the Florentine exile Palla Strozzi along with another highly talented refugee, Andronicus Callistus. One of the products of those years is a copy of the Aristotelian commentator Simplicius written for Palla by Argyropoulos (Paris gr. 1908). A colophon added by Andronicus gives details.[3] This volume, which contains the commentary on Aristotle's *Physics*, will also have given Palla a good deal of information about the Presocratics and other ancient philosophers. A few other manuscripts can be identified as Argyropoulos' work, but they lack the informative colophon which would tell us whether they were produced for Palla or at a later date.[4]

Neither of the two exiles appears to have obtained a position in Padua, even though Argyropoulos is listed in the records of the university as having taken a degree. He went back to Constantinople, where he is found teaching from 1448 until the city passed into the hands of the Turks. The details of his next few years are not clear, but once established in Florence he remained until 1471, and then after six years in Rome he came back again and stayed for another short period.

One modern authority has claimed that he was notable for his advocacy of the pagan doctrines of Plethon, but the notion seems to have little if any basis.[5] The evidence about his teaching suggests that his main concern was with Aristotle. It is clear that his courses were much appreciated and his audience included the young Lorenzo de' Medici. The foreign professor became a leading figure in the recently formed

Accademia Fiorentina, a club founded in 1454 with the object of holding daily meetings in the home of Alamanno Rinuccini (1426-99), yet another of the numerous humanists who translated some of Plutarch's writings (he later undertook the much more unusual task of making a version of Philostratus' *Life of Apollonius of Tyana*). Another sign of the cordial feelings aroused by Argyropoulos is that he was a regular guest at the house parties given twice a year by Franco Sacchetti, at which ten or a dozen intellectuals would discuss a variety of topics. And in 1466 Argyropoulos acquired Florentine citizenship. Despite this he spent the years from 1471 to 1477 and from 1481 until his death in 1487 in Rome; the reasons for his move are not entirely clear, but it has been suggested that a combination of bereavements and the election of Sixtus IV, whom he had known in his student days in Padua, may have induced him to seek a change of atmosphere.

The major part of his published work consists of translations. Among them is one patristic text, St Basil on the *Hexaemeron*; the others are Aristotelian, almost all dedicated to members of the Medici family. It is surprising that he saw fit to tackle the *Nicomachean Ethics*, since Bruni's version was in circulation and whatever criticism may have been made of it it can hardly have been regarded as a failure. The other texts are partly from the *Organon*, a fact which shows that medieval fashions in philosophy had not yet died; but he also produced versions of the *Physics*, *De caelo*, *De anima* and *Metaphysics*. There are signs in one of his prefaces that he did not share Bruni's views. In offering his work to Piero de' Medici he says that he could have translated some oratorical writings, but that this would not have been enough to demonstrate his gratitude to Piero nor a performance worthy of either of them. Philosophy is evidently a more serious subject than literature, and Argyropoulos will add just so much stylistic elegance to a literal rendering as is legitimate in the context. This statement has to be taken together with the opening sentence of the same text which runs: 'I have decided to make a more elegant translation of some treatises by Aristotle; for this will certainly be very welcome to Aristotle himself, if he is in a position to observe it. He will at last see himself appearing among the Latin races in the form in which he wished to appear among his fellow-countrymen.' Whether the two claims are coherent may reasonably be asked; but there seems little doubt that there is an undertone of polemic against unnamed predecessors. And we have independent evidence of such polemic from Filelfo, who wrote to him from Milan in November 1457 saying that his criticisms of Bruni were well known and causing some distress. Filelfo rather surprisingly praises Bruni to the extent of saying that no one in Italy has so far proved more valuable in his services to learning, an unusually warm estimate.[6]

Several introductory lectures have come down to us. They belong to the years 1457-62 and relate to the *Nicomachean Ethics* (Books I-VI), *Physics*

(Books I-III), *De anima* and *Meteorologica*. Argyropoulos dismisses doubts about the authorship of this last work by observing that the style and the manner in which the information is imparted are typical of the author, and that there are cross-references in other parts of the corpus. A somewhat scholastic approach to the texts is revealed in no less than three of the lectures, which contain what might nowadays be called a strategy for reading the text. It is laid down that there are eight questions to be asked about all texts, and this doctrine amounts to no more than a slight modification of a formula found in the Aristotelian commentators of late antiquity.[7] The questions are: the intention of the author in the work in question; the utility of it; the authorship; the title; its place in author's oeuvre; the sub-divisions within the work; what branch of philosophy it belongs to; the author's method of presentation.

Two incidental remarks are worth recording here. Argyropoulos says that he is aware of the existence of versions of Aristotle into various languages; one wonders if he had some inkling of the importance of Arabic versions that lay behind some Latin texts in circulation. And he concludes a lecture given in 1456 with an unexpectedly cordial reference to Bruni: 'Let us pass on to our commentary on and exposition of moral philosophy, which our friend Leonardo turned into Latin most elegantly and intelligently. To him are due our warmest thanks for performing a task worthy of Aristotle and the Latin language, useful to us and all speakers of Latin.' This may imply that he was lecturing on the Latin, or at least lecturing to a class many of whose members had only the Latin in front of them.[8] Two testimonies to the competence of his teaching are available. As we have already noticed in connection with Bruni the rendering of technical terms was liable to provoke discussion, and in one case a judge as capable as cardinal Bessarion preferred Argyropoulos' solution to Bruni's.[9] Another learned and intelligent judge was his pupil Politian, who was prepared to take seriously Argyropoulos' comments on Cicero's discussion of *entelecheia* at *Tusculans* 1.22, since they were supported by citations from suitably chosen ancient texts.[10] On the other hand we must hope that he did not often fall into such serious error as the belief that Aristotle had taken lessons with Socrates.[11]

The sketch given in the preceding paragraphs conjures up the vision of a scholar whose competence did not extend beyond his favourite author. It is easy to understand how a Byzantine with a philosophical cast of mind might limit his teaching in this way, since the study of Plato for any but literary reasons was not regularly undertaken in Byzantium. There are in fact occasional signs of wider horizons. During his Roman period he is reported to have given public lectures on Thucydides in the Vatican, our source being the famous German pioneer of Hebrew studies, Reuchlin. While in Florence Argyropoulos is said to have read Sophocles in Greek; one would very much like to know more about this. Perhaps he made a practice of reading a variety of authors unofficially with friends at home, for on one occasion he was found there on Sunday expounding Plato's *Meno*. His knowledge of Plato must have been at least fair. When Bessarion produced his *In calumniatorem Platonis*, a reply to George Trapezuntius, he sent a copy both to Marsilio Ficino and to Argyropoulos. The latter replied with a warm letter of thanks and appreciation of Bessarion's services in rescuing Plato from unfair criticism, and soon after composed a rejoinder to part of Bessarion's introductory matter. This rejoinder is lost, but we know that Bessarion arranged for Theodore Gaza to answer it. Before sending this answer to Argyropoulos he composed an extremely diplomatic letter, insisting on his wish to maintain good relations and saying that he would not let Argyropoulos see the reply unless he first received assurances that no offence would be taken.[12] The date of this correspondence is 1469. Ficino was already well advanced with his work, having begun to translate more than ten years earlier. It may be taken for granted that a knowledge of Platonic doctrines was being widely diffused in Florentine intellectual circles. If Argyropoulos was really interested in Plato it is reasonable to ask what his part in the process was. One notes with surprise the absence of any evidence of contact between him and Ficino, and it is also curious that at the very time of the Greek's appointment criticism from Cosimo de' Medici and Cristoforo Landino led Ficino to learn the original language in order to give his work on Plato a sounder basis. Once Argyropoulos had begun teaching it will have become clear that his approach to Plato differed from Ficino's. Extensive reports of his lectures survive in the notebooks of his pupil Donato Acciaiuoli, and it looks as if he dealt with Plato in summary and down-to-earth fashion as the forerunner of Aristotle and not as some kind of Christian before Christ. The suggestion that he saw traces of a hidden doctrine lurking beneath the surface of Plato's dialogues does not appear to be well founded. Although such phrasing is used vaguely by Acciaiuoli in a letter to Alfonso of Palencia, in other contexts it refers to difficulties of interpretation that any student is likely to meet in a careful reading of such texts. For Argyropoulos Socrates, Plato and Aristotle are the three outstanding philosophers. In a lecture given in 1460 on the *De anima* he declared that he was not interested in Zoroaster and other thinkers up to the time of Anaxagoras. It is abundantly clear that for him Aristotle was the great master of philosophy and as soon as he had revealed his opinion he and Ficino may have agreed to differ and remain at a distance from each other.[13]

Argyropoulos also knew Plotinus, since a copy of the *Enneads* now in Paris is clearly written in his hand (Paris gr. 1970). Although there is no sign in the notes made by a pupil from his lectures that he did anything to emphasise the importance of Neoplatonism, his copy of the *Enneads* does coincide at some points with notes made by Ficino in MS Laur. 87.3 as corrections of the transmitted text. These agreements could be taken as tenuous evidence of a link between the two scholars, and it is natural to infer that priority belongs to Ficino. But the question is not so simple as it appears at first sight, since the watermarks in Argyropoulos' copy suggest that it belongs to the mid-fifties and no later, a time when Ficino was at best a beginner in Greek. The puzzle needs further examination; but if it is resolved in favour of Argyropoulos one will still have to admit that he does not appear to have made striking advances in the study of a very difficult author.[14]

(ii) Ficino

We now come to one of the most influential translators of the period. Marsilio Ficino began learning Greek in 1456 at the age of twenty-three. He enjoyed the patronage of Cosimo de' Medici, who criticised him for writing an essay on Platonic doctrines based on Latin sources. The young author was advised by Cosimo and the expert humanist Cristoforo Landino not to publish on this subject until he had been able to make use of the primary sources. Although many of the books that Ficino owned and worked from can be identified among the riches of the Laurentian Library and the Biblioteca Riccardiana in Florence it is not easy to plot the course of his progress as a student. The only tangible sign of his studies is a copy of the so-called *Hermeneumata Eisiedlensia* with his ex-libris. The text was a series of *Colloquia* followed by a short lexicon of words arranged by topics. Its value was that it could serve in place of a dictionary for beginners; there was not yet any standard work of this kind, and Crastonus' lexicon did not become available until *c.* 1478, by which time Ficino's career as a translator was well advanced.[15]

Very soon he began to experiment in the art of translating. The texts chosen were for the most part little known and from the linguistic point of view none too easy; the Orphic hymns, the Orphic *Argonautica*, hymns by Proclus, the Homeric hymns and Hesiod's *Theogony*. Ficino took care not to circulate them, in case they should lead to the accusation that he was trying to resuscitate the cult of ancient gods or demons.[16] In 1462 Cosimo gave him a number of Greek manuscripts, so that he had his own copy of Plato and Plotinus.[17] At this date Cosimo seems to have used one of his own villas at Careggi just outside Florence to give hospitality to Ficino and his circle, and in the following year occurred the famous donation of a villa in the same spot where Ficino could continue his work.[18] This was also the year in which the commission was given to translate Plato and Hermes Trismegistus. Strange though it must seem to modern taste, Cosimo requested that the Hermetic corpus should be tackled first.[19] This group of treatises was a source for the theology and magic of ancient Egypt and so could be thought of as the key to a wisdom far older than that of Greece (Christian apologists had regularly made the point about the relative antiquity of the two cultures). The treatises had the advantage of being transmitted in a language more accessible than ancient Egyptian, the hieroglyphs of which commanded respect and remained a mystery. Aspersions had not yet been cast on the authenticity of the texts. If a copy had fallen into the hands of Valla, the story might have been different, but it is worth remarking that even Politian does not appear to have questioned the oddity of the Greek style, and he more than any other Italian of his century possessed the sensitivity and linguistic· competence that might have provoked suspicion.

The question of the authenticity of what passed for the work of Orpheus is another matter. Ficino, whether by ignorance or by design, did not see fit to raise it. Yet it had occurred to Bruni at the time when he was making his version of a famous passage of Homer. He stated that Homer is the earliest surviving Greek writer, since Linus and Orpheus are represented by the merest fragments, and those of uncertain status. While he did not indicate the source of his doctrine we may be fairly sure that it was a remark of Cicero, who reports the opinion of Aristotle.[20] Whether or not Ficino was aware of Bruni's reason for scepticism he may have preferred to rely on the authority of St Augustine, for whom Orpheus, Linus and Musaeus are both poets and theologians. What is more, they are the only Greeks who can claim greater antiquity than the Hebrew prophets. They are not, however, as early as Moses, and the wisdom of Egypt which Moses found there cannot be older than Isis, who is herself more recent than Abraham by two generations.[21]

The best explanation of Ficino's curiously catholic tastes in ancient philosophical and religious writing is to be found in a statement he made twice in virtually identical form. Part of the preface to his translation of Plotinus expresses the same thought as a letter to the Hungarian humanist Janus Pannonius, who had challenged him to explain how his studies were consistent with Christianity. Ficino rebutted the suggestion that he was encouraging the revival of classical paganism. He claimed that his purpose in publicising the thought of the ancients was to serve the cause of true religion. Although precise anticipation of Christian doctrine was not to be expected from the pagans, nevertheless the most acute thinkers among them understood the truth. Ficino's central doctrine is expressed as follows: 'And so through the wish of divine providence to attract to itself in wondrous fashion all men in accordance with their intellectual ability, it came about that a religious philosophy arose long ago among the Persians thanks to Zoroaster and among the Egyptians thanks to Mercury, without any discrepancy between the two. The doctrine was then sustained among the Thracians under Orpheus and Aglaophemus. It soon flourished also through Pythagoras among the Greeks and Italians. But it was finally consummated at Athens by the divine Plato.'[22] Ficino's concern with the texts that passed for the work of Orpheus and the Egyptian Hermes, whom he here calls Mercury out of deference to Latin usage, has already been noted. He also knew that Gemistos Plethon had attributed to Zoroaster the so-called *Chaldaean*

Oracles, of which some fragments survived largely thanks to the eleventh-century Byzantine intellectual Michael Psellos. They gave directions for summoning demons and contained much else that was acceptable to Neoplatonists and repugnant to Christians. Plethon's essay on them was originally included among the contents of a book owned by Ficino (Riccardiana 76).[23] He also showed his interest in Pythagoras by translating the spurious texts that circulated under his name and a number of essays by the fourth-century Neoplatonist Iamblichus which dealt with the life and doctrines of Pythagoras.[24] One understands how he came to speak of 'those ancient theologians whom we venerate'.[25] Remarks of that kind and the undeniable link with Plethon's doctrine invite scepticism about his protestations of orthodoxy. But Ficino had become a priest in 1473 and does not seem to have encountered any difficulties as a result of his views on this subject, and perhaps both men can be regarded as sincere if misguided enthusiasts. It should be noted, however, that Ficino did run into some difficulties on account of his references to astrology and magic, about which he obviously knew more than orthodox members of the church thought acceptable. Belief in these pseudo-sciences was part and parcel of Neoplatonism.[26]

Ficino's view of Plato is given in a famous letter of 1489 addressed to a German correspondent. Speaking of the two roads to happiness, one philosophical, one religious, he says: 'Our friend Plato admirably combined the two in one. At all points he is equally philosophical and religious, being a subtle disputant, a devout priest and an eloquent orator. So if you follow in the footsteps of the divine Plato, as you have begun to do, you will find and achieve happiness, God pointing the way and leading you on. This is all the more certain because our friend Plato with his Pythagorean and Socratic arguments follows the law of Moses and prophesies the law of Christ.'[27] On another occasion Ficino can be found venturing the opinion that Socrates may be treated as a forerunner of Christ.[28]

Enthusiasm for Plato was not confined to study of his doctrines. In Florence one group of intellectuals had an annual celebration over dinner. It was known that in antiquity there had been such a custom. The earliest mention is in Plutarch's *Table Talk* 8.1.1 (717B) where the day is named as the 7th of Thargelion, and among the Neoplatonists of later antiquity it was made the occasion for a lecture or reading from poetry; Proclus (410-485) records having spoken himself on the theme of how Homer might have replied to Socrates' criticism of him in the *Republic*. The Florentines identified the month Thargelion with November; in fact it more or less corresponds with May and the mistake probably arose from a belief that the penultimate month of the Athenian calendar corresponded to that of the Julian calendar. Ficino's introduction to the *Symposium* tells us about the restoration of the ancient custom.

Plato, the father of philosophy, died at the age of 81, on the 7th of November, his birthday. He was relaxing at a dinner-party after the dishes had been removed. This dinner-party, by which his birth and the anniversary of his death are both marked, was repeated annually by all the early Platonists up to the time of Plotinus and Porphyry. But since Porphyry's time, for 1,200 years, this annual banquet has been in abeyance. Finally in our own time the great Lorenzo de' Medici, with the intention of restoring the Platonic banquet, appointed Francesco Bandini Master of the Feast. So when Bandini began to prepare the celebrations of the 7th of November he gave a royal reception to nine Platonic guests at the estate of Careggi: Antonio Agli, bishop of Fiesole; Ficino the doctor; Cristoforo Landino the poet; Bernardo Nuzzi the orator; Tommaso Benci; Giovanni Cavalcanti, our close friend whom the guests called 'the hero' because of his moral virtues and outstanding intellect; the two Marsuppini, Cristoforo and Carlo, sons of the poet Carlo. Bandini asked me to be the ninth and last, so that by the addition of Marsilio Ficino to the others the full number of the Muses should be made up. After dinner Bernardo took Plato's book entitled *Symposium or Concerning Love* and read all the speeches made at that dinner-party. After the reading he asked the other members of the company to expound the speeches, each taking one. All agreed; lots were cast and it fell to Giovanni Cavalcanti to expound that first speech by Phaedrus. Pausanias' speech went to Antonio the theologian, Eryximachus the doctor's to Ficino the doctor; Aristophanes the poet's to Cristoforo the poet; the young Agathon's to Carlo Marsuppini; Socrates' discussion was given to Tommaso Benci and Alcibiades' to Cristoforo Marsuppini. A division of this kind was approved by all. But the bishop and the doctor being forced to leave, one for the cure of souls, the other for that of patients, handed over their parts in the discussion to Giovanni Cavalcanti. The others turned towards him and sat ready to listen in silence.

The patronage of the young Lorenzo de' Medici appears from this account as the main stimulus. The date is presumed to be 1468, since an autograph copy of Ficino's story is dated July 1469 (Vat. lat. 7705), and Lorenzo was then eighteen. But appearances sometimes deceive. It is perhaps suspicious that in the version just given above there are nine participants apart from Lorenzo, whereas one would expect him to be included. However that may be, another text has been found (Laur. Strozzi 98), not autograph but exhibiting occasional corrections in Ficino's hand, in which there are several erasures affecting the main facts. The chief difference is that Lorenzo and the estate of Careggi are not found in the original wording. It was Bandini who had the idea of reviving the ancient usage. Ficino must have had diplomatic reasons for revising his story in order to give greater glory to his patron.[29]

Translating Plato occupied Ficino for about six years, at the end of which he wrote commentaries on the *Symposium* and *Philebus*.[30] Then about 1470 he set to work on a lengthy study entitled *Theologia platonica de immortalitate animorum*, completed in 1474. Apart from dealing with the topic indicated in the title he aimed to prove that Christianity and

Platonism could be reconciled. A printed edition appeared in 1482. But it was the printing of the translation in 1484 that should probably be regarded as a more important event. It had a great success despite a large number of typographical errors. On the whole it was a faithful and accurate version, even if occasionally when confronted by delicate issues such as the pre-existence of the human soul the translator yielded to the temptation of rendering the Greek in a fashion more acceptable to Christian susceptibilities.[31]

A print run of just over a thousand copies was sold out within a few years and many reprints were issued. It was a long time before Greek texts in the original language enjoyed such popularity. But the market had been prepared for Ficino by the controversy over the relative merits of Plato and Aristotle. Ficino wrote a brief introduction to each dialogue explaining its purpose. In two cases, however, the *Symposium* and *Timaeus*, he decided that a much more extended analysis, chapter by chapter, was required. Both were of great importance, especially the latter, to those whose approach to Plato was coloured by Neoplatonist thinking; on the other hand it can be noted that Ficino did not see fit to make *Alcibiades I* the opening text in his collection, which would have been the choice of many Neoplatonists. In his general preface he begins with the observation that religion has to be made to appeal to the more educated classes, and it was by a divine dispensation that Plato was sent into the world to spread the light of religion among its peoples. One notes with some surprise how different this attitude is from that of the Byzantines; perhaps it is another sign that Ficino was under the influence of the highly untypical Plethon. He continues by remarking that the sun of Platonism has not yet shone among the Latin nations and so Cosimo de' Medici asked him to perform the necessary task. He produced ten dialogues for Cosimo, then after his death another nine for Piero, after which he was deflected from his enterprise by various misfortunes. But Lorenzo de' Medici, to whom the work as a whole is dedicated, helped him to resume his activity. There is an odd implication that Cosimo disregarded the work of Bruni, who had continued in office as chancellor of the republic until his death in 1444 and does not appear to have fallen from favour. Yet there are clear signs that where a version by Bruni already existed Ficino was not above borrowing some ideas from it.[32] In the interests of flattery towards his patron and emphasis of his own importance this honourable debt is denied a mention.

Ficino's amazing energy next led him to make a version of the basic text of Neoplatonism, the *Enneads* of Plotinus (205-269/70), to which he added a commentary of his own. He was urged to undertake this task not by Lorenzo de' Medici but by Giovanni Pico della Mirandola. The drafting of the translation occupied him during the years 1484-6, revision and the preparation of the commentary most of the time from then until 1490.[33] Publication of both in print followed in 1492. It seems that he was already giving lectures on this extremely abstruse author; according to a plausible combination of incomplete reports in our sources he was able to assemble a large audience in the church of Santa Maria degli Angeli in 1487. He had previously lectured on Plato's *Philebus* but public lectures on Plotinus are a more remarkable indication of the character of Florentine intellectual life. It may be worth noting that some of Ficino's writings were in such demand that they were already being translated into the vernacular by himself and others. One modern expert has commented very favourably on Ficino's deep understanding of the difficult texts of the Neoplatonist writers, in particular the complex argumentation of Proclus' *Theologia Platonica*.[34]

His last years, although affected by troubled political conditions and religious strife in Florence, were not inactive. In 1490-2 he worked at a translation with commentary of two of the essays by pseudo-Dionysius the Areopagite, whom he described as 'the culmination of Platonic teaching and a pillar of Christian theology', a verdict which would certainly have delighted the unknown author of these treatises. And in 1492 he was able to benefit from one of the recent acquisitions of the Medicean Library. A considerable quantity of books was brought back from Greece by the refugee scholar Janus Lascaris, and among them was a hitherto unknown commentary by the Neoplatonist Proclus (410-485) on Plato's *Republic* (Laur. 80.9). Ficino sent a friend some notes on it. The last major work, left uncompleted, had as its subject the Pauline Epistles, on which he lectured in Florence cathedral in 1497.

(iii) Scholar-printers: Chalcondyles and Janus Lascaris

Argyropoulos was not the only learned refugee who contributed to the great period of Florentine culture. There were three others of note, who held in succession a post at the university. Andronicus Callistus, a very productive copyist who had previously lived in Padua, Bologna and Rome, came to Florence in 1471. During his stay, which lasted until 1475, he included among the texts on which he lectured the Hellenistic epic poet Apollonius Rhodius. The choice of a post-classical author is noteworthy. Although he had already lectured on the *Idylls* of Theocritus during his days in Bologna, the new departure may have impressed a Florentine audience. Certainly the young Politian took note, as will be seen.[35]

Both the other exiles spent one significant stage of their very long careers in Florence. Demetrius Chalcondyles (1423-1511) had lived for a while in Bessarion's circle in Rome and the cardinal's patronage led to his appointment to a chair in Padua in 1464. There he seems to have taught without great distinction, if the uninspired character of his inaugural lecture is any guide. It may however be noted as a sign of his dedication to the task of teaching that he produced his own version of the *Erotemata* text-book for beginners, which was sufficiently popular to be printed several times. In 1475 he came to Florence and stayed until 1491. Although he cannot be shown to have made much impact in intellectual circles, one notable achievement stands to his credit: in 1488 he supervised the production of the first printed edition of Homer. The significance of this publication needs to be set in its proper context.

Printing in Greek may be said to have begun in Venice in 1471 or the following year, when one Adam of Ammergau issued an abridged version of the Chrysoloras-Guarino *Erotemata*.[36] The text is only partly in Greek; the first entirely Greek volume is probably the similar handbook of Constantine Lascaris issued in 1476 in Milan.[37] While for a decade or more a slow trickle of grammars and dictionaries appeared, texts for reading were few and far between and it is clear that professional scribes did not suffer any great decline in the demand for their services. The first signs that their monopoly was about to be seriously infringed appeared in 1478-81, when a press in Milan working for Bonus Accursius of Pisa extended the range of its products with three titles. Aesop's fables, with an appendix in which some were repeated with a word-for-word Latin version, were aimed at a market of beginners and schoolchildren, as the colophon declares. A Psalter will also have served the needs of students, as was noted in an earlier chapter. Less expected is a text of Theocritus *Idylls* 1-18 and Hesiod's *Works and Days*; it must have been a rather speculative enterprise. But whereas the majority of the major Latin authors had been issued in print in the years between 1465 and 1475, and many Greek authors were becoming available in Latin dress,[38] the first edition of a substantial and popular Greek text was Chalcondyles' Homer of 1488. Chalcondyles' own interest in printing may go back some years if we are right to accept an ingenious suggestion made recently. His handwriting is suspiciously like the type designed for a book printed in Vicenza *c.* 1475.[39] However that may be, a different type was used for the large and very handsome Homer, which included the *Hymns* and *Batrachomyomachia*. Chalcondyles confessed that the text of the last two items left much to be desired owing to the corrupt state of the manuscripts. But he will not have had much difficulty in preparing an adequate text of the epics. He tells us that in order to determine the correct reading where there was uncertainty he took the trouble to read through the enormous commentary compiled by the twelfth-century archbishop of Thessalonica Eustathius. This procedure will have enabled him to satisfy contemporary requirements for a reading text. After leaving Florence in 1491 to go to Milan, where he spent the remainder of his career, he continued his useful work as the editor of printed editions. His next venture was an Isocrates issued in 1493. Although two or three of the essays of this author had enjoyed a certain popularity, the book was not a success. Indeed it became something of a notorious case in the history of bibliography since in 1535 there were still unsold copies, and it was decided to print fresh title and colophon pages in order to offer to the unsuspecting public what passed for a second edition.[40] Undeterred by this failure Chalcondyles set about the much larger task of publishing the Byzantine lexicon known as Suidas or the *Suda*.[41] As a dictionary with many additional articles more characteristic of an encyclopaedia it had real value for students at all levels. The result was a very large book of over 1,000 pages, and the editor urged the potential reader not to be deterred by the high price of three gold coins. He gives evidence of having performed his task conscientiously when he notes that he had collated several manuscripts and corrected numerous faults common to most or all of them, and he candidly admits once again that some passages cannot be properly understood. He claims also to have added to the utility of the book by inserting a number of words that were not included in the original text. These prove on investigation to come from two sources, the later Byzantine lexicon which circulated under the name of Zonaras and the seventh-century doctor Paul of Aegina.

Modern scholars who have had to take account of these three editions suggest that they deserve to be regarded as competent rather than brilliant performances. As a teacher Chalcondyles, partly no doubt through the good fortune of holding a chair in a great centre during its best years, had a number of distinguished pupils, among them the Englishmen Grocyn and Linacre, while the Italians included Pico, Politian and the future pope Leo X. In Milan too there were good students, since Castiglione and Trissino followed his courses. Aldus Manutius paid him the compliment of calling him the leading scholar of his day. Since Aldus also had very close relations with Marcus Musurus one is bound to express mild surprise at this extravagant judgment. Presumably it is to be explained by the enthusiasm of friendship. Convincing evidence has yet to be found in the verdict of other contemporaries or in his own writings. Perhaps the highest compliment he received is the fresco portrait in Santa Maria Novella in Florence in which Ghirlandaio showed him in the company of Ficino, Landino and Politian.

To complete the picture of Chalcondyles two other reports must be noted. The first concerns a little-known episode from his Milanese period. The jurist Alciato, better known for his book on emblems, records having heard Chalcondyles give an opinion about the Greek words that needed to be supplied in the text of the *Digest* at 41.3.30 pr. Most manuscripts omitted the Greek and the Florentine Pandects were not accessible. The passage dealt with the distinction between objects composed of a single substance and those that are compounds. Chalcondyles proposed φυσικόν and τεχνικόν, which is intelligent enough, but in fact the words in the Florentine manuscript are ἡνωμένον and συνημμένον.[42]

The minor humanist Pietro Alcionio (1486-1527) composed a dialogue in which Chalcondyles appears as one of the speakers. The assertion is put into his mouth that the church authorities destroyed copies of Greek love poetry and substituted for it the poems of St Gregory of Nazianzus, presumably in the school curriculum, though that point is not made explicitly. While it is certainly true that Gregory was the most popular of the great Cappadocian fathers of the fourth century throughout the Byzantine era, and his poems were quite well known, there is good reason to think that the part of his oeuvre found worthy of inclusion in the school syllabus was a selection of sixteen of his orations. Chalcondyles' assertion is not supported by other evidence, and it looks as if he either had a rather inaccurate vision of the cultural history of late antiquity or is being made the mouthpiece of a Renaissance humanist's conception of a dark age clouded by ecclesiastical bigotry.[43]

The third refugee was Janus Lascaris (1445-1535). Although he did not have a chair until he succeeded Chalcondyles he seems to have taken up residence in Florence at an earlier date, perhaps *c.* 1475.[44] Certainly he was active in the service of the Medici from 1490 onwards, making two successful journeys in Greek lands in search of manuscripts. We have already seen how one of his acquisitions was of immediate interest to Ficino. According to Lascaris himself the number of volumes added to the Medici library was 200, and they provided eighty texts hitherto unknown. These figures entitle him to rank as second only to Aurispa as a collector.[45]

He held his chair during the years 1492-5. An inaugural lecture from his second year is extant.[46] It reveals that in his first year he had read Sophocles and Thucydides, two of the more difficult authors, and was proposing as a programme for his second year Demosthenes and Greek epigrams. This brings us to one of the high points in his career, for in 1494 he issued the first printed edition of the collection of epigrams known as the *Greek Anthology*. One is tempted to think of him as a predecessor of those modern academics who lay down the principle that teaching and research complement each other. Various observations can be made about the edition. One is that it gives the text in the form imposed on it by the Byzantine monk Maximus Planudes in 1299, not the earlier extant version of the collection known as the *Palatine Anthology*.[47] Planudes' autograph still exists (Marc. gr. 481), but although it had been part of cardinal Bessarion's collection and was by now in Venice, the books were rarely if ever accessible, and Lascaris used another copy. This form of the text was adopted by all subsequent editors until the second half of the eighteenth century. Another striking fact about the edition is its typography. Lascaris explains in his letter of dedication that current Greek typefaces are unattractive and difficult for compositors, so that he has gone back to letter forms used in antiquity. In the *Anthology* and two smaller volumes that soon followed he used an upper-case fount based on the forms seen in inscriptions. One is reminded of Filelfo's *litterae Atticae*. Opinions may vary about the aesthetic merit of this experiment in purism which Lascaris extended even to Latin. He soon found himself needing to make some concession to conventional practice, and volumes issued by the same press about the time of his departure from Florence, while retaining capitals for the main text, employ an ordinary lower-case fount for the commentaries printed in the margins. His radical innovation did not find favour with other printers.[48]

When printing the *Anthology* Lascaris does not seem to have excelled as an editor. In 1798 one of his successors passed a rather negative verdict, noting that Lascaris prints many lines with metrical faults, even when a solution was ready to hand. The inference is that his aim was to present the text as it appeared in a tolerably good manuscript. His own metrical knowledge was respectable enough, to judge by his own compositions in the same genre.[49] More positive judgments have been given about two of his other productions, the *Hymns* of Callimachus and the *Argonautica* of Apollonius Rhodius. The best modern edition of Callimachus, which records in exemplary detail textual difficulties and progress made in solving them, demonstrates that Lascaris made a fair number of necessary minor adjustments both to the poetic text and to the small body of ancient and medieval notes that accompany the *Hymns*.[50] In his Apollonius Rhodius the same appears to be true at least in the scholia.[51]

The choice of the three texts mentioned so far may invite us to sense in the background the influence of Politian, who revelled in the composition of Greek epigrams and put some emphasis on the study of Hellenistic poetry. He and Lascaris were not on the best of terms, judging by three epigrams that Lascaris wrote about him.[52] There is also a tradition that Lascaris had accused him of plagiarising ancient authors in his lecture on Homer. But Lascaris would hardly have been able to let that factor weigh seriously when the delicate financial implications of printing Greek were under discussion. The *Anthology* may have been popular; at any rate a pocket-size reprint was issued by Aldus in 1503, incorporating a few improvements made as a result of collating another manuscript. The other texts issued by the Florentine press were mostly safer propositions from a financial point of view. The most risky was Euripides. Lascaris selected four plays, the *Hippolytus*, *Medea*, *Alcestis* and *Andromache*. None of these was included in the basic Byzantine curriculum nor apparently had they been the subject of courses in the university. But in adding Lucian to his list the printer could hope for reasonable sales, as the popularity of the satirist showed no sign of waning. There were also three smaller books. Chrysoloras' grammar, being still in use, merited a new impression. Cebes' *Pinax*, a philosophical dialogue in which a painting is interpreted allegorically, was also a very suitable and edifying text for beginners. Lastly Lascaris' choice fell on a collection of moralising verses known as the *Gnomai monostichoi* which he printed with a little hexameter poem by Musaeus on Hero and Leander. The latter was not yet seen to be a product of the early Byzantine era. Lascaris could follow in the footsteps of Ficino and regard it as the work of the mythical associate of Orpheus, entitled to respect for its exceptional antiquity. It is in any case a work of a certain charm.[53]

The two Greek professors put Florence on the map as a centre of printing in their own language. It is probably only due to political circumstances that the enterprise came to an end. Similarly in the next decade the Venetian Greek press was obliged to suspend its operations because of the wars. Since Aldus was able to resume his activity his firm produced enough to justify its outstanding place in the history of publishing. That uncontested place should not tempt us to deny full credit to Lascaris for what he achieved during his time in Florence. Later when he took up residence in Rome he was able once again to perform useful services as editor and printer.[54]

12

Politian

The outstanding figure in Florentine literary and scholarly circles from the mid-seventies until his death was Angelo Ambrogini (1454-1494), generally known as Politian, a name derived from his birthplace Montepulciano. As a poet in both Italian and Latin he was first-rate, and his scholarship proved even more convincingly than Ficino's that the Italians could master and make advances in the subject which the Byzantine refugees expected to dominate. Politian had attracted attention at the age of fifteen when he presented Lorenzo de' Medici with a Latin version of the second book of the *Iliad* in hexameters, and he soon afterwards continued with Books 3-5. Although the choice of text was conventional, as was to be expected from a young student, Politian did not take long to demonstrate how broad his interests were, and of all the scholars discussed in this book he is second to none in the breadth of his reading. His Greek interests are perhaps least evident in the area which for modern students is of primary importance, the literature of Athens in the fifth and fourth centuries BC, a fact which is surprising in view of his talent as a poet. His scholarship can be understood if we consider five principal facets of his activity, his study of Homer, Aristotle, Hellenistic literature, and the Greek texts in the *Digest*, and his attempt to imitate the epigrams of the *Greek Anthology*.

One can treat the authors in chronological order and begin with Homer. Practical concerns or a desire to study Greek philosophy had not removed Homer from the curriculum, and we still have a general introductory lecture by Politian (1486), a Latin poem by him in praise of Homer (1485), and a later introduction for a course on the *Odyssey* (1489), together with notes on the first two books of the poem.

The lecture on Homer begins with a *captatio benevolentiae*. The Florentine audience is assured that all learning has long since disappeared from Greece and been transferred to their own city, to such an extent that one might think Athens had been moved wholesale from its site to Florence. Florentines are now themselves professors of Greek. Politian does not bother to mention any others and one may ask how many had in fact received the honour of such appointments by the year of his death. The next remark is a curious claim: the sons of noble families are said to speak Attic with a purity and ease which has not been witnessed within the last thousand years. One would not expect to find emphasis on the spoken command of the ancient as opposed to the modern language, even if the educated elite of Byzantium had attempted to maintain up to the very end of the empire the habit of speaking an archaising language based on the ancient classics.

A brief account of the poet's life follows. Politian stresses how remarkable it is that a blind man should have been able to learn so much that he is a treasure-house of instruction on every topic. A passing remark, which one would have liked to see expanded, alludes to the poet's facility of composition. 'Those most beautiful poems, justly admired in every age, poured forth easily and extempore, one might say flooded in a swirling eddy, whereas Varus (*sic*) informs us that the poet of Mantua composed very few verses in a day.' But the next sentence, rather obscurely phrased, appears to be an allusion to the stories in the so-called Herodotean life of the poet which speak of his powers of extempore repartee, and not about the composition of his great works.[1] Politian passes on to the style of the *Iliad* and *Odyssey*, citing short passages as examples of the three styles known to ancient critics, high, medium and low. He soon turns to philosophical themes, claiming that almost all significant ideas have their origin in Homer. A section follows on the gods, fate and the soul, in which notions of famous philosophers are cited. There is a long quotation from Quintilian on Homer's skill in eloquence, while Dio Chrysostom is quoted for the view that he offers much to readers of every age and for his portrait of the ideal king based on quotations from Homer. Politian's encomium begins to wear thin when he extols Homer's understanding of medicine. The indebtedness of many philosophers to the poet forces him to consider the exclusion he suffered from Plato's ideal state on account of the unflattering stories he told about the gods. Politian thinks this question requires a longer investigation and contents himself with remarking that Plato quotes Homer very often and calls him *magister vitae*, adding that those who spend their lives studying him can be considered fortunate. Antiquity would not have allowed children to read him closely in their formative years had there been any potential for harm in his poems, nor would jurists quote him as the father of virtues.[2] Still less would the most eloquent of the church fathers, Basil the Great, say that Homer's poetry is all an encomium of virtue.[3]

The fame and influence of Homer have spread to the north and east, continues Politian. As evidence he adduces the Borysthenites and the Indians. The former are reported as having had great admiration for Homer – a past tense is used – and the Indians 'although they are unable to see some of the stars that are visible in our part of the world, nevertheless meditate on the disasters of Priam, the laments of Hecuba and Andromache, and the brave deeds of Hector and Achilles, just as much as we do'. They are credited with having a translation of Homer into their own language.[4]

The passage reads very oddly until one realises that it is confection of unacknowledged material from a classical source.[5] Dio Chrysostom, an important representative of the Second Sophistic who was not yet very well known in Politian's day, says in his *Borysthenitikos* (9-10) that the inhabitants of the region north of the Crimea are enthusiastic in their admiration of Homer, while in his short essay *On Homer* (6-7) he states that the Indians have made a translation, also noting that they do not see all the stars that we see, such as the Bears. Naturally one has to be sceptical about both suggestions. As far as the Indians are concerned, modern scholars have wondered whether Dio had obtained a garbled report from merchants in Alexandria who knew of the recitation in India of epic poetry somewhat resembling Homer.[6]

The observation of Politian's plagiarism does not exhaust the interest of the passage. The past tense used in connection with the Borysthenites might have prompted an acute listener to ask at what date they had achieved such a high level of culture, and the modern reader may be entitled to feel some surprise that Politian did not ask the question himself or make some unflattering comparison about contemporary inhabitants of the same region. His analogy drawn from India exposes him in a similar and more pointed fashion. The audience was invited to think that the observation referred to the present. But could Politian seriously have thought that the circumstances described by ancient sources were still valid in his own day? We need not criticise him for his lack of scepticism about Dio. But when he puts forward Dio's view without modification, the implicit lack of historical understanding does not do him credit.

If he expected to escape detection, there is a tradition that he was disappointed. The story goes that after his lecture Janus Lascaris took him aside and criticised him for passing off ancient learning as if it were his own. The tale is known in two versions, neither faultless in detail, but not perhaps devoid of foundation. The earlier is found in Guillaume Budé's notes on the *Digest*. He says that Politian produced without acknowledgment information derived from the life of Homer ascribed to Plutarch, exploiting the fact that it had not yet been made generally available in Latin. Lascaris is not mentioned as the source of the story, but as they were friends it is an easy inference. The mistaken identification of the Greek text in question is perhaps not very serious. The other version of the episode is later but more specific. It comes from the jurist François Duaren (b. 1509), who says that Budé used to tell it. He adds the useful detail that Budé had heard it frequently from Lascaris. In this version the Greek source laid under contribution is Herodotus, the supposed author of another life of the Greek epic poet. Lascaris took Politian to task for quarrying in a text that was not available in Latin or in a printed version.[7]

Politian's course on the *Odyssey* was given three years later. His opening lecture begins with the proposition that one ought to discuss first the life of Homer and give an appreciation of his work, but as he has already done that in his previous course and has published a poem on the same theme, he can spare himself the trouble. He reminds the audience in the briefest terms of the merits of Homer and says of his lectures on the text 'dabo operam, ut non his dumtaxat qui graecam litteraturam affectant, sed et his pariter consulatur, qui sunt latinitate contenti.' 'I shall take care to meet the needs not only of those who are tackling Greek literature but equally those who are content with Latin.' This seems very odd, not simply because it suggests that he was attempting to lecture to two different types of student at once, but also because the remnants of his commentary which survive in the same manuscript are of a highly detailed and linguistic character and leave the impression that Politian's instruction had all the drawbacks of schoolroom pedantry. The main part of the introductory lecture is devoted to the concept of a unitary, as opposed to episodic, plot. It owes much to Aristotle, as the author acknowledges without giving the precise reference; in fact he is drawing on Chapter 23 of the *Poetics*, which regards it as a merit of the *Iliad* and *Odyssey* that the action centres on a well-defined theme.[8]

As a pendant to Politian's annotation of Homer one may draw attention to a curious puzzle. Prefixed to his version of Books 2-5 of the *Iliad*, undertaken in the years 1470-5, is a note about allegorical interpretation. It refers to a short work by the Byzantine scholar Demetrius Triclinius dealing with the first four verses of the fourth book of the *Iliad*. Politian gives a résumé of the text. He appears to be in general sympathy with the tendency of the essay, and cites in addition the authority of Proclus' commentary on Plato's *Timaeus* in support of its position. The allegory is of the physical rather than the moral type. What is strange is that although we know a good deal about the work of Triclinius there is no other trace of an essay on this subject, and it would be rather odd if a reference in Politian were the only evidence for it. I have toyed with the idea that Politian's memory failed him and that he was referring to similar works by other Byzantines such as Michael Psellos and John Diaconos Galenos. But it has to be said that neither of these texts corresponds very closely with what Politian reports of the contents, and one is left wondering whether he had access to a codex now lost which contained an essay on this theme attributed, perhaps wrongly, to Triclinius. If so, this is one of the rare cases in which a Renaissance scholar may have read a text not available to us.[9]

The note on allegory is the most interesting of the notes, mostly very brief and without significance, which Politian wrote to accompany his version of the *Iliad*.[10] A few of them demonstrate the application of the principle. For example at *Iliad* 5.384 he interprets the wounding of

Aphrodite by Diomedes with the help of a concept drawn from Plato's *Symposium* and certainly well known in Florentine Neoplatonist circles: 'Venus in manu vulneratur quoniam celestis illa venus Platonis cum in sensu tangendi polluitur vulgaris evadit.' ('Venus is wounded in the hand because Plato's celestial Venus, when corrupted by the sense of touch, becomes vulgar.') Similar influence is doubtless at the root of the explanation of 5.149: 'Nube quadam circumsepta anima divina sapientia purgatur puraque in luce refulget.' ('The soul, encircled by a cloud, is cleansed by divine wisdom and gleams in pure light.') The notes also reveal a few errors by Politian, presumably to be explained by his youth. At 5.722 he failed to read in the scholia the words ἡ Δημώ correctly and inferred the existence of a person called Hedemo. Another mistake of word division at 2.760 led to the creation of the name Geleonteus and at 2.751 he confused the adjective and noun in the phrase ἱμερτὸν Ταρτησσόν.

I now turn to Politian's dealings with philosophical texts. Despite the revival of Platonism it is important not to lose sight of the evidence which shows that Aristotle was far from being pushed into the background. One might reasonably say that Politian was in the heart of Neoplatonist territory, and yet he provides plenty of evidence. His lecture *Panepistemon* is an introduction to the philosopher, and he gave a course on the *Nicomachean Ethics* in 1490-1. He has even been thought to be the first person to own the *Poetics*, and although that claim now has to be abandoned, one may still suspect that he was the first Italian to have a good understanding of this difficult text.[11] The *Praelectio de dialectica* contains a passage which shows that he had studied Aristotle with the help of ancient and more recent commentators. The effects of these studies are sometimes seen elsewhere. In lecturing on Ovid's letter of Sappho to Phaon (*Heroides* 15) he seems to take over a statement of the method to be used by a commentator which he could have found in writers such as Ammonius. Their view was that an introduction must deal with certain questions: the life of the author, his intention, the utility of the work, the quality of the style, the title, and whether the attribution to the author is correct.[12] Further evidence of Politian's close study of Aristotle is provided by two chapters in the *Miscellanea*. In 1.1 he reports the opinion of John Argyropoulos, his former tutor in philosophy, that Cicero made a mistake at *Tusculan Disputation* 1.22 when he used the word *endelecheia* of the fifth element which accounts for the activities of the mind. This word should refer to continuity or continuous action. The right word is *entelecheia*, indicating perfection. Argyropoulos was able to quote other passages to support his view from later Peripatetic authorities. Politian accepts that his opinion has to be taken seriously, but thinks that even weightier authority can be found to vindicate Cicero's reading. First he cites at some length the various later authorities who had a very high respect for Cicero's philosophical writings, a procedure not strictly relevant to his case. Then he comes to the confusion of the two words. What is the right reading? Politian asserts that the text of Aristotle has been exposed to corruption, citing the extraordinary story from Strabo of how the original texts of the Aristotelian writings were kept in a cellar for generations and only came into circulation in the early years of the first century BC. Politian thinks that their editor Apellicon, being anxious to restore damaged passages, made bold alterations to the texts. As far as the passage in question is concerned, there is so little difference between the two readings that one may easily take either view, and it is safer to follow Cicero, since he is far earlier than Alexander of Aphrodisias, who can be placed in the reign of the emperor Severus (222-235). What is there against the supposition, continues Politian, that Cicero may have seen the original Aristotelian manuscript, perhaps not in pristine condition, but scribbled over by Apellicon? He could have determined that the word coined by Aristotle should be given a meaning that would bring his view into harmony with Plato's doctrine as expressed in the *Phaedrus* about the perpetual movement of the soul. Various later commentators assert the identity of Platonic and Aristotelian doctrine on this subject.

The defence of Cicero is remarkable for its ingenious reconstruction of a plausible sequence of events. Politian elsewhere shows that he knew how to handle the concept of the hypothetical missing archetype of surviving manuscripts (1.25); here he combines it with textual history. He also does his best to gain external support for Cicero's interpretation. One may doubt whether he is successful on the point at issue; modern scholars seem to uphold the opposite view. Argyropoulos had quoted from other Aristotelian writings; would Politian have claimed that all such passages had been corrupted identically? Perhaps he would. But if he had been in the habit of using the principle of 'interpreting Homer by means of Homer' he might have been given pause.

Less far-reaching in its implications but significant for the proof it gives of Politian's intelligence in restoring texts is a discussion in *Miscellanea* 1.90 of a lapse in Theodore Gaza's version of Aristotle's *Problemata* (953a18). The passage speaks of Heracles' madness, which caused him to murder his children. Theodore was wrong on two counts. A phrase referring to the outburst is quite inadequately handled, and in fact scarcely makes sense. Politian understood the text rightly. Equally serious is Gaza's treatment of the next phrase in the Greek, where the wording is corrupt. He produced a version mentioning 'the inflammation of ulcers which sometimes precedes death'. Politian saw that the transmitted text must be adjusted so as to include a reference to Mount Oeta, which can be achieved by the addition of two letters. His idea is confirmed by the best manuscripts, which seem not to have been available at the time.[13] It may be worth noting that Politian's discussion is not designed as a polemic against Gaza.

A different kind of skill is displayed in the handling of another text of post-classical philosophy, the *Enchiridion* of Epictetus. Politian made a version of it in 1479. This is dedicated to Lorenzo de' Medici, and Politian tells us that he had recently taken the opportunity to browse in the riches of his patron's library, as a result of which he selected this text as a suitable offering. The library had two copies of it, both seriously defective, and Politian claims to have heard that other copies were no better (one wonders what inquiries he could have made to assure himself on this point). The copies have not been identified; if they are no longer in the Medicean library, perhaps one has to infer that they were thrown away, being too badly damaged to satisfy librarians with a strong aesthetic sense. More important for our purpose than such questions of identification is to note how Politian set out to remedy the defects in the material available to him: he used the commentary by the Neoplatonist Simplicius to fill the gaps, recognising that, while the exact wording could not be restored in every passage, the general sense was reasonably clear.

Politian's most interesting departure from what might be termed the conventional areas of scholarship is his concern with Hellenistic poetry. As early as 1482-3, in the second year of his tenure of a chair in the university, he had lectured on Theocritus' *Idylls*. The copy he annotated (Laur. 32.46) while preparing his course may justify the inference that he did not yet feel entirely at ease with the language of this poet. Many difficult words are glossed with explanations from the scholia or the *Suda* lexicon.[14] An alternative view would be that Politian did not need all this information himself but was anxious to have the right answers ready to hand when his pupils asked for guidance. Certainly at a later stage of his career when he came to do some work on Callimachus he acquitted himself very well. The chosen text was the fifth hymn, in honour of Pallas Athene and describing a rite performed in Argos. In *Miscellanea* 1.80 he presents the Greek text accompanied by a Latin version of his own in elegiac couplets, the metre of the original. This chapter of the *Miscellanea* opens with a quotation from Propertius (4.9.57-8) and its title is 'A little-known story about Teiresias and Pallas, by which the meaning of Propertius is revealed'. A learned discussion of the myth follows, with references to various parallels, including another rare poetic text, the *Dionysiaca* of the early Byzantine poet Nonnus.[15] The passage immediately following the quotation from Nonnus contains a surprise. It turns out that Pico della Mirandola persuaded Politian, when his book was just about to be printed, that the Callimachean poem should be added, with a translation. Politian felt he could not refuse his friend's request, although he was very short of time. He warns us that he thinks there are still some faults in the Greek as it stands, which he has hesitated to correct, whereas he has supplemented the incomplete line near the end of the poem. Perhaps he did not have the time to solve all the puzzles to his satisfaction. He refers to his manuscript source in the plural (*exemplaria*), and I am inclined to take the word literally.[16] The chapter continues with a criticism of his enemy Domizio Calderini (1446-1478) for maintaining that Propertius wrote in imitation of Callimachus, since there is so little of the latter's work extant and none of it deals with themes of love. Calderini could have replied that he was taking Propertius at his word. Finally Politian states that he intends to print the Greek in the ancient fashion, without accents, an attempt at historical accuracy in which he has found very few followers, though it is worth recalling that Janus Lascaris a few years later made another gesture of the same kind when he designed a Greek type face in capital letters so as to imitate inscriptions of the classical period. It should be added that Politian's Callimachus text is printed without even the breathings on initial vowels, and if he thought that was also historically correct he was partially mistaken.

His knowledge enabled him to make a number of minor corrections to the text which are recorded in the apparatus of modern editions. He understood enough about the Doric dialect in which the poem was composed to restore the forms of some words which the manuscripts wrongly gave in the vocalisation of Attic Greek (lines 4, 84, 93). A more subtle point of dialect usage was his ability to recognise that two verb forms should be interpreted as future rather than present tenses (lines 107 and 130).[17] A metrical detail is put right (line 137) and Politian may share with the corrector of one of the manuscripts the credit for a small improvement at line 49. Apart from two lacunae few serious problems remained for the general understanding of the hymn, although quite a number of details had to be sorted out by scholars of more recent generations. Nevertheless the Greek is of a difficulty that tests the capacity of the average modern student, and Politian's achievement is considerable.

An important inference is to be drawn from Politian's presentation of the Callimachean hymn. He does nothing to suggest in this chapter of the *Miscellanea* that it was his deliberate policy to change the direction of Greek philological studies by adding Hellenistic poetry to the curriculum. There was no special fascination for him in the ancient scholar-poet; the parallel between the two of them is a coincidence rather than the result of studied imitation. It was Pico who asked him to provide the full text of the Greek source of the myth. The edition of the hymn was an afterthought. Neither it nor the use of Callimachus to correct a corrupt passage in Catullus (66.48)[18] should be pressed too hard. What they prove is that Politian was a polymath. This is consistent with a passage near the end of the *Lamia*, in which he says that the grammarian's task is to examine and elucidate all types of writers, whether they are poets, historians, orators, philosophers, doctors or lawyers.[19]

Although the specialist literature of the last two professions named in the list was often neglected by philologists (and still is), Politian lived up to his promise. He shows some signs of interest in medicine, as is proved by the notes he made in two volumes of Galen (Laur. 75.8 and 75.17) and by the evidence that he was engaged in translating medical texts. These versions, which may not all have been completed, do not survive.[20] His polymathy also extended to the law. Thanks to the intervention of Lorenzo de' Medici he was given a chance to work on the Florentine Pandects. Several chapters of the *Miscellanea* refer to the Pandects, and in 1490, a year after the publication of the first *Centuria* of this work, he made a collation of the ancient manuscript, working during the summer at great speed. During some of his operations he appears to have been assisted by Scipione Forteguerri, a future member of the Aldine circle.[21] Among other things Politian made a transcript of the sections of the *Digest* which are in Greek. He also remarked on the Greek epigram in honour of the emperor Justinian which is found in the Florentine codex.

In order to appreciate Politian's observations correctly we need to revert briefly to an episode which had taken place a few years earlier. In 1486 Marsilio Ficino and Cristoforo Landino had been allowed to consult the precious relic and, what is more surprising, to write a note in it recording the occasion.[22] They looked at the Greek epigram, which is found in two places. Seeing it on folio 442 recto of volume I, where it had been added about a century earlier by Leonzio Pilato, they noted that it had also been written on folio 10 verso by one of the original scribes of the manuscript. They came to the strange conclusion that the manuscript was 'composed and not merely transcribed by Justinian himself'. This is phrased in such a way as to suggest that a need for verification had arisen. A dispute might have occurred in legal circles if the text of the Pandects had been generally known and available for comparison with the vulgate text of the *Digest*. But the Pandects were not regularly accessible, and this suggestion must remain a very uncertain hypothesis. The second half of the verdict given by Ficino and Landino is equally puzzling. The notion that Justinian himself transcribed the text looks like a naive interpretation of the statement in the epigram that 'Justinian produced this book', taking the words literally, in disregard of the next phrase which refers to the efforts of the jurist Tribonian. One hesitates to suppose that such expert scholars seriously imagined that the emperor had acted as a copyist even for the production of the first official copy, and it is tempting to advance the alternative that they meant to say 'Justinian had the volume compiled and copied'.[23] But one feature of the wording of their note is against such a translation. The Latin is as follows: *quapropter perspicuum iudicamus hoc volumen proprie fuisse ab ipso Justiniano compositum neque solum transcriptum.* What are we to make of *proprie*? Is it no more than the modern Italian *proprio*? And why did they not use the common and natural construction of *curare* and the gerundive if they meant what is alleged?

With this in mind one can proceed to Politian's palaeographical observations. In *Miscellanea* 1.41 he provides one of the most intriguing demonstrations of his skill in this field. He gives a description of the *Pandects* leading to the inference that the volume is *dubio procul archetypum*. The last word has various shades of meaning, and the authoritative modern view of what Politian meant here is that the Pandects are one of the official copies distributed by order of the emperor.[24] One may try to pursue the question a little further. The palaeographical description includes the following statement:

> quibusdam etiam saltem in praefatione, velut ab autore plane et a cogitante atque generante potius quam a librario et exceptore inductis, expunctis ac superscriptis, cum graeca epistola graecoque etiam pulcherrimo hoc epigrammate in prima fronte.

This may be translated: 'There are also in the preface at least some words crossed out, deleted or rewritten above, as if by the author directly or a person thinking out the wording and drafting it, rather than by a copyist or shorthand writer; in addition there is a Greek letter and this very beautiful Greek epigram right at the beginning.' Politian appears to be making here the observation that modern palaeographers make about the traces of redrafting left by an author in a master copy, alterations of a kind that one would not expect to be made by anyone else.[25]

The plot thickens when we find almost identical comment in Politian's note on Suetonius' life of Nero (ch. 52) where the ancient biographer speaks of autograph papers of the emperor which he has handled and identified as such:

> ut facile appareret non tralatos aut dictante aliquo exceptos, sed plane quasi a cogitante atque generante exaratos; ita multa et deleta et inducta et superscripta inerant.

> (As a result it was easily apparent that they were not transcribed or taken down from dictation, but clearly written as if by a person thinking and composing – so numerous were the erasures, corrections and additions above the line.)

It is obvious that Politian has borrowed the idea and the phraseology from the ancient author, and the main part of his note on this passage of Suetonius runs as follows:

> unde re vera creduntur Pandectae istae Florentinae eo tempore fuisse scriptae quo Iustinianus eas primum composuit: nam in prohemio multa videmus deleta, multa inducta, multa item superscripta. quod autem haec sint tantum in prohemio, in reliquum autem operis non sic, hoc ita evenit quia scilicet prohemium ex se composuit Iustinianus, reliquum autem

operis ex aliis iureconsultis assumpsit, et ideo in his nihil cogitabat, sed omnia certa ponebat.[26]

(Hence the famous Florentine Pandects are truly believed to have been written at the time when Justinian first composed them; for in the preface we see many words deleted, many crossed out, many also written above the line. As to the fact that this happens only in the preface and not in the rest of the work, this results because Justinian presumably composed the preface by himself but took over all the rest from other jurists, and so in those parts he did not have to think for himself but put forward an established text.)

A clear distinction is drawn between preface and text. If the inference made about the first seems exaggerated, is the same true of what he says about the latter? Obviously he means that the text was stable, but he appears to make Justinian the copyist, not noting the differences between the hands of the various copyists. But that is to attribute a very crude error to him and one would be happier to suppose that the verb *ponebat* means 'laid down' without implying that he transcribed himself.

To return to the Greek aspect of Politian's inquiries: his view that the epigram deserves the epithet *pulcherrimum* seems a disappointing error of taste to modern readers who are used to reserving such praise for the best products of the Hellenistic age. An attempt to excuse him on the ground that the evolution of this literary genre was not understood seems to fail. In view of his knowledge of the *Greek Anthology* he must have read some of the best specimens of the genre.

Besides the *Digest* Politian studied the Greek paraphrase of the *Institutiones* made by Theophilus. He read enough of this to realise that it had its uses. Some concepts expressed with brevity in the Latin texts were expanded in the Greek for the benefit of students who did not have the advantage of a western education. Politian gave as an example the definition of the various categories of freedman.[27] It argues great patience on his part that he should have been willing to go through a paraphrase of this kind, and one wonders whether he was using it as a convenient method of improving his Greek. Aldus Manutius asserts that Politian was one of the humanists who used the comparison of text and translation as a means of learning the language.

We now come to the last noteworthy feature of his Greek scholarship. Politian was one of the very few humanists who composed a substantial number of Greek epigrams.[28] According to his own testimony he began at the tender age of seventeen. The year is therefore 1471, which happens also to be the year when Andronicus Callistus arrived in Florence and John Argyropoulos left. There is reason to think that Politian owed his interest in the *Greek Anthology*, witnessed by the collection of epigrams in MS Vaticanus gr. 1373, to the stimulus provided by Andronicus.[29] A letter which could usefully have served as a preface to the published collection reveals two motives for Politian's activity.[30] He begins by remarking that the Greeks have not produced anything worth while in verse for six hundred years. The figure is not perhaps to be taken literally, given that Latin idiom used this figure for any undefined large number and Politian probably did not know or wish to praise the latest Byzantine products that would have fallen outside the limit, the verses of Theodore Studites. He adds that he had heard rumours of one or two people about to produce good poetry, and as nothing has actually appeared he hopes by publication to stimulate them. A second motive is revealed a little later in the same letter. Politian did not write in the expectation of outdoing the ancients in their own field. His intention was to learn by the practical experience of composition more about the nature of the originals. In this he puts in a nutshell the reason which for so long influenced Anglo-Saxon practice; it is only in recent years that verse composition has been largely abandoned, whereas earlier generations of British scholars acquired through it an understanding of ancient metrical practices which served them well. Understanding of metre had not made any significant progress in Politian's day; at best scholars might appreciate the efforts of Demetrius Triclinius to restore metrical faults in the texts of Greek drama. Politian's verses, whether hexameters or elegiacs (there is also one experiment in iambics and one in hendecasyllables), have many faults. There are numerous errors of prosody and offences against rules of caesura. A feature of note is that several pieces are in Doric dialect, presupposing an acquaintance with Theocritus. The earliest of these is no. 11, composed at the age of nineteen, and addressed to John Argyropoulos. Are we to infer that Politian had read Hellenistic literature on his own initiative? Or did a tutor offer a course on Theocritus? The tutor in the years in question appears to have been Andronicus Callistus, who is known to have lectured on Theocritus in Bologna. When he arrived in Florence he gave a course on another Hellenistic poet, Apollonius Rhodius.[31] It is an obvious inference that he introduced Politian to the delights of the best work of the post-classical period.

Politian, like most of the other figures in this history, was also employed at times in translating. But it is obvious that though he had begun his career in this way his best efforts were devoted to other projects; and part of the reason for this is no doubt that by the time of his maturity as a scholar the great majority of the principal texts were accessible to readers of Latin. What may be his most important contribution in this field resulted from his participation in a Florentine diplomatic mission to Rome in 1484, during which Pope Innocent VIII commissioned him to make a version of the history by Herodian. This is an account of the Roman empire from the death of Marcus Aurelius in 180 to the accession of Gordian III in 238. Politian duly performed the task, which he claims to have despatched with ease in a few days, and produced Latin of the highest quality. But what distinguishes him from other scholars of his generation is his *Miscellanea*, a series of short notes on an enormous variety of topics. The first *centuria* was printed in 1489, and a manuscript draft of part of the second, containing only 59 chapters, came to light in 1961.[32] In the preface he acknowledges that the format owes something to two classical miscellanies by Aelian and Aulus Gellius; the latter will have been generally known to his readers and was closer in spirit to his own work. More recent examples were the collection by the Byzantine statesman Theodorus Metochites (*c.* 1330) and the much slighter one by Guarino, but it may well be that he did not know of either. The chapters which serve as the best guide to an appreciation of what Politian's learning and scholarly method could achieve in the field of Greek studies have already been quoted above. Comparable displays of acute erudition can be found in the writings of Valla and Bessarion, and no doubt they would have been matched by Musurus if he had chosen to publish his results in the same form. But Politian's adjustment of an existing literary genre so as to concentrate on problems of scholarship was a new departure which did not quickly find any close imitators. Arrogant though many humanists were, they knew that they could not compete.

13

Padua, Bologna, Ferrara and Messina

I now turn to the study of Greek in various other cities, most of which have not so far appeared in this history. For chronological and other reasons Padua deserves to be treated first. As is well known, its ancient university made it the centre of intellectual life in the Venetian Republic, of which it had become part in 1405. But though it had been the home of the circle known as the pre-humanists, a serious interest in Greek seems to have begun only with the arrival of the Florentine exile Palla Strozzi in 1434, whereas in Venice itself, where there was no university, Barbaro and a few others had taken up the subject. Palla, who was born c. 1373 and was old enough to have had a hand in the appointment of Chrysoloras, had also had a major part in bringing Filelfo to Florence in 1428. On being exiled he lived in Padua until his death in 1462. For nearly thirty years he was in contact with Byzantine refugees and no doubt gave them a great deal of help. It is possible that he built up a large library.[1] Unambiguous but necessarily very sporadic evidence of his activities comes from two manuscripts in his hand and others with an informative colophon.[2] With John Argyropoulos, who taught in Padua in 1441-4, he collaborated in transcribing Simplicius' commentary on Aristotle's *Physics* (Paris gr. 1906, and cf. nos. 1907-9). Another refugee, Andronicus Callistus, who was in Padua in the years 1441-4 and 1459-62, was involved in their partnership (he wrote the colophon in Paris gr. 1908). Callistus was a very prolific and intelligent copyist, of whom there will be more to say shortly. Yet another famous copyist, Joannes Scutariota, whose career lasted from 1442 to 1494, far longer than the average, did some of his work for Palla.[3]

Soon after Palla's death another effective patron of the subject made his mark in Padua. The visit of cardinal Bessarion led to two notable events in 1464, which must have raised hopes that the university was about to enter a new phase of vigorous intellectual life. A decision was taken to appoint a professor of Greek and the choice fell on one of the cardinal's protégés, Demetrius Chalcondyles, whose later career has already been noticed in connection with the development of printing in Greek. His inaugural lecture has come down to us. It naturally acknowledges his debt to his patron. But what the new professor had to offer was sound learning rather than the capacity to inspire. He rightly makes something of the possibility of reading Aristotle in the original instead of being at the mercy of poor and clumsy versions. But otherwise he does little more than deal in rather general terms with the achievements of the Greeks in the arts.[4] Two years later we find him partnering an Italian in the transcription of a copy of the *Greek Anthology* (Laur. 31.28). On the whole, however, it had to be said that his presence did not make a great impact.

Simultaneously Bessarion had brought to Padua Regiomontanus, the German mathematician and astronomer whom he had met during a diplomatic mission to Vienna in 1461. A lecture given by Regiomontanus in 1464 makes it seem as if he were about to take up an appointment. In fact he does not appear to have stayed and by 1467 he had left Italy altogether. The lecture is interesting, since it enumerates the leading authorities in various fields which were of concern to him, and though it might be an exaggeration to call the lecture a historical introduction to mathematics, one should give the author credit for a degree of historical awareness.

Although there is not much to report about Padua for a while, some signs of the vigour of Greek studies can be noted. The first is the activity of Pietro da Montagnana, a teacher of grammar who died at an advanced age in 1478. He had a library which included both Greek and Hebrew manuscripts, an unusual achievement at that date. He is credited with translations of Greek tragedy, the *Ajax* and *Hecuba*, and comedy, the *Plutus*, in each case the first play from the Byzantine syllabus, and also parts of Herodotus, Theocritus and, rather surprisingly, Philostratus. A few autograph notes survive in the margins of his copies; they do not give a very flattering impression of his attainments and have in fact led to some scepticism about his authorship.[5]

Further tantalising evidence is provided by one Nicola Passera Della Porta, who is described in a colophon as doctor and philosopher of Padua. At the age of thirty-three in 1488 he made a copy of several poetic texts (Wroclaw, Rehdiger gr. 35): the *Orphic Argonautica*, Dionysius Periegetes' poem on the geography of the world, Apollonius Rhodius, Hesiod's *Shield* and *Theogony* and Aratus' *Phaenomena*. None of these texts was a rarity in Byzantium, indeed most of them were common enough; but as a selection of reading matter for an Italian they are impressive by their range and quantity. Our opinion of this man rises still further when we find that he owned another volume of poetry (Ambr. S 31 sup.) ranging from Homer and Pindar through Callimachus and Moschus to Musaeus and Proclus' *Hymns*.

Another reliable indication comes from the end of the century. The professor of Latin eloquence, Calphurnius, who had been appointed in 1486, found the time to lecture on a rather out-of-the-way Greek author. Aldus' preface to his Herodotus of 1502 tells us that Calphurnius was reading with his pupils Cicero's *Letters to Atticus* and Pausanias. This guide to ancient Greece, of great value to archaeologists, had attracted Aldus' attention some years before, and perhaps he hoped Calphurnius would edit it. If so, his plan was foiled by the humanist's death in the following year and publication was delayed until 1516. Though Calphurnius is known chiefly as a Latinist, he was also the owner of a substantial library of Greek texts.[6]

In 1497 the university took a step forward by appointing Nicolaus Leonicus Thomaeus, who was required to lecture on Aristotle. It is alleged that he was the first Italian to lecture on the Greek text of the works in Padua. As a young student he appears to have attended the courses of Chalcondyles and he may have seen himself as continuing the work of his master. But it has to be said that he is still a rather obscure figure, and it remains to be proved that his appointment made a substantial and immediate impact.[7]

One of the refugees whom we have encountered in Padua moved on to Bologna. Andronicus Callistus is important both as a copyist and as a teacher, and while he cannot be described as a neglected figure there are reasons for thinking that he deserves to be the subject of further research. Although his career cannot be traced in detail we know that he reached Padua by 1441 and the last report of him in Italy is that in 1475 he left Florence for Milan. Several years in the 50s and 60s were spent in Bologna; he was known to Bessarion; and he taught in Florence in 1471-5, where he won the admiration of Politian.

We are fortunate in having from his years in Bologna some information about his teaching which is very valuable. In one of a pair of letters he wrote to Demetrius Chalcondyles *c.* 1465 he lists the lecture courses he is currently giving. He names Pindar, the epistles of Phalaris and Theodore's grammar as texts being studied in Greek. One may venture the guess that the three books named are the syllabus for three separate classes, advanced, intermediate and elementary.[8] The same letter reports classes on Aristotle's *Politics* and *Economics* in Latin, a fascinating proof that the market for Greek culture was wider than the circle of those who could master the language. Andronicus adds that he is planning to go on to another work of Aristotle on nature, by which he may mean the *Physics*, but the phrasing of the letter is consistent with the view that he had not yet decided which of the scientific works he would deal with.[9]

The class on Pindar may be the first serious attempt to read a poet whose fame in classical Latin literature made him an object of curiosity. He had also been one of the authors included in the Byzantine curriculum. The letters of Phalaris are a more surprising choice, since they are not particularly prominent in Byzantine collections of letters, a genre much studied in that civilisation. But probably Callistus believed them to be genuine, and if they passed for the work of the tyrant of Acragas in the sixth century BC they would have ranked as the earliest such collection. Perhaps his judgment coincided with the view expressed in 1692 by Sir William Temple: 'I think the epistles of Phalaris to have more race, more spirit, more force of wit and genius than any others I have ever seen, either ancient or modern.'

What is most striking about Callistus' instruction in Bologna is a fact not previously used in this context. From a report by his pupil Merula it emerges that he lectured on Theocritus. The particular point mentioned by Merula is the name of the river Crathis, which occurs at *Idyll* 5.16. The importance of the information is that while Theocritus was an author familiar to anyone brought up in the Byzantine tradition, it has sometimes been suggested that Hellenistic literature aroused no great interest in Italy until Politian lectured on Theocritus and edited one of Callimachus' *Hymns*. We can now see that the credit for this enlargement of the literary horizon should be given partly to Callistus.[10]

Callistus' choice of texts for reading with pupils can be compared with other contemporary information on the subject. It looks as if he had devised in Bologna a progression from a textbook of grammar to simple prose and then to poetry. This type of approach to the subject is seen also in a letter of Alamanno Rinuccini to his son dating from 1473. After expressing the view that the study of Greek is to be treated as if it were the dessert at a meal, he tells his son that when he has been through the elementary linguistic drills he should choose an orator or a historian as a text to read. The poets are to be held over until later, because their style almost constitutes a different language owing to the number of dialects they employ. This advice is sound and is a further reminder of the difficulties facing the beginner.[11]

But not all lecturers studied the needs of their pupils so well. One of Chalcondyles' pupils in Padua was the German Hartmann Schedel, who records that he began his course with *Erotemata* and then passed to Hesiod, which will have been rather easier than Pindar but by no means a simple introduction to the delights of Greek poetry.[12]

Callistus the copyist perhaps merits further study, because a number of the books he transcribed are notable for good readings which may be the result of his intelligence in grappling with corruptions. Since he was extremely active as a scribe – presumably he was often forced to earn his living in this way – the number of books to be examined is very large. My own impression after examining some published data is that though he was intelligent and sometimes made the right corrections, there is no proof of exceptional talent. Theoretically it is possible that some good ideas in the opening pages of Aristotle's *Poetics* are due to him – they are found in his transcript Paris gr. 2038; but there is an alternative explanation, which is that he had access to one of the two key witnesses (Riccardianus 46) in its undamaged state.[13] It also has to be noted that if Callistus were of exceptional ability he would not be expected to stumble when it was necessary to interpret abbreviations; yet it looks as if there were two texts where he failed in this way.[14]

After Callistus' departure from Bologna the subject seems to have languished for a while. It was taken up again by Antonio Urceo Cortesi, generally known as Urceo Codro (1446-1500), a pupil of the younger Guarino. His original appointment in 1482 required him to teach grammar, rhetoric and poetry. From 1485 onwards his contract was varied by the addition of a clause that he was to teach Greek on public holidays, and this formulation is repeated annually until the end of his life.[15] One is reminded of Sir Winston Churchill's remark that he would let clever boys 'learn Latin as an honour and Greek as a treat'. It is hard to know how many holidays the Bolognese allowed themselves in the last two decades of the century, but unless they were exceptionally frequent one is forced to the conclusion that the demand for Greek was limited, and despite the undeniable enthusiasm of the professor, whose annual introductory lectures are liberally interlarded with Greek quotations, no pupil could have received enough public instruction to make much progress. The professor's first course was devoted to Homer, to whom he often returned, his second to Hesiod and his third to Theocritus.[16] Quite a number of other authors are mentioned as texts adopted for a course. Apart from Aristotle we may note in particular Euripides and Aristophanes,[17] Plutarch on education,[18] Hippocrates' *Aphorisms*,[19] and there is an offer to deal with a wide variety of medical and mathematical authors if requested. This interest in medical matters is to be noted. One would like to know if it owes anything to his elder contemporary Leoniceno, professor in Ferrara. It is of course not certain that the offer was taken up; professors of medicine seem to have needed some convincing that the study of Greek could bring them dividends that were not to be had from the usual sources.[20] Though it is plausibly conjectured that his auditors may have included Copernicus,[21] neither the Pole nor the others are likely to have learned anything out of the ordinary, if we are to judge from the preserved formal lectures. His remarks on Homer are conventional in the worst sense; he treats the poet as a source of knowledge of every kind, after the fashion of the less intelligent critics of antiquity. His praise of Greek studies is no more exciting, as it discusses in a pedestrian manner the Greek origin of the liberal arts and medicine. The speaker ends by saying that it would be a disgrace to go off like merchants to learn German or Spanish instead of improving one's mind with Greek.[22] The audience are invited to read Homer with him this year in order that they may, when the need arises, be able to write, declaim and speak in public in Greek. Even in a world which valued literary accomplishments far higher than is easily conceived in our own day this manifesto has an oddly hollow ring.[23]

Whereas Codro's attainments can only be described as modest, Niccolò Leoniceno (1428-1524) was a man of real distinction who taught for many years in Ferrara. In the late forties and early fifties he studied in Padua, where he could have met Palla Strozzi and Callistus. He had a number of distinguished pupils – Bembo and Linacre are notable among them – and he was a source of valuable help to the publishers in Venice at the turn of the century. We know that he was in touch with Aldus at the time when the editio princeps of Aristotle was being prepared, and he allowed his text of Theophrastus' botanical works, which is in Callistus' hand (Paris gr. 2069), to be copied for Aldus so that the edition could proceed. When Callierges and Vlastos produced their volume of Galen in 1500 it was again Leoniceno who made texts available from his library.[24]

His best efforts were devoted to Greek medicine, especially Galen. The first humanist version of any work by this standard authority had been due to Giorgio Valla, who published *De sectis* in 1483-4 and followed this with versions of other treatises in 1498. Despite this chronological priority Leoniceno has a better claim to be regarded as the first Italian to come to grips with some of the problems posed by the Galenic corpus. He translated a few of the works in it, including the commentary on the Hippocratic *Aphorisms*, and this version earned the approval of Politian. Leoniceno had written to Politian to express his admiration of the *Miscellanea*, which he appreciated greatly despite having long since abandoned what he calls *politioris humanitatis studia*.[25] The remark is significant, for even if Scaliger was later to praise Leoniceno for his achievement both as a philologist and as a student of medicine, we may suspect that Leoniceno's modest words reflect his aims accurately.

The printed text of his translations of Galen is preceded by an introduction. Although this is not a general account of Galen it merits attention. It begins with a discussion of a passage in Aristotle's *Historia animalium* about rabies (604a5-8). Here Leoniceno found that Gaza's version was nonsensical, because it made Aristotle say that men do not die from the disease. A modern rendering of the passage runs as follows: 'Rabies drives the animal mad, and any animal whatever, excepting man, will take the disease if bitten by a dog so afflicted; the disease is fatal to the dog itself, and to any animal it may bite, man excepted.'[26] Leoniceno proposed to correct the text by making a small change in the Greek, involving only two letters, at both points where the exception is referred to. After the change the text asserts that the animals suffer more quickly than man.[27] Curiously enough Leoniceno does not claim to have found his proposed reading in a Greek manuscript, and perhaps he did not possess the text in his own library; but he does not even suggest that a search be made. In fact the known manuscripts have the reading presupposed by Gaza's rendering and one modern editor has defended it by arguing that Aristotle wishes simply to say that, in contrast to what happens to the infected animals, human beings do not necessarily die of a bite.[28] One is inclined to reply that if this was Aristotle's meaning he would have made it explicit. Before the invention of modern treatment it was quite exceptionally rare for any victim of rabies to survive, and one can understand why Leoniceno did not wish to leave a grossly implausible statement in the text.

To return to Leoniceno's argument: the point of his opening paragraph is to show that in some places the text of the classics needs to be corrected. One imagines that he had been confronted with unreasonable conservatism in the form of attempts to defend the correctness of a transmitted text at the cost of impossibly complex and subtle interpretation. He passes on to a consideration of two passages in Galen's *Ars parva*, and explains his reasons for emending the text. The argument is obviously that of a man fully familiar with his subject, and it is interesting to note that the two proposals are both recorded in the margin, with an attribution to Leoniceno, in one of the extant manuscripts (Paris gr. 2273).

Interpretation of Galen also earned Leoniceno a small place in the history of philosophy. He wrote an essay on Galen's scientific method. It is a discussion of a complex and obscure statement made at the beginning of the *Ars parva* which had puzzled a number of medieval commentators. The solution offered is to see a distinction between one method suggested by Galen as a means of investigating a given problem, whereas there is another suitable for organising the established facts of a subject when they have to be taught to pupils.[29]

As an eminent authority who offered the public improved versions of the medical classics of Galen he was among those asked for an opinion about the most pressing epidemic of the times, the new plague of syphilis which broke out in 1494 while the French army of Charles VIII was camped around Naples. The disease was commonly known as the *morbus Gallicus*, except among the French, who chose to name it after the place where it first occurred. A meeting of doctors was held in Ferrara to discuss the intractable new disease, and shortly after Leoniceno wrote a booklet on the subject, published by Aldus in 1497. In his view the disease was not a new phenomenon. Searching in ancient literature and applying the doctrine that a disease does not appear in one form only but in a number of variant versions, he finds a classical precedent in Hippocrates, citing *Epidemics* 2.1 and 3.2-3. The second passage is the more important; it is one which to some modern scholars has seemed to be another description of the famous plague of Athens recorded in Thucydides 2. Leoniceno does not see the analogy. With a triumphant but misplaced devotion to antiquity he asks the question 'Who would not recognise from Hippocrates' words an epidemic similar to that of our own times?' It is worth noting that some modern authorities believe that a number of medieval cases of leprosy may in reality have been syphilis, but this thought does not seem to have occurred to Leoniceno.[30]

One of the least fortunate refugees was Constantine Lascaris, who grew up in Constantinople and was a pupil of John Argyropoulos when the city was captured by the Turks in 1453. Somehow he managed to escape to freedom, and after a few itinerant years he found employment in Milan from 1458 to 1465; but then after a very short stay in Naples he was unable to do more than make a rather uncertain living in Messina.[31] There he remained from 1466 until his death from the plague in 1501. Cardinal Bessarion attempted to help him by nominating him to a chair of Greek with the duty of teaching the monks of the local monasteries of what is sometimes referred to as the Basilian order. A stipend of 80 gold coins was attached to the post, but the payment of it seems to be have been highly erratic. Although Lascaris' existence was sometimes relieved by the arrival of excellent pupils from elsewhere – a notable case being the visit of the young Bembo in 1492 – he was not always content with his lot. A surviving letter gives eloquent expression to his feelings, and though one cannot rule out the possibility of it having been composed in a fit of depression, the grounds for complaint were probably neither imaginary nor limited to the short term.[32] The letter is a bitter tirade against the poverty and neglect he suffers under the present government. He thinks nostalgically of Milan and says he would even contemplate going to Britain. But a few lines later, cataloguing the unhappy fates of other learned men, he notes that Andronicus Callistus had died there friendless. Even John Argyropoulos lived in poverty in Rome, obliged to sell off his library, while Theodore Gaza ended his days at Policastro in Calabria. Lascaris makes it clear that Rome and Naples are both equally distasteful to him.

The move from Milan was occasioned by the marriage of his pupil Ippolita Sforza to the Neapolitan prince Alfonso, duke of Calabria. A copy of one of his textbooks transcribed for his pupil in his own hand still survives (Paris gr. 2590). Although Milan was not the best place for a refugee to profess Greek, especially as Filelfo had been settled there for many years, Lascaris appears to have obtained a regular position after waiting for some time. While in Milan he came across two unusual texts, one being the post-classical epic poem of Quintus of Smyrna, the other, which perhaps stimulated him more, the Orphic *Argonautica*. He wrote a brief introduction to it, from which we can infer that he read the text with his pupils.[33] He begins with a typical scholastic procedure of the *accessus* type, comprising in this case only four sections, the poet's life, the purpose of the text, its title and the metre. The last three are speedily dealt with; the purpose of the work is declared to be narrative poetry. But on the poet's life he enlarges with all the details he could find in a variety of sources. It is perhaps not surprising to find him accepting all ancient traditions about the mythical author. But there were evidently some people who did not believe in the existence of Orpheus, since Lascaris takes the trouble to insist that their view is unreasonable because poets, historians and geographers mention him. Although it is easy to be censorious in the face of such naiveté, in fairness one has to allow that the required degree of scepticism about the ancient biographical tradition relating to the Greek poets is a recent phenomenon.[34] Yet Lascaris might have considered whether the surviving text could really be a genuine work of exceptional antiquity. His devotion to it may have extended to preparing the editio princeps of 1500.[35]

Lascaris' chief claim to fame in his own day was the authorship of various works on Greek grammar, one of them being a textbook for beginners printed as early as 1476. As such it was one of the first products of the new technology to serve the needs of students of Greek.[36] It is curious to see how a man who had by now spent ten years isolated on the periphery of cultural life achieved this distinction for his work. He continued to receive recognition, as is shown not only by Bembo's period of study with him but also by Aldus' publication of a later edition of the grammar. Probably he maintained regular contact with the mainland by correspondence, and it is unfortunate that very little of it has come down to us.

While in Messina he will have had the opportunity to search for manuscripts in the local libraries. Several areas of southern Italy and Sicily had had flourishing bilingual communities during the middle ages, and some of the monastic libraries had been well stocked, though it may be doubted whether they had many texts of pagan literature outside the range required for maintaining the usual reading programme in the schools. By the second half of the fifteenth century, however, the Greek element in local culture had been very much reduced. It was probably necessary to search in neglected libraries and it does not appear that Lascaris made any startling discoveries. A few commentaries on the ancient handbooks of rhetoric seem to have been his only substantial reward.[37]

Although he possessed a large personal library – 83 volumes given by him to the city of Messina have found their way via the duke of Uceda to the Biblioteca Nacional in Madrid – this collection was formed with great difficulty. It is quite likely that he did not bring the whole of his existing library to Messina when he first arrived, since it was not his original plan to settle there, and in fact a number of books written or owned by him have been identified in places other than Madrid. In the main block of 83 there are 25 entirely copied in his own hand, and no less than 43 others have had missing sections restored by him. He several times notes that he had trouble in finding a text.[38] Once he had the extraordinary luck to find in Messina a volume that he had owned many years earlier in Greece (Madrid gr. 127 (4677)). But the most telling proof of the difficulty which he faced in his work as teacher and scholar is found in a note at the end of a copy of Herodotus which he made on paper of poor quality (Madrid gr. 25 (4568)): 'Constantine Lascaris wrote out the text for himself and others in Messina in Sicily, having long wished to possess it and not finding any better paper in the city. He copied very quickly because the owner of the exemplar was a visitor and wished to leave; in the year 1487 from the incarnation, on the 30th of August.' If we find Lascaris' overall achievement less than outstanding, the conditions in which he worked make it remarkable that he could do anything useful at all.[39]

14

Venice

(i) Ermolao Barbaro and Pietro Bembo

The Barbaro family played an important part in Venetian affairs, and one member of it has already been mentioned in an earlier chapter. His contribution to humanistic studies is more than matched by that of his grandson Ermolao Barbaro (1453/4-93), who at the age of twenty already had a considerable achievement to his credit: the first translation into Latin of an Aristotelian commentator, in this case the paraphrase by the fourth-century sophist Themistius. It was a new departure to make available to a wider public the ancient exegetical material. For some years Barbaro lived in Padua, and it might seem more logical to have dealt with him in the preceding chapter; but there are two reasons which make it equally satisfactory to give a brief account of him here. One is that he returned to Venice in 1484 and spent most of the rest of his life there; the other is that his teaching in Padua was perhaps not always at the highest level. It seems that in 1474-6 his courses on the *Nicomachean Ethics* and *Politics* were based on the Latin text, not the Greek, and that it was the medieval versions, not the more recent alternative provided by Bruni or Argyropoulos, which served as the basis for his lectures, even if he occasionally shows awareness of Bruni. Such at any rate is the inference to be drawn from a copy with autograph marginalia (Columbia University, Plimpton 17).[1]

While still in Padua he translated the *Rhetoric* (1478-9). But it is the work undertaken in the following years which has made his reputation. In Latin he made valuable contributions to the Elder Pliny and the geographer Pomponius Mela, and in Greek his energies were devoted to the important botanist Dioscorides. An interest in matters scientific is apparent, and it was perhaps an ambition dating back to his student days to work in these fields, since he says in his preface to Themistius that he had been struck by the quality of Gaza's translations. Several of these were of scientific treatises.

Dioscorides, who wrote in the middle of the first century, compiled the most famous of all herbals. Its value as a pharmacological reference book was uncontested for centuries: translations were made into Arabic and Latin and fine sets of illustrations exist in several manuscripts. Barbaro made a version and equipped it with a large supplement of his own, in which he assembled as much information as he could about each plant from other classical sources. He lists 1,018 items; while most entries are short, a few make substantial paragraphs.

It is tempting to suppose that Barbaro matched his concern with Dioscorides by maintaining a botanical garden. The two notions seem to be mentioned in the same breath in a letter of 1484 which describes his daily routine at Padua.[2] At a certain hour he visits a neighbour's garden and his own; 'we contemplate the plants in each and think about Dioscorides, whom we must certainly edit one day', an ambition achieved a few years after his death by Aldus.[3] Barbaro's own work had to wait still longer before being published; it did not appear until 1516. Another translation of the herbal appeared almost at once in 1518. It was due to the Florentine humanist Marcello Virgilio Adriani. One does not know if he was surprised by Barbaro's publication when his own researches were well advanced and determined not to let his own efforts be wasted; at all events he acknowledges the value of what Barbaro had done, and asserts that he himself has collated five copies of the Greek text, an unusually exhaustive operation at that date and one that could not be performed at all in most academic centres owing to the relative poverty of the libraries. If Adriani had begun to study Dioscorides independently it is a sign of the growing interest in the Greek scientific legacy.

Barbaro's contribution to Dioscorides seems not to have been studied closely.[4] It may be worth pausing for a moment over one remark which has attracted attention. In his *Corollarium* he is concerned with the authorship of the pseudo-Aristotelian treatise *De plantis* and reports a current opinion according to which the extant Greek text is due to a certain Maximus. The source of this conjecture is not known; the Maximus in question has been identified with the learned and versatile Byzantine monk Planudes, and presumably the author of the conjecture realised that a translation from Latin back into Greek was not likely to have been undertaken except in Planudes' circle. An attentive reading of the preface to the treatise reveals, however, that if Barbaro or some other humanist argued in this way he was on the wrong track, since a clue in the preface reveals that the scholar responsible for the Greek text was probably from one of the Italo-Greek communities.[5]

Another member of the Venetian aristocracy makes his appearance in our story just after Barbaro's death. Pietro Bembo (1470-1547), who was nominated librarian of San Marco in 1530 and later became a cardinal, is best known for his achievement as a writer of perfectly Ciceronian Latin and for his advocacy of an archaising standard in the Italian literary language. His views on Greek are to be found in a youthful essay written in Greek in 1494 and never published.[6] Bembo had travelled to Sicily in May of 1492 and stayed until the summer of 1494, studying with Constantine Lascaris, whose *Grammar* he brought back with him to

Venice where it was printed by Aldus. Lascaris is at first sight an odd choice of mentor. Venice had a professor of classical languages in Giorgio Valla (1447-1500), who took up his appointment in 1485 and owed his position at least in part to Barbaro. But as he was not of outstanding talent and his interests were less literary than scientific, Bembo may have had sufficient reason for looking further afield. Yet one is surprised that he did not consider going to Padua or Milan or Florence, especially as his father had been ambassador in Florence and Politian had stayed with the family during his visit to Venice in 1491. Whatever his reasons – he says in a letter to his Latin tutor that he was attracted by Lascaris' fame as a teacher, by the prospect of escaping from distracting obligations in Venice and, much less intelligibly, by the idea that Messina still maintained a pure form of Greek – it has to be said that his time in Messina was not badly spent. The Greek of his essay of 1494 is fluent and passable as an imitation of the classical language. One can tell that the writer has a close acquaintance with Demosthenes, the obvious Greek model for a speech. In both the extant copies there are corrections and it looks as if Bembo asked for help in making improvements; but they do not appear to be in Lascaris' hand. The text purports to be an address to the Venetian senate, the speaker's first appearance before that body. One wonders if the Greek reflects a maiden speech given at an unusually early age or is simply the product of an attempt to revive the ancient educational practice of the imaginary speech (*suasoria*): in the present case he would be responding to the challenge, 'Imagine what one would say if trying to persuade the Republic to help Greek studies.' Bembo thought of Greek composition as a game[7] but we are not obliged to treat the sentiments expressed in the essay as frivolous. It is more interesting than other compositions of the same kind. Bembo at once confronts a difficulty which may have been more acute in Venice than in some Italian cities: he has heard merchants saying, 'Why do we need Greek literary studies? It is enough, quite enough if we preserve Latin.' He notes that the Greeks themselves are in no position to do much. He takes the highly unusual step of estimating that we now possess barely one per cent of Greek literature, and even that risks being lost if no action is taken. This statement indirectly confirms that Bessarion's donation of his great library, designed to meet this objective, was not yet having any effect. A long encomium of the role of *logos* in the development of civilised society follows: here Bembo may conceivably have taken a hint from a passage in Gorgias' *Helen*, which he had translated during his stay in Messina.[8] It should be easy for Venetians to obtain copies of texts; the Republic has many possessions in Greece, and in general the Venetian towns are well developed with industries and schools. The value of education as a means to providing the necessary skills in a society leads to the formulation of a dilemma: either one decides not to be a first-rate power or not to neglect education. And then the speaker passes to the task of justifying Greek, which he does in terms more or less conventional for the period, noting the difficulty of attaining to the highest levels in many arts and branches of learning without Greek, and criticising in particular writers in philosophy who tried to do without. But he does not single out individual Greek authors as specially rewarding or undeservedly neglected, and since there was already a teacher of the classical languages employed by the Republic he does not have to make out a case for the establishment of a chair. It remains quite unclear how much effect his views had, even in the circle of his friends, and though the essay could be regarded as a promising beginning to a scholarly career Bembo did not go on to make his mark as a Hellenist.

(ii) The Aldine publishing house, the Neakademia and Forteguerri's manifesto

Much the most important publishing house of the Renaissance was the firm established in Venice by Aldus Manutius (*c.* 1450-1515).[9] It owes a good deal of its fame to the high proportion of Greek texts in its list. The founder's early career is obscure. He had been brought up in and near Rome, and after continuing his education in Ferrara he spent some years as a tutor to the family of Alberto Pio, prince of Carpi, a small town just north of Modena on the way to Mantua. In 1489 or 1490 he went to Venice to set up his business, but it was not until 1495 that the first book appeared under his imprint. The timing was not propitious, for it was in 1494 that the French had made their first invasion of Italy. Aldus' fortunes were frequently affected by the turbulent political conditions of the period. Even if Italy had been less troubled at the time, the financial success of the new firm would hardly have been guaranteed, since the market for texts in the original Greek, as opposed to the increasing number of versions, remained limited. The choice of Venice as the headquarters of the firm could not be justified by the presence of the best contemporary scholars. On the other hand the city was already a great centre of printing. Aldus must also have known that Greeks from Crete and the territories of the former Byzantine empire normally arrived in Italy at Venice and he doubtless had some information about the community of exiles in residence there. A third factor which may have moved him was the donation of cardinal Bessarion's library; but if he had hoped to be able to exploit its riches, he was soon to be deceived, for all the evidence is that he was obliged to look elsewhere for copies of Greek texts.

At the time of his move to Venice Aldus was not yet a leading figure among humanists. His activities for the next few years remain almost entirely unknown. A rare glimpse of his preparations for one of the earliest publications of his firm, the Theocritus of 1495, is afforded by a letter from the professor in Bologna, Urceo Codro. It appears that Aldus had asked for some Greek texts, and Codro replied that there would be a delay because his Greek copyist Nicholas was occupied with other commissions. Aldus had also asked about a verse in Theocritus which he could not understand (18.14), and Codrus tells him that his manuscript is faulty. Codrus' own copy of the text, written by Andronicus (Callistus?), has the true reading, and he goes on to explain it by reference to parallel expressions in Aristophanes and the lexicographer Pollux. In fact Codrus' advice is incorrect, but the episode suggests that despite the lack of reliable manuscripts Aldus was doing his best to issue a respectable edition.[10]

Another letter from Codrus is valuable for the light it throws on an important aspect of Aldus' activities. It is generally believed that Aldus frequently issued books in large impressions ranging from 1,000 to 3,000 copies, and it is an easy assumption that he made his name by ensuring not simply that texts were accessible but that they were relatively cheap and accurately printed. On these last two points Codrus is critical. In a long letter sent to Battista Palmieri on 15 April 1498 Codrus begins with a complaint about Aldus' stinginess in his business transactions. He adds that the style of publication is wasteful in its use of paper and announces his intention of not buying any more of Aldus' books until the price has come down to a tolerable figure. It is all very well for Aldus to talk of the great labour and expense involved in printing; the labour involved in earning money is equally great. Prices have never been so high. He admits to being very glad that he has bought the Aldine Aristotle, so as to be able to answer questions from philosophers who have doubts arising from the translations in circulation. But his joy is outweighed by the thought that for the same sum of money he could have acquired ten excellent Latin books of substantial size. And the Aristotle contains many errors which leave him uncertain how to answer questions about particular words. While recognising that all printers make mistakes, when the sense is ruined by the wrong word one is bound to feel hard done by; and he quotes some examples from the *Historia animalium*. In the first passage the word 'veins' was printed by mistake for 'diaphragm'; Codrus thinks it amazing that the Greeks in Aldus' circle did not notice. In another passage he suggests an alteration to the text which should probably be treated more as an emendation than the detection of a misprint. The effect of the letter as a whole is to show that contemporary admiration for Aldus was not unbounded.[11]

Yet Codrus' comments do not do justice to Aldus. The design of Greek type really was difficult and expensive, with not much prospect of recouping the outlay from big sales. Over the years Aldus, aided by the expert designer Francesco Griffo, produced four founts. Although these types have shortcomings, Aldus' influence was such that they set a pattern for a long time. As models Aldus used contemporary scribal hands. It has been suggested that the source of his first fount was the hand of the calligrapher Immanuel Rhusotas, and that the second was a reduced version of the same hand, perhaps influenced by a member of the Gregoropoulos family, who belonged to Aldus' circle. The third may have been based on the script of Marcus Musurus, of whom there will be more to say shortly, and the fourth is extraordinarily like the hand of Aldus himself.[12]

Mention of Aldus' friends and associates brings us to the important topic of his Greek club, known as the New Academy or Neakademia. Its aim and character are not easy to define precisely. One recent definition of its main function is that it intended 'to select the Greek authors to be printed and to seek solutions to the various philological and literary problems involved'.[13] That is certainly correct as far as it goes. The existence of such a society is proved by various references, the earliest of which appears to be the colophon of the first edition of Sophocles, issued in August 1502. Difficulties of interpretation arise when we look closely at the evidence, especially the so-called constitution of the Neakademia, from which one modern authority infers that it held periodic banquets 'in imitation of the Platonic symposia'. What this last phrase means is far from clear, and it looks like a mistranslation, as we shall see. But that is not the main difficulty raised by the curious document in question.

Only one copy of it survives, pasted into the front cover of a binding. A good deal of the empty space in the margins is occupied by brief notes on a variety of topics in a hand which has been recognised as belonging to Scipio Forteguerri, the author of the text.[14]

In my opinion it can only be understood satisfactorily if we assume that it suffers from an internal inconsistency, since on one level it is no more than a set of rules for a scholars' dining club, whereas on another level it is concerned with much grander aspirations, which are clearly implied but not spelled out in detail. The best interpretation of it hitherto, which does not claim to be a full solution, has the great merit of seeing that there is more in it than meets the eye and of drawing attention to other relevant evidence, provided by a letter written by Johannes Cuno to Willibald Pirckheimer on 21 December 1505. This states clearly that Aldus is planning to move to Germany and found there a New Academy, where a staff of men learned in Greek and Hebrew will see to the printing of important books and lead a new educational movement. Such grandiose plans explain a phrase in the constitution, to which we can now return.

The text begins: 'Since serious lovers of education derive much benefit from Greek conversation, it has been decided by the three of us, Aldus Romanus, John the Cretan and thirdly myself, Scipio Carteromachus (i.e. Forteguerri) to pass a law that it is not permitted to speak to each other except in Greek.' Anyone who does otherwise for any reason whatsoever is to be fined one small coin, without possibility of postponement; failure to pay will lead to the fine being doubled, quadrupled, etc. in geometric proportion, ultimately leading to expulsion from the club. The money is to be put into a special purse or box, entrusted to one of the three founders, and sealed. When it is decided to open it, the cash is to be counted, and if it is enough for a symposium, it is to be handed over to Aldus, so that he may 'entertain grandly and not in the style reserved for the printers, but in a fashion worthy of men who are already dreaming of the Neakademia and have already in a Platonic sense almost established it'. If there is not yet enough money collected, it is to put back until the sum is sufficient for a feast.

Apart from the obvious hint that Aldus' treatment of the printing staff was not normally generous, this last sentence allows an important inference. The mention of the academy is in a form which means that the document cannot be treated as the foundation charter, and the title 'Law of the New Academy' (Νεακαδημίας νόμος) is a mistake due to a confusion in the mind of Forteguerri, who extended the concept of a law from the rules of the dining club to the further ambition of its members.

Qualifications for other members are then outlined in such a way as to show that the group sought people sympathetic to Aldus' grand schemes. Visitors and foreigners were to be eligible on the same terms as others. Failure to observe the rules was to lead to expulsion without possibility of readmission unless there was repentance accompanied by an offer of guarantees of future good behaviour. A clause in this section seems to indicate that an offender will be expelled as unworthy of the New Academy, in other words those who cannot follow the rules of the club are not suitable as prospective members of the more august association that is being planned (τῆς Νεακαδημίας ἐκδεδιώχθω ἀνάξιος ὤν). A sensible further provision is that those who are learning Greek and do not yet speak it may be admitted as members after a test of their progress.

In imitation of the formulae used in Athenian public documents of the classical period the text states that the law has been proposed by Scipio Cartermachus 'of the tribe of readers', and put to the vote by Aldus Romanus, the founder of the New Academy, and John the Cretan 'of the tribe of correctors'. All three are given the classical title of *prytaneis*. Approval by all the members is recorded, four of whom are named, after which comes the phrase 'and many others who are already anxious to learn and desire a new academy, attracted by the name alone.'

The interpretation which seems to do full justice to the wording of the document is that it proves the existence of a plan for a new academy, and the plan is to be promoted in the meanwhile by forming a club of like-minded enthusiasts who will dine together from time to time. In formulating a judgment it is important to take into account what one eminent modern authority has termed 'the evidently facetious style of the document'. Even in Rome at this time men were increasingly unwilling to speak Latin, let alone Greek; so an obligation to speak only the latter cannot be intended seriously. In addition one should note that several Latin texts issued by Aldus, such as his Statius (1502), Valerius Maximus

(1502) and Ovid (1504), are stated to be products of the Academy.[15]

These two considerations are not to be lightly dismissed, and one may accept the conclusion that there is a touch of academic humour in the document. Yet it does not follow that we must treat it as entirely frivolous. Humour and serious purpose are not irreconcilable. There are other signs of Aldus having thought seriously about the advancement of learning, to be achieved if need be by moving to Germany.[16] As to the colloquial command of Greek, Politian's remark on the subject should be recalled, and the topic had arisen a few years before in the Aldine circle, since Musurus in his preface to the Aristophanes of 1498 alludes to it. It is clear that Greeks and some Italians claimed to set store by this accomplishment.

One way of gaining further insight into the aims of Aldus and his friends is to analyse the inaugural lecture given by Forteguerri, published by Aldus in 1504.[17] It opens with a long and not very specific encomium of the Greek language as an instrument of expression. The speaker makes some use of the oration by the second-century sophist Aristides in which Athens is celebrated for having secured the adoption of her language by all civilised peoples, an achievement treated as a victory won without any blood being spilled.[18] This is a learned reference to an impressive passage in a text not yet printed in 1504, but it would be more appropriate in a lecture designed as a history of Greek culture. Next the speaker turns to the achievements of the Greeks, which are declared to be superior to those of other nations in the same ratio as an elephant is to a gnat. Philosophy is the first example given, and it is pointed out that even non-Greeks have chosen to use that language in preference to their own. The test cases of Aulus Gellius, Musonius, Favorinus and Philo are not badly chosen, but they are not improved by the addition of Anacharsis, whose spurious letters are said to be very elegant and no less rich in moral teaching (*perquam elegantes nec minus praeceptis refertae*). The speaker shows himself aware of the traditional debate as to whether the Greek philosophers owed much to the wisdom of the Egyptians. He is not disposed to deny such a debt, but suggests that the concepts in question are those which had been previously brought to Egypt by the Jews. As such they are theological, part of the *Hebraica veritas*, which is not the speaker's concern. This is an evasive way of dealing with an objection to the claim being made for the overriding importance of Greek culture in all spheres. In this part of his lecture he is dealing with patterns of thought common in Christian apologetic literature.

Then follows a paragraph on the similarity of the Greek and Latin languages, a notion he reverts to later in the hope of persuading his audience that Greek is an easy language. All good poetry derives from Greek, he claims; one wonders what view he took of Dante. There is an emphatic statement of the inadequacy of the Latin versions of Aristotle, a view in which he would have been fully justified had there been no alternative to using the medieval versions, but which seems unfair to the more recent work of Bruni and others. He adds that Platonic philosophy is more sublime than Aristotelianism and is consistent with the Christian religion. That claim might well have been contested by members of his audience, as it had led to violent controversy some fifty years before. Modern philosophers, he continues, have neglected Platonic philosophy, knowledge of which is desired rather than possessed by many people. Once again there is clear exaggeration; it is disturbing to note that Ficino's popular translation of Plato is either implicitly condemned or wilfully ignored.

Not surprisingly the sciences provide some good arguments for the speaker. Greek is essential for the mathematician. The audience are invited to consider how inferior Campano's version of Euclid appears when compared with Theon's edition and the commentaries of Proclus. The version in question had been produced c. 1255-9, and Forteguerri was probably entitled to pass this unfavourable judgment on it, since he is known to have made a copy of the Greek text of Euclid (Vat. gr. 1295).[19]

Medicine is also mentioned, but without any telling example. Last come the superior sciences of law and theology. Jurists can benefit from a knowledge of Greek. Forteguerri claims on the authority of his teacher Politian that Justinian inserted a good deal of explanatory material into the Greek wording of laws, designed to make clear matters which were obvious to anyone brought up in the Latin tradition but not to students educated in the eastern half of the empire.[20] Forteguerri's argument is flimsy here; he is not concerned with students of Greek upbringing, but attempting to suggest reasons for the study of Greek which will appeal precisely to those educated in Latin and well able to appreciate the connotations of Latin legal terminology. He ends this section with a claim to have inspected the Florentine Pandects, a fact not noted by modern authorities on legal humanism. Perhaps one should not assume that he implies any thorough examination; it may be enough to suppose that he had been present when Politian was working on the manuscript.

As to theology, he first mentions several of the Greek fathers as authors worth reading and then adds a remark in the tradition of Lorenzo Valla, to the effect that the whole of the literary tradition about Christ, with the exception of St Matthew's Gospel, was originally composed in Greek, so that for certain matters recourse to the Greek source is essential. 'Quid quod omnia quae de Christo literis mandata sunt graece primum composita feruntur, excepto Matthaei evangelio? quare fieri non potest ut nonnullorum fides a graeco petenda non sit.'

In the concluding paragraphs there is a justification of the appointment of an Italian to the post of teacher, as if there had been some pressure for the appointment of a native speaker, followed by praise of Venice and in particular of Aldus for ensuring a supply of books. It becomes clear that the lecture was a prelude to a course on Demosthenes and one may note that the editio princeps of that author appeared in November of the same year with a colophon indicating that it was a product of the Neakademia.[21]

While our verdict on this lecture may be moderately favourable, there is no cause for treating it as an exceptional or revolutionary statement. Some well chosen examples are counterbalanced by exaggeration or faulty argument. Large claims are made, and in some sense these coincide with Aldus' wide range of publications. To these we must now turn.

(iii) The publications of the first ten years

As we have seen, there had been very little printing in Greek before Aldus set up his business. In 1498, 1503 and 1513 he issued lists of his publications; the first of these is confined to his Greek books, in the others the Greek titles precede the Latin (Paris gr. 3064). This arrangement is a clear sign of the policy of the house. Almost every title is the editio princeps of a classical author. By making so many texts available, even if the price was not always as modest as some members of the academic public hoped – in the list of 1498 the Aristophanes costs two-and-a-half gold pieces and the five-volume set of Aristotle eleven gold pieces – Aldus transformed the position of contemporary scholars and students, not to mention copyists, who began to find their services in demand mainly for the provision of out-of-the-way texts. The modern scholar is bound to ask whether the quality of the Aldine product matched the fame of the house. Obviously much depended on having access to manuscripts relatively free from corruption. It used to be assumed that Bessarion's splendid legacy to the Venetian Republic was readily available, but all the evidence about manuscripts used as copy in the printing house indicates the opposite.[22]

Although there were also private collections, these too might be jealously guarded. In the preface to the *Thesaurus cornucopiae et horti Adonidis* (1496) Aldus gives a fairly clear indication of this. He reports that he is now beginning to be respected for his services to the literary public, and many of those who had buried their books – he uses the Greek word βιβλιοτάφοι – are now bringing out their treasures and offering them for sale. At one time he had not even been able to borrow Greek manuscripts for an hour; now they are freely available, and some have been sent to him.

Yet the supply remained erratic at best. Aldus' remarks on the subject are too frequent and too specific to be treated lightly. Sometimes it was a case of having only one copy at his disposal, as happened with Theophrastus and Aristotle's *Eudemian Ethics*; on other occasions the editor's difficulties were not resolved by collating the various copies, and Aldus despairingly comments in his preface to Theocritus that one needs the divinatory powers of an Oedipus to understand what the author meant, while Musurus, the most expert of his collaborators, notes that the manuscripts of the letters by the sophist Alciphron were so corrupt that he had to leave some passages in an unintelligible state. These instances are all earlier than 1500 and imply an urgent need to furnish texts to an expectant public even if the result achieved was far from perfect. The preface to the Thucydides of 1502 reveals a different attitude: Aldus tells us that he would have included in the same volume Xenophon's *Historia graeca* and the history by the late Byzantine author Gemistus Plethon, but has postponed publication because he does not have at least three copies.

The other determining factor was the level of scholarship achieved by Aldus himself and the members of his circle. Learned men are not always good at the textual criticism required of editors, and very few learned men of Aldus' day were expert enough in Greek to tackle all the puzzles presented by an ancient text in a typical manuscript copy. Several of the Aldine editions, however useful they may have been to that generation of scholars, left nearly all the problems unsolved, and cannot properly be described as contributions to an improved understanding of the classics.

Before trying his hand at a major enterprise Aldus issued two small volumes which he described as a prelude. One was Musaeus' *Hero and Leander*, the short and indeed attractive poem which owed some of its vogue to the mistaken belief in its exceptional antiquity, although it is in fact a product of the fifth century AD. Perhaps Aldus did not know that Janus Lascaris had just issued an edition in Florence. Having referred to his forthcoming Aristotle he commends Musaeus as a pleasant and celebrated poet, and as the source of Ovid's *Heroides* (18 & 19). Most of the preface harps on a financial question: he needs to sell many copies if he is to raise the capital necessary to ensure a supply of the texts in demand.[23]

Aldus claimed to be responding to a demand by issuing Constantine Lascaris' grammar in February 1495. It too is presented as a prelude to more substantial titles. The copy was provided by Bembo and his companion Angelo Gabriele, who had just returned from a period of study with Lascaris. Later in the year Aldus printed the text-book which was most likely to compete with Lascaris' work, the grammar by Theodore Gaza, to which he surprisingly and almost certainly mistakenly chose to add a very difficult text, four books on syntax by the ancient grammarian Apollonius Dyscolus.

What is usually known as the Aldine Aristotle was a five-volume series issued between November of 1495 and June of 1498. To refer to it as Aristotle is misleading, insofar as the *Poetics* and the *Rhetoric* were omitted, while most of Theophrastus apart from the *Characters* was included, as were a few other items of less importance. A little of the printer's copy has survived; Aldus did not use early and important manuscripts, and yet his edition provided the Greek text that was a basis for most if not all subsequent work until the beginning of the nineteenth century. The reception granted to the edition by one expert contemporary has already been recorded; one can only speculate on what he might have said if he had been able to foresee the influence that Aldus' product was destined to have.[24]

As the first Aristotelian volume was going through the press[25] Aldus and his friends somehow found the time to put together a composite volume of poetry, in which the first item is a fuller collection of the *Idylls* of Theocritus than had previously appeared. The most important of the remaining texts are Hesiod and Theognis.

Although the New Academy had not yet been formed, it must be inferred that Aldus' friends and acquaintances were giving him much essential help. One name which perhaps deserves special mention is that of Francesco Cavalli (d. 1540), a native of Brescia who taught medicine in Padua from 1492 to 1510. Aldus acknowledges his help in determining the order of the Aristotelian writings and declares that he will publish Cavalli's essay on the subject. For reasons which are not known his plan failed and the essay appeared under another imprint.[26]

The enormous effort required for the production of five volumes of Aristotle does not appear to have exhausted Aldus. Several more titles were issued before the end of the century, some of them before the completion of the Aristotle. Of these further titles three may be described as educational, since they were aimed at the student of the language, two were partly or wholly scientific, and two, edited by Musurus and discussed in section (v) of this chapter, were literary.

The scientific texts raise an interesting question: is it possible that Aldus had been inspired by the experience of editing Aristotle's zoological treatises to formulate a project to issue a wide range of other Greek scientific works? Such books were still in many fields the best source of information. But if Aldus had any such thoughts, he must soon have abandoned them, since no more scientific texts appeared under his imprint. Yet one of the two texts he issued ought to have earned a warm welcome. It was the herbal of Dioscorides, which had enjoyed wide circulation both in the original and in various translations during the Middle Ages. Its value in medical practice meant that it was far better known than Theophrastus' scientific treatises on botany. However, though this herbal clearly played an important part in the development of medicine, there does not appear to be any evidence that Aldus' edition of the original Greek text made a significant contribution. As a kind of appendix he added the two didactic poems on snakes and antidotes by Nicander. These Hellenistic texts are so difficult that it is hard to imagine them being exploited, even if the information they contain has any practical application.

The other volume with some scientific content was not wholly Greek; it began with the Latin texts of Firmicus Maternus, an astrologer, and

Manilius, the author of a difficult poem on the same subject. Astrology and elementary astronomy were not clearly distinguished in antiquity, and Aldus shows his adherence to this traditional attitude by including the astronomical poem of Aratus, giving the Latin versions followed by the Greek text. A very large body of scholia had accumulated around the Greek text, and Aldus printed them. Such extensive commentaries are usually a sign of a text having been used for instruction in schools, and there is reason to think that Aratus had indeed been the text used in Byzantium to impart the elements of astronomy to schoolchildren. Aldus' Greek associates without any doubt knew enough about the Byzantine tradition to give him this information; what use he expected his Italian readers to make of it must remain unclear. Similar considerations apply to the short treatise which stands as the last item in the list of contents, the *Sphaera* of Proclus (the attribution to the Neoplatonist philosopher is not quite beyond doubt). This was an elementary introduction to astronomy, filling only six-and-a-half pages; Aldus printed it with a Latin rendering by his English friend Thomas Linacre.[27]

Turning now to the publications designed to help students, we may first deal with the volume entitled *Thesaurus cornucopiae et horti Adonidis*, which has a colophon dated August 1496. The main part of it is a lexicon occupying folios 1-77. Aldus tells us that it was originally the work of Favorinus Camers and the Florentine Carlo Antinori, who made a compilation of material derived from Eustathius' commentaries, the *Etymologicum Magnum* and other grammarians. Politian helped them. A letter from Camers giving this information is printed. It includes a revealing statement of his intention. The compilation was made so that 'students of the poets and especially Homer shall not offend the ears of their tutors and perpetually trouble them by asking every day "What is the tense of this verb? Could it be a first aorist, or a middle perfect, or even pluperfect?" and so forth.' Aldus worked through the material, aided by his friend Urbano da Belluno. Despite his efforts it is still very difficult to use, because all the explanations are in Greek; one needs to be quite a good scholar already in order to derive any benefit from it. The rest of the volume is a selection of writings by various Greek grammarians, and though some of them are of value, they are not easy to use owing to their technical vocabulary. Once again if Aldus hoped to be of assistance to students of modest attainments he will have been disappointed.

Perhaps some readers conveyed this message to him, for next year he issued another lexicon. This was a fresh version of Crastonus' lexicon, which had been published in Milan *c.* 1478 and subsequently reprinted. Crastonus' name is not mentioned, which seems unfair until one sees how much revision has taken place. Musurus is sometimes said to have been involved in the process, but there seems to be no firm evidence for this apart from the presence on one of the preliminary pages of Greek epigrams by Musurus and Forteguerri. There is a curious difference between the Aldine production and Crastonus, which reduces the impact of any charge of plagiarism. Whereas Crastonus had sensibly arranged his work in parallel columns of Greek words and Latin equivalents, Aldus' lexicon reverts to the practice of giving Greek synonyms or explanations and adds as a kind of appendix a Latin key. As a result it is still some way from providing the improved reference book that was felt to be needed. Aldus probably performed a better service with the Greek grammar which he had commissioned from Urbano da Belluno, issued in the same year.

At the beginning of the new century we find a great flurry of activity in the first four years. It is not clear whether Musurus continued to have a substantial part in the enterprise; he had produced two great volumes in 1498 and 1499, the Aristophanes and the epistolographers, but the details of his biography are obscure, and it rather looks as if he spent a good deal of his time in Carpi during the years 1499-1503. It also needs to be noted that in 1499 he was not completely committed to the Aldine circle, since he had some link with the press of Zacharias Callierges, contributing a letter to its publication of yet another Byzantine dictionary, the *Etymologicum Magnum*. But even if Aldus for the time being could not count on the regular collaboration of his most gifted associate, the first years of the century marked a very notable stage in his career, because his productions included several of the most central texts of classical literature.

The first book to be set up in type was not one of the most significant. It is difficult to know why Aldus interested himself in Philostratus' *Life of Apollonius of Tyana*. His introduction to it is the opposite of what one expects in a publisher's blurb, and he declares that he cannot remember reading anything worse. *Nihil unquam memini me legere deterius lectuque minus dignum*. Aldus' verdict is probably typical for his time; about thirty years later Sir Thomas More in his *Dialogue concerning heresies* has this to say: 'What labour took Philostratus to make a book full of lies, whereby he would have had Apollonius Tyaneus in miracles match unto Christ? And when he had all done, he never found one old wife so fond to believe him.'[28]

Neither Aldus nor More could be expected to take much interest in an ascetic Pythagorean of the first century, who presents an intriguing figure for students of the history of religion in antiquity. For some reason the publication seems to have been delayed until 1504, a curious fact when one considers Aldus' well-founded observations about the cost of locking up so much capital in a hazardous enterprise.

Next came another text which might be expected to appeal to a relatively narrow section of the market, the lexicon of Pollux, issued in 1502. Aldus' objective must have been to supplement the range of lexicographical works available to students. Pollux provided a wide survey of Attic usage, with a good deal of information about the culture of classical Athens. He wrote at the height of the Atticist movement in the second half of the second century, and his attempt to guide his contemporaries in the niceties of the Attic idiom which they all wished to write, besides being fine evidence of the archaising movement, has its uses for the modern scholar. But it is scarcely an instrument to put into the hands of beginners.

The three volumes which followed mark a change of tack. There can have been no shortage of readers wishing to acquire a first-hand acquaintance with the two greatest historians, Thucydides and Herodotus. Both were already available in Valla's Latin versions, and it will be recalled that Valla had complained of the difficulty of the task that Bessarion had set him with the commission for the Thucydides. With this version, whatever its imperfections, the reader had some help in his struggle with the more difficult of the two authors. Neither edition appears to be important for its contribution to the textual criticism of the author.

The third important publication of 1502 was Sophocles, an author who falls into a slightly different category. Despite some professions of enthusiasm for Greek tragedy by the Italians, who can have been left in no doubt by their teachers about the importance of the tragedians in the Byzantine curriculum, it is not likely that many Italians were able to read the plays. Sophocles is in any case a more subtly difficult text than is sometimes realised. What sales Aldus can realistically have expected must remain uncertain. One may speculate that for this and some of the other titles he ventured to issue he may have hoped to find some purchasers in the fairly substantial Greek émigré community in Venice or even to export a few copies to Crete. He would have been flattered by Sir Thomas More's suggestion that his books reached Utopia, where the inhabitants have the poetical works of Aristophanes, Homer and Euripides, plus Sophocles in the small Aldine type.

The edition itself, like those of the two historians, is a modest achievement from the textual point of view. Part of the printer's copy survives (St Petersburg gr. 731). It was seen through the press by John Gregoropoulos, a regular member of the Aldine circle. This volume happens to be the first to mention in its colophon the Aldine Academy, giving a glimpse of life in the publisher's household, 'as we sat in a semicircle round the fire with our Newacademicians in the cold of winter'. It is in the handy pocket-size format which Aldus had used for the first time in 1501 for his Vergil. No scholia were printed with the tragedies, but the preface expresses the intention of issuing them shortly, and adds that they would have been helpful in dealing with some problems of colometry in the choral lyrics. The edition remained important for some time; as with many other authors the best manuscripts were not fully exploited until the nineteenth century.

The Aldine is probably best known for the editor's intervention at

Antigone 572. He appears to be the first scholar to propose that the line be given to the heroine, whereas the manuscript tradition is unanimous in assigning it to her sister Ismene. In such cases the question must be decided in the light of the context, since the manuscripts have no authority, a surprising fact overlooked until quite recently, although it was appreciated by an ancient or early medieval commentator on *Ajax* 354.[29] The *Antigone* passage has been much debated; influential English commentators of the Victorian period were inclined to follow the lead of the Aldine editor, but the division of opinion has not coincided with national or linguistic boundaries. Recently strong grounds have been given for accepting the text as it stands in the manuscripts: the heroine maintains an unyielding silence, while her more normal sister can no longer control her feelings.[30] The Aldine editor's proposal now seems to have been an influential mistake.

The one remaining Greek book produced in the year 1502 was Stephanus Byzantinus, a recondite text dating from the sixth century AD. It is a kind of gazetteer of ancient geography. However necessary reference books may have been to the student, one feels that Aldus was a trifle optimistic in recommending it to a humanist in charge of a school in Brescia. The dedicatory letter does not give us much more information. Aldus notes, no doubt moved by uneasy feelings about his future prospects in the medium and longer term, that he had set up his business in the year when Italy first began to be troubled by foreign invasion. What manuscript was used as the basis of the edition is not clear, and whoever was responsible for preparing the text seems to have followed his source pretty closely.

An undated volume which has been assigned to this year contains substantial works by Constantine Lascaris on grammar and syntax. A Latin translation was produced in such a way that the sheets could be interleaved with the Greek if required, and so the original and the version were on facing pages. As a kind of appendix 48 pages were added, giving a variety of brief texts. One of these is a key to understanding ligatures and abbreviations used by scribes and printers, and is a further reminder to us of the obstacles in the way of the learner. The last of the supplementary items is notable: it is an introduction to Hebrew script, the significance of which will become apparent later in connection with another publication.

1503 was a year of great activity. Two of the texts Aldus chose to issue had already been printed by Lascaris in Florence. They were popular authors, likely to have gone out of print quickly, so that Aldus might hope for good sales. One was the *Greek Anthology*, issued with the title of *Florilegium*, this Latin word being a translation of the Greek *anthologia*, perhaps devised by Aldus for the occasion.[31] The other was Lucian, whose popularity seems to have remained steady for a long time. The colophon indicates it was ready in February, but for some reason Aldus decided to add several other texts of much less obvious appeal, making a very large volume, ready for issue in June. One would like to know more about the commercial or other considerations which led to the change of plan. The additional texts are by authors of the Roman imperial period, scarcely of interest to anyone outside the ranks of professional scholars: Philostratus' *Lives of the sophists*, published in the thirties of the third century, which could offer welcome biographical information about a number of ancient personalities from Gorgias and Protagoras in the fifth century BC down to prominent figures of the Second Sophistic; the same author's *Heroicus*, a dialogue about the cult of dead heroes; his *Imagines*, a set of descriptions of paintings in a gallery in Naples; two other small sets of such descriptions by his grandson, also called Philostratus, and Callistratus, a fourth-century writer otherwise unknown. In antiquity the description of a work of art, commonly a painting or sculpture, had been recognised as an opportunity for the display of literary skill; as in so many other matters the tradition went back to Homer, who set a precedent with his long description of the decoration on the shield of Achilles in *Iliad* 18. The tradition survived into Byzantine times, a notable example being Paul the Silentiary's account of the wonders of Haghia Sophia in Constantinople. It was less deeply entrenched in Latin literature. Was the importance of these texts urged on Aldus by the Greek members of his circle, who automatically accepted Byzantine criteria in literary appreciation and could therefore enjoy such specimens of formal prose without ever setting eyes on any of the works of art being described? One would like to think that the marvellous development of Italian art had led Aldus and his friends to ask whether comparable masterpieces had been produced in the ancient world, and to treat literary descriptions as a source of information about the originals, so few of which had been recovered by the early archaeologists. Since Aldus wrote no preface to the volume we can only speculate on his thoughts.[32]

Two other titles issued in 1503 relate to previous publications of the house. There may have been requests for commentaries to assist readers of Aristotle. At any rate Aldus now produced some help for students of the Organon by assembling works of Ammonius and two Byzantine scholars, Psellos and Leon Magentinos, on the *Categories* and *De interpretatione*. This is only a fraction of what could have been made available to the public, but rather than continue the series he may have preferred to concentrate on primary texts. He took the opportunity to redeem a promise, made a year earlier in his preface to Thucydides, by issuing Xenophon's *Hellenica* and the brief résumé of later Greek history by Gemistus Plethon. The publication had been held up because he had not had enough manuscript copies to work from; in order to have a fair chance of eliminating corrupt passages he felt it was desirable to have at least three copies. To this volume he added Herodian, the third-century historian of the Roman empire, previously translated by Politian into

Latin, and the scholia on Thucydides, which despite being very brief notes might have been quite useful to the average reader at that time.

The real novelties of this year were two in number. Looking forward perhaps to his plan to publish Demosthenes he printed first the commentary on the orations which goes under the name of Ulpian, and as this did not make a large volume he added the lexicon by Harpocration, which was designed as a guide to the technical terms found in the Attic orators.[33] This volume has no preface or dedication. His other fresh venture was Euripides; the text filled two volumes in small format. For most of the plays this is the editio princeps. Curiously it omits the *Electra*, for which the public had to wait until 1545. The title indicates the inclusion of some scholia and the preface says that the reader will soon be able to read the scholia to seven plays; again the public had to wait for a while, their need being met by Arsenius of Monemvasia in 1534.

Part of the printer's copy has been identified (Paris suppl. gr. 212 and 393). It was written by a member of the Gregoropoulos family, to judge from the handwriting. There is little doubt that the person chiefly responsible for the edition was John Gregoropoulos, who had an important position in the printing house. Though the result was undistinguished from a scholarly point of view, it remained important, like the Sophocles of the preceding year, until the end of the eighteenth century.[34]

Aldus does not indulge in a eulogy of the text now being offered to the reader. Instead he laments the destruction of books, both in antiquity and in his own day. As a crumb of comfort he reports that his firm is selling a thousand or more copies of various good authors every month: *mille et amplius boni alicuius auctoris volumina singulo quoque mense emittimus ex Academia nostra.*

The output of 1504 again included one of the principal authors already printed elsewhere and sure to sell, Homer, issued now in a pair of volumes in small format. But the major contribution of the year was Demosthenes, accompanied by the explanatory material attributed to Libanius and by Plutarch's *Life*. There was also another commentary to help students of Aristotelian logic, John Philoponus on the *Analytica posteriora*. With it there is an interesting admission by Aldus: he confesses that he does not dare adjust the transmitted text, and is content to record variants, marking each passage with an asterisk. His statement can be taken as a sure sign that the average scholar felt extremely hesitant in matters of textual criticism.

This is the appropriate moment to mention a venture by Aldus into another field. Since the first year of the new century he had interested himself in Christian poetry. The first two volumes, issued in 1501 and 1502, consisted almost exclusively of Latin authors. The earlier of the two was mainly devoted to Prudentius, but had as a kind of appendix the Greek hymns of St John Damascene and some lesser authors; a Latin version was also provided. When so much remained to be done for the central areas of Greek literature the choice of such texts can only be characterised as eccentric. The same applies with perhaps even more force to the second part of the series. In a miscellany of Latin texts we find the Homeric centos, edited by the Camaldolese monk Pietro Candido, who wanted to be able to present the book to Pietro Delfino, the head of his order. It is difficult to see what spiritual enlightenment could have been obtained by reading stories from the New Testament told in hexameters, each verse of which was constructed from parts of two or three lines of Homer.

The third part of the series, dated 1504, was more substantial. It was a bilingual edition of the fourth-century Cappadocian father Gregory of Nazianzus. This is not such a strange choice as had been made for the previous volumes. Gregory had been one of the favourite authors of the Byzantines, and though their enthusiasm had been shown mainly in admiration for a selection of sixteen of his sermons, it is clear enough that his poems also enjoyed some popularity, and Aldus' advisers were justified in drawing his attention to these skilful compositions with their edifying contents. Gregory later earned praise from one of the most persistent critics of all things Christian. Gibbon says:

> Gregory's Poem on his own Life contains some beautiful lines, which burst from the heart, and speak the pangs of injured and lost friendship ... in the Midsummer Night's Dream, Helena addresses the same pathetic complaint to her friend Hermia:
>
> > Is all the counsel that we two have shared,
> > The sisters' vows, etc.
>
> Shakespeare had never read the poems of Gregory Nazianzen, he was ignorant of the Greek language; but his mother-tongue, the language of Nature, is the same in Cappadocia and in Britain.[35]

The erratic nature of the criteria used in the Aldine circle in questions of value and aesthetic merit is made clear once again by the last instalment of these poetic texts. A slim volume of great rarity, not dated and sometimes thought not even to have been released into circulation, contains a hexameter paraphrase of St John's Gospel by the early Byzantine poet Nonnus. An epigram by Scipione Forteguerri in Greek elegiacs adds little to our understanding of why Aldus bothered with this eccentric production. The editor was probably Pietro Candido, judging by a letter of Forteguerri which reports him as being in Rome with a codex of Nonnus in his possession.[36]

One other publication relates to the church. It is the Hours of the Virgin, accompanied by the seven penitential Psalms, in Greek but according to the Roman use. The date is 1497 and there was a reprint in

1505. It falls outside the scope of this study except that it serves as a reminder of the presence in Venice of a sizable Greek community. Aldus employed a few of them in his business and may have known quite a number of others. It is possible that there were among them members of the Uniate church which accepted Rome's primacy, for whom the Hours would have been welcome. At all events we must reckon with this colony as a factor which will sometimes have weighed with Aldus in his calculations of what could and could not be printed.

At this point we should pause to take note of a project which would have been extremely remarkable if Aldus had been able to realise it. In the first few years of the century he appears to have planned a trilingual edition of the Bible. It is tempting to suppose that Aldus had heard of cardinal Ximénez's recent decision to found a new university with a view to encouraging the study of Latin, Greek and Hebrew. Whereas the cardinal's enterprise flourished and led to the production at Alcalá of the Complutensian Polyglot Bible, printed in 1514-17 (but not put on sale until at least 1520), Aldus made little progress, and apart from a few allusions in correspondence there is no tangible evidence of his plans except for a single experimental page which survives in two copies.[37] The resources of the firm were evidently not equal to the challenge. One imagines that Erasmus must have discussed the matter with Aldus during his stay in 1508. At all events it was left to Erasmus to achieve the distinction of producing the first Greek text of the New Testament in Basle in 1516.

The year 1505 saw a reduction in Aldus' activity, followed by a cessation of all work in Greek in the two following years. What he managed to issue in 1505 is of relatively little account. There is a volume of the post-classical writers of epic, Quintus of Smyrna, Triphidorus and Colluthus; these are obscure authors who have remained the province of specialists and had no claim to more extensive circulation in Aldus' day; a fact which may have drawn attention to their existence is that the first and third were known to have been recovered by cardinal Bessarion in the course of his attempt to form a complete collection of ancient literature, and the find had been made in Apulia, presumably by an agent working on his behalf, at the monastery of St Nicholas just outside the remote town of Otranto, in a district which had been a great centre of Greek culture throughout the middle ages and even at the end of the fifteenth century retained its importance, only to suffer a terrible blow when the Turks invaded and briefly captured the town in 1480.

The other volume dated to this year is a most curious miscellany, and a modern reader is bound to ask why the publisher did not make any effort to compose the equivalent of a blurb in order to increase sales. The contents begin with the least surprising item, Aesop's *Fables*, preceded by a quite substantial – and needless to say fictitious – biography of Aesop. There were various such biographies, and the one used by Aldus is a recension due to the eminent Byzantine scholar and teacher Maximus Planudes. Fables were much used as school texts in the medieval period, both in the west and Byzantium, and Aldus remained true to the scholastic tradition by printing a Latin version to go with the Greek for the benefit of less advanced students. After Aesop come the fables of Babrius, whose name is here distorted to Gabrias, and the text in fact is not in its original form, which was recovered only in the nineteenth century. Then follow two short compilations of Greek mythological tales by Cornutus and Palaephatus, both obscure authors, the former of the first century AD, the latter of uncertain date. Such texts could be serviceable as sources of information in an age sadly deficient in handbooks. Next comes the Hellenistic treatise known as Heraclitus on Homer. Aldus used one of the manuscripts which attributed it instead to Heraclides Ponticus, one of Aristotle's most distinguished pupils. It is an interesting essay on allegory in Homer. Of course the modern reader does not find any, but there was a long tradition stretching back almost to the archaic period of classical Greece and given respectability by the Stoics, which used the method of allegorical interpretation to remove what seemed objectionable aspects of certain episodes in Homer, such as the moment when Hephaestus catches Aphrodite and Ares *in flagrante delicto*. There follows a very recondite and mysterious work, the *Hieroglyphica* of Horapollo, thought to be a product of the fifth century AD, allegedly translated from Coptic into Greek by a certain Philippus. It is meant to be an explanation of Egyptian hieroglyphs; modern experts say that the author had only the most limited knowledge of the subject. We have had occasion to note, both in connection with Christian apologetics and with Ficino's view of the history of the philosophical tradition, how the antiquity of Egypt exerted a special fascination over the minds of intellectuals. Ficino had not failed to notice the passage of Plotinus (5.8.6.1) which refers to hieroglyphs, saying that when the Egyptian priests wished to convey divine mysteries, they did not use the shapes of letters but whole figures of plants, trees and animals. An essay which claimed to explain one of the oddest features of an enigmatic civilisation would therefore be of some interest to the educated public, and in fact during the sixteenth century there were some thirty fresh editions or translations of it.[38]

The last significant item is a collection of some 1,300 proverbs, one of the collections made in late antiquity. The text is based on a manuscript now in Florence (Laur. 80.13); it belonged to Janus Lascaris, who served as the French envoy in Venice 1503-09.[39]

The volume closes by reverting to the topic of the first item, offering a few brief excerpts from a variety of authors who concerned themselves with the fable.

(iv) Interruptions

The years 1506-7 are a blank for our purposes. Aldus produced nothing in Greek and very little in other languages. It appears that he was in some financial difficulty. Activity was resumed in 1508 and lasted into the following year, when on 9 May the Venetian army suffered a serious defeat at Agnadello between Milan and Crema. The forces of the League of Cambrai had succeeded in their aim of reducing the power of the Republic. Aldus left the city for three years.

The brief period during which he had been able to operate was marked by important events. The most famous might be reckoned strictly speaking to fall outside the scope of this book – Erasmus' stay in the Aldine household which resulted in a vastly expanded edition of his *Adages*. In its new form the already popular book became one of the best-sellers of the age. Though it is not exactly a work of Greek scholarship it deserves a mention here. The original edition of 1500 had been a small book of 152 pages, dealing with 818 proverbs; the book which emerged from the Aldine press in 1508 was a folio of over 500 pages dealing with 3,285 proverbs. The Greek element was vastly increased, Latin translations being provided to help the reader. In the adage *Festina lente* Erasmus acknowledged his debt to the Aldine circle. He had been able to exploit a much wider range of Greek texts, many of them not yet in print, and to discuss them with leading experts such as Musurus. Erasmus did not compile a dictionary of proverbs, which might have been an arid production; he brought a learned and cultivated mind to bear on ancient expressions of popular wisdom, which he treated in the manner of an essayist. In subsequent editions the collection was expanded still further; but the Aldine without question represents the most important phase in its evolution.[40]

The other major production of this year was a pair of volumes designed as a corpus of Greek rhetorical theory. In the Byzantine educational tradition handbooks on the art of public speaking, mostly dating from the Roman Empire, had been of great importance, and the Aldine collection begins with the two staple texts by Hermogenes and Aphthonios. It also includes Menander Rhetor and Sopater, texts of a certain interest which were not inflicted on every Byzantine schoolchild. But the range of the Aldine corpus is wider: it adds a text attributed to Dionysius of Halicarnassus and Demetrius *On style*, and it makes good a surprising omission in the Aristotle issued in the previous decade by printing the *Poetics* and *Rhetoric*.[41]

What may seem odd about this Aldine initiative is that the Greek orators other than Demosthenes and Isocrates had yet to be printed – Aldus himself supplied the need in 1513. Probably we have here one more example of the influence of Byzantine taste. Refugee scholars such as Lascaris and Musurus had been brought up in a tradition which assigned little importance to Lysias and the lesser Attic orators, and once Demosthenes and Isocrates had been made available it might have seemed natural to treat the publication of the handbooks as the next priority.

The task of editing fell to another Greek member of the Aldine circle, Demetrius Ducas.[42] He wrote a letter of dedication to Musurus, which is warm in its praises of his success as professor of Greek in Padua. We learn incidentally that in preparing the text of Hermogenes Ducas had the benefit of being able to work with Aldus himself.[43] Perhaps we should infer that the rest of the task was performed by Ducas unaided, the head of the firm being unable to find the time. Curiosity is roused by a compliment he pays to Aldus: in giving thanks for the invention of printing which now prevents further losses of literature he notes that Aldus, having laid hands on a single manuscript copy, usually obtained with difficulty, can manufacture a thousand. This may be good evidence of the print-run for some texts; one would very much like to know if it was the regular procedure of the house.[44]

The rhetoricians were soon followed by another substantial work for which Ducas had the main responsibility, Plutarch's *Moralia*, a massive volume of 1,050 pages. He is thought to have been helped by Erasmus and the promising young Italian scholar Aleandro. The latter contributed to the preliminary material an epigram in Greek elegiac couplets. Aldus' letter of dedication is not very revealing; Ducas in his dwells on the lessons to be learned from a close study of Plutarch. He admits that in some passages the Greek text is corrupt to the point of being unintelligible, and he says he has decided to leave them as they stand.[45] This policy was perfectly sensible. The volume had a mixed reception; it was by no means free from misprints, and some users may have been disappointed by the number of difficult passages which the editor had failed to improve, a rather unreasonable attitude when due allowance is made for the nature of Plutarch's style and the resources available to Ducas and his colleagues.[46] Although Ducas may not have been an outstanding scholar, he clearly was making a contribution of value to Aldus' objectives, and it is a great pity that scholarly enterprises had to be suspended in the middle of 1509. Ducas next appears in Spain, where he held a chair at Alcalá from 1513.

By that time Aldus had been able to resume business. He began with two textbooks. One was a reprint of his undated issue of Constantine Lascaris of *c.* 1502; for this printing he added to the supplementary material by including some matter, essentially Byzantine in date, on the dialects of the classical language. The other was the *Erotemata* of Chrysoloras, issued on the advice of Musurus, who had moved from Padua to Venice. This recommendation from the most learned and intelligent of his Greek associates is one of the best possible proofs of Chrysoloras' skill in devising a manual that reduced the difficulty of the language for beginners. It may be worth noting in passing that Aldus reports a widely held belief that Chrysoloras taught for many years in Florence – which is of course inaccurate but reflects the importance of his achievement. The 1512 edition is accompanied by some supplementary texts; no doubt these too had the stamp of Musurus' approval.[47]

In January of the following year appeared a pocket-sized edition of four poets, Pindar, Callimachus, Dionysius Periegetes and Lycophron. The second and third of these had already been printed elsewhere, the former in Florence before the turn of the century, the latter in Ferrara in 1512.[48] Pindar was such a famous name that there must have been demand for a printed text. He is, however, a difficult author, and it was not to be expected that the first editor would do much more than reproduce a current text with all its faults. Even if Musurus had devoted his energies to the task, it would probably have made little difference; but there is no sign that he was closely involved with the edition. This Aldine is not a notable contribution to scholarship.[49] Of the other texts it offers, Callimachus probably appealed to advanced students only, while Dionysius and Lycophron are further proofs of Byzantine influence in the formation of literary taste. Both had been popular in the middle ages, the first as a text-book of geography, the second as a series of riddling prophecies by Cassandra. With the exception of Callimachus all these authors had been accompanied in most of the medieval copies by a substantial commentary written in the margins, and it would have been useful to readers if Aldus had printed such scholia, but he failed to do so. The only remaining feature of the book which requires comment is that Aldus reveals in the preface once again his ambition to publish a Hebrew Bible.

The next venture was a corpus of Isocrates and the minor Attic orators,[50] together with a few brief rhetorical pieces by sophists of various dates[51] and two more substantial essays from the Second Sophistic, Aristides' *Panathenaicus* and *Encomium of Rome*. Though Aristides had been a great favourite of the Byzantines, the earlier humanists had not devoted much attention to him. But the two pieces selected for inclusion in the Aldine were aptly chosen, since they amounted to a celebration of the two ancient cities which occupied the thoughts of any intellectual reflecting on the progress of civilisation. While Musurus may have given the publisher advice during the manufacture of the volume, he does not appear to have participated actively, and the quality of the editorial work has been severely criticised by modern experts, one of whom went so far as to say that 'the efforts of three centuries were spent on purging the text of the Aldine'.[52]

Aldus' remaining publications are best treated in the next section, which is devoted to Musurus. He was responsible for some important editions that were issued at the end of Aldus' career or just after, and the publisher's other collaborators fade into the background. Since Musurus had been a member of the Aldine circle before the turn of the century, it will be necessary to retrace our steps in order to deal with his youthful achievements.

(v) Musurus

The early career of Marcus Musurus (c. 1470-1517) is not well documented. In the verses he wrote to accompany his edition of Plato he acknowledges a debt to Janus Lascaris, under whom he studied in Florence c. 1490. One notes that he has nothing to say of Politian, whose lectures should have been if anything an even greater attraction. The enthusiasm of the young student can be seen in the elegiac couplets he composed on completing a transcript of the minor Attic orators (Burney 96): even if the reader has no previous initiation into the mysteries of oratory, after becoming acquainted with the ten orators of the canon he will be an influential speaker in public; Musurus has sat up late at night making his copy, sticking to the task although his eyes were tired, anxious to reach his goal.

In 1503 he took up an appointment in Padua, and we learn that in 1508 his stipend was raised from 60 to 100 florins.[53] Erasmus tells us that he lectured at seven in the morning, taking only four days' holiday in the year, and in winter Raphael Regius, the professor of Latin, aged about 70, would come regularly to hear him, whereas younger students could not bear the cold.[54] Among his duties in Padua was the translation of Greek letters coming from the sultan in Constantinople.[55] Not a great deal is known about his teaching; while we must presume that he lectured on the usual authors, it is clear that at some stage in his career he included in his programme a text more typical of the Byzantine than the Italian curriculum, selected orations by St Gregory of Nazianzus.[56]

In 1512 he was made professor in Venice. We do not know when and why he left Padua. It is likely enough that he was induced to move by the advance of the forces of the League of Cambrai in 1509. He had been lecturing on Pindar, *Olympians* 1-5, and his audience included the German scholar Johannes Cuno.[57] Since some modern authorities believe that on taking up his new chair he was able to consult the manuscript collection of cardinal Bessarion for his edition of Plato, one might consider the hypothesis that the prospect of access to the collection had been a reason for moving. Loans were occasionally made from it, and unfortunately the surviving documents do not cover the period when the Aldine house would have benefited from this facility.[58] But even if access was granted on one occasion for the loan of a Plato, this will have been an exception to the rule as far as the Aldine press was concerned. From Sanudo's diary of political affairs we know that in 1514 the captain-general asked that the books of the cardinal of Nicaea, which were locked up, should be put in a library in Terra Nuova, because they were Greek books and Musurus was in Venice to lecture on them. In May of the following year the request was repeated.[59] It is safe to infer that nothing had been done in the meantime. One might hazard the guess that failure to act was one reason for Musurus to move to Rome in 1516.[60]

His relations with Aldus go back to the editio princeps of Aristophanes which he produced in 1498. At one time this book was regarded as a considerable scholarly achievement, because it offered a text of the comedies free from many blemishes characteristic of most of the medieval manuscripts. But this verdict has proved to be too favourable. While it is true that Musurus worked hard to make a fresh and reasonably coherent set of marginal scholia out of the rather disparate material available to him, for the poetic text itself he simply accepted the revisions made by the Byzantine scholar Demetrius Triclinius.[61]

Though the edition itself is less of an advance than was claimed in the past, the editor's preface or dedicatory letter is more interesting than many and casts light on the Venetian milieu. It begins by saying that after the mainly factual Aristotle Aldus offers the reader a text of some literary charm which can relieve his exhausted intellect. The playfulness of the comedies, however, should not be seen as entirely lacking in serious quality, and some moral questions arise in them. Readers will also gain from the great variety of vocabulary, and if someone were willing to follow Aristophanes' style in conversation with his neighbours he might succeed in giving the impression of having been brought up in the heart of Greece. The reference to conversation shows Musurus thinking about Greeks who might buy the volume; shortly afterwards he draws a contrast between refugees from Byzantium and those who are condemned to pay taxes to their Turkish overlords, and expresses the hope that he has performed a useful service at least for the refugees. At first sight the claim that a classical text could be of any value for conversational purposes must seem bizarre. But the Byzantine tradition, which laid emphasis on reading the classical authors in order to improve one's written style, also had some effect on the spoken word, as we learn from a letter of Filelfo, dated 1451 but no doubt drawing on his experience as a visitor to Constantinople much earlier in the century. Filelfo claims that Greeks whose speech has not been corrupted speak the language of Aristophanes, Euripides, Plato and Aristotle. He adds a more informative paraphrase, saying that the court circle retained an old-fashioned elegance and dignity in conversation.[62] There is no reason to doubt that he is describing correctly one aspect of the almost incredible archaism characteristic of Byzantium.

Musurus next turns to the scholia, observing that a great deal of time and effort was needed in order to arrange them clearly. Despite the energy he brought to the task there was barely enough time, as the material was complex and corrections had to be made to the proof sheets. The printers' errors were worse than Hydra's heads and required the attentions of an Iolaus. This allusion to a classical myth is presumably designed to convey the impression of modesty; he could hardly compare himself to Hercules cutting off the Hydra's heads and implies instead that he took the humbler role of Hercules' companion Iolaus.

In the final paragraph Musurus addresses himself to the Italian readers of his edition and claims that Aristophanes will be welcome to the Venetian nobility because of his picture of Athenian society. Venice is in some ways a copy of Athens, he adds. This remarkable assertion may strike us as inappropriate flattery. Yet it is preferable to the gaffe committed some decades earlier by George Trapezuntius who suggested that Venice was modelled on the state described in Plato's *Laws*, a singularly tactless notion if he had stopped to think about it.[63]

A year after editing Aristophanes Musurus produced a corpus of Greek letter-writers. It is in two parts, with colophons dated March and April. His task was complex: thirty-five authors were included, ranging in date from Plato and the classical orators Isocrates and Aeschines through to the end of antiquity. Leading figures of the fourth century AD such as Julian the Apostate and St Gregory of Nazianzus are included, and there are even two later writers of very slight interest, Procopius of Gaza and Theophylactus Simocatta. The resulting collection once again reflects Byzantine taste. Many Byzantines had practised the art of letter-writing, and as usual they studied the precedents set by ancient authors, setting aside religious prejudice to the extent of including the emperor Julian among their models. The Aldine is therefore a collection similar to those found in some medieval manuscripts but rather more comprehensive.[64] It was not replaced by an equally useful collection until 1873, the date of R. Hercher's *Epistolographi graeci*. One point from a brief statement by Musurus may be noted. He complains that for the letters of the second-century sophist Alciphron the manuscripts were in such bad condition that he did not feel able to print a legible text, and he did not have the courage to make conjectures to restore it. Yet he adds that he can boast without bad taste or exposing himself to Momus, the eponymous god of blame, that no other scholar of his day could have done more with the material at his disposal. There is little reason to doubt that the claim was justified.

Also from the year 1499 is a letter Musurus wrote in Greek to the students of Padua as a preface to the lexicon known as the *Etymologicum Magnum*. This was a Byzantine compilation, much more useful to its original intended public than to foreigners learning the language. The book was not issued by Aldus and it is not thought that Musurus took the lion's share in the task of editing; but some of his remarks are worth citing. He makes a riddling allusion to the *Pinax* of Cebes, a dialogue on education in which a painting is interpreted as an allegory. There may be an implication that it was being used as a reading text for beginners; and Aldus in 1502 included it in the supplementary material to one of his handbooks of grammar and syntax. The *Pinax* enjoyed considerable popularity from now on; whether it had already done so in Byzantium is an open question, as the manuscript tradition is far from rich. To return to the preface to the dictionary: Musurus tells us that it is meant to serve as a reference book for the reading of poetry, especially Homer. He notes that the correction of the text has been made difficult by the lack of a suitable manuscript copy; although there were old and apparently trustworthy manuscripts available, they were full of obscurities which in his opinion would have required the skill of an Oedipus to solve them. If one asks what puzzle they could have presented that might be compared to the riddle of the Sphinx, it seems best to suppose that there were many abbreviations, some of them used rarely if at all in other types of text, which the editors could not read with confidence. Musurus himself, given enough time, could probably have worked out the puzzles they offered; certainly his later work on the lexicon of Hesychius suggests great skill in dealing with such technical points of palaeography. But the lexicon issued in 1499 was mainly the work of lesser scholars, Nicholas Vlastos and Zacharias Callierges.

Musurus' relations with Aldus during the first decade of the sixteenth century have already been mentioned in the preceding section, and so we can here pass directly to his first major task after taking up residence in Venice, the editio princeps of Plato. It appeared in 1513 and was dedicated to the Medici pope, Leo X. In certain respects it may be thought to differ from other Aldines. In the first place the transmitted text, though by no means perfect, was in a much better state than that of most authors, and therefore did not invite editorial intervention on the same scale. In the *Laws* Musurus is thought to have made few if any alterations to the text.[65] Most unusually, it looks as if his source could have been one of Bessarion's manuscripts (Marc. gr. 187). Not that this book was used in the printing-shop; it had to be returned to the library in good condition. A similar picture emerges from his work on the *Republic*.[66] For the rest of the corpus it is to be presumed that he used another copy from Bessarion's library (Marc. gr. 186), occasionally taking readings from other copies (such as Paris gr. 1810). If this view is correct, it means that for some reason the usual obstacles to borrowing from the library no longer existed. But since it appears in all other cases that Aldus was unable to use its resources, one should probably look for another explanation of the facts. *Entia non sunt multiplicanda praeter necessitatem*. Here perhaps it is necessary to posit the existence of copies made from Bessarion's manuscripts before he donated them to Venice. Whichever solution we prefer, we are obliged to view with much scepticism the claim of the publisher that his editor had collated the text against very old copies. Bessarion's own manuscripts were not old books, but manufactured for his personal library.

The text was issued in two volumes, of 501 and 439 pages. The only additional material was the author's life by Diogenes Laertius and the brief treatise known as Timaeus Locrus, a Hellenistic paraphrase of the *Timaeus* in Doric Greek. What is most remarkable about this edition is that it appeared almost thirty years after Marsilio Ficino's Latin version had been a best-seller.

Completed in 1513, but held over until the next year because the publisher hoped to be able to include some additional material, was another volume of the Aristotelian commentator Alexander of Aphrodisias. Once again a work forming part of the Organon, the *Topica*, was the subject of the commentary. We have here further evidence that Aristotelian studies of the most traditional type showed no sign of disappearing from the university curriculum. This Aldine has not won great admiration from the only modern editor.[67] The publisher took the opportunity to announce that he would continue with such texts once he had dealt with other more immediate concerns, for which he alleges there is popular demand. He names the authors: Strabo, Athenaeus, Pausanias and Xenophon. The first three were soon issued by his house, but the fourth appeared in 1516 under the Giunta imprint.

Another relatively minor production of 1514 was a fresh issue of the *Suda* lexicon. It appears to be little more than a reprint of the editio princeps.[68] But this final year of Aldus' activity is made remarkable by the issue of two recherché authors edited by Musurus, who shows for the first time an exceptional capacity in dealing with the difficulties of the texts as they had been transmitted. These two editions have earned him the reputation of being the ablest textual scholar that Greece has ever produced.[69]

One of them is yet another lexicon, by an otherwise unknown Hesychius, who lived in Alexandria in the fifth or sixth century. It lists many rare words found in poetry and sometimes preserves a correct form that has been lost in the primary tradition of an author. With 51,000 entries it is rather larger than the other comparable dictionaries, and this fact may have seemed a strong reason in favour of publication. Only one manuscript survives (Marc. gr. 622), which the owner kindly lent to Aldus. Musurus went through it with exceptional thoroughness in order to prepare it for the printer. The script was neat and clear, and as it had been written relatively recently, perhaps *c.* 1430, there was little risk of the type-setter being puzzled by a script that differed much from current scripts. On the other hand there were many abbreviations, and Musurus marked most of them, giving in the margin the full form of the word. Though this was partly a clerical task, it also required a knowledge of a wide range of compendia. Few of Musurus' contemporaries would have been able to perform it equally well. None of them could have equalled his other feat, which was to correct an extremely large number of faults in the text; it has been calculated that as many as a quarter of the entries need some adjustment, and while many of these changes are details of orthography, others are more substantial and in some cases depend on uncommon learning or ingenuity.[70] It is possible that Musurus was enabled to make some corrections by consulting a copy of the lexicon attributed to St Cyril of Alexandria, a book much used by the Byzantines and listing many of the same words. Even if this is so, it need hardly reduce our admiration for his skill; and it should in any case be noted that existing editions perhaps fail to give him full credit for all his improvements to the text.[71]

The other text issued in August of 1514 could scarcely appeal to any readers who did not think of themselves as professional scholars. Athenaeus' *Deipnosophistae*, a compilation made *c.* AD 200, is an extraordinary collection of information about food, drink and social customs in antiquity. It consists of little more than quotations from an enormous range of authors, most of them now lost; the writers of comedy are particularly well represented. But it offers little or nothing to readers who look to classical Greek literature for intellectual stimulus. Aldus commended it to his readers on two grounds. He describes it as a storehouse of miscellaneous learning, which it undoubtedly is, and he notes the value of its quotations as a means of correcting faulty texts. As instances he gives some passages of Theophrastus' *Historia plantarum* Book 4 cited in Athenaeus Book 3.[72] This second reason for attaching value to Athenaeus' work is also perfectly sound, but it is one that appeals to specialists only, and is in any case valid for no more than a very small proportion of the quotations.

Athenaeus is a very big book and Musurus edited it with great skill. Aldus says he collated the Byzantine epitome and numerous copies of the full text, which lacks the first two books and a small amount of the third. There is reason to doubt the second half of his claim, as there were not many copies in circulation.[73] There is no doubt he did a good deal for the text, and his ability to restore the metre in the quotations from poets is much in evidence. A particularly good example is the long quotation from the elegiac poem by Hermesianax (597-9), in which he was able to make quite a number of the corrections necessary to heal the text.[74] Some of his proposals were easy enough for an intelligent and attentive reader, though it should be said that Byzantine scribes had been surprisingly lazy or reluctant to intervene with adjustments of orthography and syntax. In the calculation of what he achieved there is an element of uncertainty: in the standard edition a number of emendations are assigned to him although they appear in a manuscript written a few years earlier than the Aldine edition. This is Heidelberg, Pal. gr. 47, signed and dated by Paolo Da Canale in Venice in 1505-6. The assumption has been made that the corrections derive from classes or lectures given by Musurus, who was still teaching in Padua at the time.[75] Though the choice of Athenaeus as a text to read with pupils is odd, the assumption is almost certainly justified, because the capacity to correct the texts with success seems to have been such a rare gift.

After Aldus' death early in 1515 Musurus moved to Rome. While keeping in touch with the Aldine firm he had dealings with Filippo Giunta in Florence. So we find him collaborating in the first printing of a didactic poem in five books on fishing, the *Halieutica* of Oppian, who lived in the second century. The ancient and medieval taste for absorbing factual information in versified form was destined to continue for some time. The book does not appear to be important otherwise; if the publisher's preface is to be trusted, both he and Musurus had three manuscript copies of the Greek at their disposal, on the basis of which the text was to be constituted; and as the text was not rare in Byzantium, the publisher's statement may be taken at face value.

In Rome there was more than one press capable of dealing with Greek, and two leading scholars whom Musurus had known in Venice were active there. One was Janus Lascaris, who in 1517 edited the ancient notes on Homer commonly but erroneously known as the Didymus scholia. The other was Zacharias Callierges, who in 1515 had made the intelligent decision to reprint Pindar with the accompanying scholia in order to give the reader some help with a difficult text. One of his other, less important, productions concerns us here because it tells us something interesting about Musurus. In 1516 Callierges undertook a reprint of Theocritus and the other bucolic poets. In Bion's *Lament for Adonis* a lacuna after line 92 was filled by six verses which can be stated with some confidence to be a supplement by Musurus, who knew the genre well enough to be able to indulge in a little free composition. In making up his own supplement he went further than editors usually do; nowadays they never do more than indicate a suggestion made *exempli gratia*. Musurus was quite skilful, and there are other signs of his willingness to fill a small gap in a text. The fourth *Hymn* of Callimachus is a case in point; it seems fairly certain that he is responsible for two supplements, one of which is excellent.[76]

Meanwhile in Venice the Aldine press completed one of the projects it had previously announced by printing the *Geography* of Strabo. It had been begun at a time when Musurus was at hand to give advice, and it is possible that he had some part in the production; but the publisher's preface makes no reference to him at all, and the question is unresolved. The manuscript used was Paris gr. 1395, a poor copy, and the edition does not appear to have been a great achievement. It is noteworthy that the Latin version by Guarino had been printed as early as 1469.[77]

Musurus' last edition was another proof of his methodical and competent scholarship. The Aldine press issued Pausanias' *Periegesis*, a description of ancient Greece in the style of a guide-book. At this time there was no possibility of travelling to Greece for what would now be called tourism. Despite this fact, or perhaps because of it, admirers of the ancient world could ponder nostalgically over the wealth of monuments visited by a tourist of the second century AD. They can hardly have failed to learn a good deal of ancient history from the digressions and background information provided by the author; it is harder to say how they will have reacted to the detailed descriptions of works of art or the frequent indications that such and such a temple was no longer in good repair or that a city was deserted. But the publisher was hardly misleading his readers when he assured them that the book was a treasure house of classical learning. He rightly claims credit for a useful innovation, running titles at the top of each page to give the reader an idea of the contents. He also thanks Musurus for his contribution, again rightly for it is clear that this is one of the best of the editiones principes. The corrections made in the text are quite numerous. On average there is one for every four pages of a modern printed edition. The majority of these improvements can be categorised as necessary adjustments of syntax or the restoration of proper names to their correct form. Some of the latter required unusual knowledge: at 1.10.2 the obscure tribe of the Nestioi is restored to the text by means of redividing the words transmitted. Ingenuity is occasionally displayed; examples occur in a remark about Theseus' return from Marathon at 1.15.3, and at 5.25.9, where part of the correction was to remove a mistake arising from one of the abbreviations known as *nomina sacra*. But the majority of the changes are fairly simple and obvious. It is interesting to observe that many other corrections of similar faults were not made by Musurus and had to wait for the attention of more recent scholars. Musurus was a pioneer; but he left much for his successors to do, and it has to be said that a good deal of what he left undone does not look any more difficult than what he was able to achieve. Perhaps we should infer that he was unable to give of his best because he was working under the pressure of a strict schedule in the publishing house.

Before leaving Musurus note should be taken of one more Aldine edition of 1516. It contains sixteen selected orations of St Gregory of Nazianzus. Musurus may have been responsible for seeing them through the press; at all events he wrote the letter to the publisher which serves as a kind of preface. The texts had been favourite reading of the Byzantines, but in Italy they had made little impact, as other patristic literature had greater claims on scholars' attention. Musurus tells us that he had included this author in his syllabus for students. In so doing he reasserted a Byzantine tradition in a way that other refugee scholars probably had not. The editing of the text will not have been a particularly difficult task. The writings of the fathers were mostly better preserved because they had not been exposed to the hazards of copying for so long and they were not the products of a different cultural world. The editor's task, then as now, was not so much to restore sense to what could not be understood as to choose between minor variations that in general made no difference to the author's message. For Musurus, if indeed he was the editor, it will have been relatively easy to ensure that a satisfactory text emerged from the printing shop.

I conclude this section by drawing attention to a remark made in a letter to the French bibliophile Grolier, which serves as the preface to an issue of Aldus' Greek grammar dated November 1515. Musurus is clearly in pessimistic mood, owing to the incessant wars in Italy. He thinks texts need to be printed in order to ensure their survival, and he asks Grolier to encourage the new head of the firm Andrea Torresano to proceed with a programme of authors. The list he gives is: the Old and New Testament; commentaries on the poets and on Aristotle; Galen; Strabo; Pausanias; Dio (he may mean Dio Cassius rather than Dio Chrysostom); Diodorus Siculus; Polybius; Plutarch's *Lives*. Within ten years a good many of his demands had been satisfied, in one case by his own efforts; but Polybius had to wait until 1530, Diodorus Siculus (16-20) until 1539, Dio Cassius (36-58) until 1548. The list may be taken to reveal Musurus' vision of the tasks awaiting scholars. The range is wide. Notable features are the renewed concern with the Bible; the reappearance of an interest in Roman history; the realisation that the supreme authority in medicine had been neglected. There is little sign of merely antiquarian concerns.

15

Conclusion

The almost simultaneous blows of fate which removed Aldus and Musurus from the scene mark the conclusion of one stage in the history of scholarship. The reasons for this judgment will become clear if we attempt to take stock of what had been achieved since 1397 and what tasks remained for the future.

Much of the Greek legacy had been made available to the educated public. In 1528 Castiglione was to recommend in *The Courtier* (1.44) the study of both the classical languages, with Greek included 'because of the abundance and variety of things that are so divinely written in it'. Several major university cities had a chair of Greek, and even if continuity of instruction could not be guaranteed in each individual centre, in the country as a whole there was now a continuous tradition, which had not been true in the Middle Ages. If the holder of a chair was gifted as a teacher, he could do much to reduce the difficulty of the student's task. Chrysoloras' grammar went some way towards meeting the need for an improved manual, and the dictionary associated with the name of Crastonus was another step in the right direction. But much remained to be done in this department, and since many educated men still found the language too hard to master, translations into Latin or the vernacular assumed notable importance, both in the classroom and for private reading. Modern readers are aware of the hazards of relying too closely on translations, since there is inevitably some loss of the finer points. Renaissance readers were in a different position; few of them can have failed to see the drawbacks of the medieval versions of Aristotle and other authors, and there was widespread pleasure at the increased degree of understanding that resulted from applying Chrysoloras' principle of trying to convey the meaning of whole sentences in idiomatic fashion. Delight in the literary quality of versions by Bruni and others may have given the average reader too high a degree of confidence in their accuracy as reflections of the original author's meaning. This is not to imply incompetence on the part of Bruni, though it should be noted that such charges can be made against George Trapezuntius and Rinuccio Aretino. There is a more serious reason for expressing reservations about the versions. It is that they were based on manuscripts which in many

157

passages of many authors were affected by scribal error and therefore not fully intelligible. The majority of Byzantine readers had not possessed the knowledge and skill to remove such corruptions. Most texts as a result contained a number of passages which could not be satisfactorily interpreted. Presumably the Byzantine reader had resorted to guesswork or suspended the rules of syntax. This is what the translators were obliged to do. By the application of intelligence to the context they could often make a good guess about the author's intention. This method of approximation had its uses, but any scholar could see its limitations. The art of textual criticism was urgently needed. In the preceding chapters we have seen that few scholars, whether Greek or Italian, were in a position to make a substantial contribution to the improvement of corrupt texts. It is tempting to speculate that Musurus, had he been granted a long life, would not only have demonstrated his skill in dealing with other authors, but also might have taught enough gifted pupils to establish a tradition. As it was, many ancient texts, which circulated widely by the early sixteenth century thanks to the efforts of Aldus and other printers, were marred by much the same number of incoherent passages as they had been for generations.

The quantity of ancient literature now accessible to the public was considerable. Of the major literary authors only Aeschylus had yet to be printed. An attempt was soon made to fill the gap. The Aldine press issued the Greek text in 1518; but its linguistic difficulty was so great that many passages defied the editor's efforts to make the poetry intelligible. Aeschylus had been included in the Byzantine school curriculum, and to a large extent it was the authors with a place in that curriculum who acquired a similar status in Italian schools and universities. This was the inevitable result of importing Byzantine teachers. It meant that Italian students of the fifteenth and early sixteenth centuries continued to devote attention to a number of authors who have little or no place in a modern syllabus for a degree in classics. This does not mean that the Italians failed to express their own taste or ask new questions. In one important case they effected a change. The interest in Plato generated by Bruni and Ficino, though it did not lead to the disappearance of Aristotle from the universities, created a quite new situation. In Byzantium Plato was a well known author, who nevertheless had to be studied with care because his doctrines were in conflict with those of the church, and the authorities had issued an edict in 1082 denouncing the Platonic theory of forms and allowing the study of Plato only as a model of good prose style. In Italy means were found to overlook or minimise any possible danger to orthodoxy.

Concentration on the Byzantine school curriculum entailed an emphasis on the classics of pagan literature which provoked occasional hostility from representatives of the church. In Byzantium a modest concession had been made to the wishes of the church: it seems that the

Psalms were used as a reading text in the lower forms of schools, and in the more advanced classes the pupils often read a selection from the orations of St Gregory of Nazianzus, one of the great Cappadocian writers of the fourth century. This concession does not appear to have become a regular Italian practice, even if Musurus read Gregory with his pupils and occasionally other students used the Psalms as a text to be read in the early stages of learning. Greek patristic literature in general could not interest the Italians for the same reasons as it had the Byzantines. But in international relations religion was an important factor, and so some Italians made it their business to find out what the leading authorities of a schismatic church had written.

One major author who was important in Byzantium but fell outside the range of any school reading list was Galen. In the west some of his work had been known in medieval Latin versions, chiefly by Burgundio of Pisa and Nicholas of Reggio. Though these were not of the highest quality, it is interesting to note how little further work had been done by 1515 to improve access to the Galenic corpus. Only a few fresh translations had been produced, and a very small part of the corpus was in print. The other pillar of Byzantine medicine, Dioscorides, had been printed, but there is reason to suspect that the exploitation of his work was delayed by a couple of decades or more.

If we look forward to the progress of Greek studies in the generation that followed Aldus and Musurus we shall find some change taking place. The activities of Musurus' successor in the chair at Venice are a good example. Though he gave courses on some standard authors, he was chiefly famous as a naval architect designing new ships for Venice. He claimed to use classical authors as the sources for some of his innovative ideas. It is far from certain that he was telling the truth; but if he was, one such source was a chapter in the *Mechanica* wrongly ascribed to Aristotle, which deals with the efficiency of oars mounted in various positions. This is not a text which had been of much concern to the Byzantines and certainly it was never used in the schoolroom. The best of ancient science and technology had not made much impact on the fifteenth century. It was about to be exploited more fully, with the natural consequence that it was soon overtaken and made obsolete. The question of the relative merits of the ancients and the moderns posed itself with greater insistence than before. Not that it was new: it had occurred even at the end of the fourteenth century, when Giovanni Dondi dall' Orologio (d. 1389), a friend of Petrarch, wrote a letter on the subject. By the middle of the next century it was possible for Benedetto Accolti, Poggio's successor as chancellor of Florence, to make his own view clear in the title of his *De praestantia virorum sui aevi dialogus*,[1] while in 1473 Alamanno Rinuccini, writing to Duke Federigo of Urbino and presenting him with a Latin version of Philostratus' *Life of Apollonius*, took a balanced view, reckoning that in many fields the moderns now equalled anything that antiquity could offer. For the fine arts he cited a dozen famous names from Giotto and Cimabue to Brunelleschi and Alberti, and when it came to Latinity, he was willing to claim that Valla and Tortelli had done wonders. The argument continued, and it may well be that it was not at once settled decisively in favour of the moderns because there was a steady trickle of fresh knowledge emerging from Greek authors. But as the sixteenth century wore on, this defence of the ancients also ceased to be effective, and the short book on the subject published in 1539 by the Spaniard Cristóbal de Villalón may well have marked a new stage in the establishment of a consensus. Certainly the speed with which ancient learning might be overtaken can be seen in the case of Galen. The Aldine house issued a substantial corpus of his writings in 1525. Already in 1543 Vesalius exposed the limitations of his anatomy by proving that it was based on animal rather than human anatomy. In fact even before the publication of the Aldine the writing was on the wall; in Bologna on 17 May 1520 Berengario of Carpi demonstrated at a dissection held before an audience that Galen's anatomy could be corrected.

But for a generation or so ancient texts not yet printed could be published with advantage. The most important publications related to mathematics and astronomy. Ptolemy appeared in Greek in 1533; but his works had been studied in translation in the preceding century. Less effort had been devoted to Euclid, whose *Elements* appeared in 1533 at Basle, and Archimedes, published in the same city in 1544. These first editions coincided with the maturity of highly competent mathematicians such as Tartaglia and Commandino. In the fifties or sixties Bombelli read the still unprinted text of Diophantus and as a result was able to take a step forward in the development of algebra. Though Euclid had been read in Byzantium as an introduction to one part of the quadrivium, these texts in general had been regarded as the preserve of experts and not the constituents of a curriculum in secondary or higher education. The age in which the Byzantine school programme was nearly synonymous with the Greek legacy was over.

There is a hint of this change in Musurus' latest editions. He and Aldus may have begun to realise that they were dealing with texts that had been very little appreciated in the middle ages. Pausanias' guide-book was attractive to students of ancient history with a wider perspective than the Byzantines were usually capable of. Athenaeus' *Deipnosophistae* with its vast array of fragments of mainly lost authors satisfied antiquarian concern with ancient food, wine and social customs, again topics rather beyond the horizon of most medieval readers. It is not difficult to believe that if the Aldine circle had had access to the library bequeathed to Venice by Bessarion, other editions could have resulted which would have changed the balance of the Aldine publishing programme still further. Two instances may be cited. The best manuscript of Homer's *Iliad* is one of the treasures of the collection, and one reason why it is so highly valued is its unique corpus of marginal scholia. When these were finally printed in 1788 they gave a fresh insight into the nature of ancient scholarship on Homer and stimulated a new phase of scholarly inquiry into the origins and transmission of the Greek epic. Another fascinating work in Bessarion's library was Photius' *Bibliotheca*, of which he owned the two most important manuscripts. This extraordinary collection of résumés of texts, pagan and Christian, preserved and lost, could scarcely have failed to fascinate Erasmus and Musurus; it might even have stimulated someone to invent the genre of the book-review, of which it is the nearest medieval analogue.

In any survey of a cultural or intellectual movement it is easy to point to missed opportunities. Yet the effects of an injection of Greek influence can be observed in most areas of literature, art and philosophical thought. The exceptions test the rule and are worth considering. The one which may surprise is architecture. Here Vitruvius held the field. When Raphael painted *The School of Athens* it was Roman architecture that he painted, not Greek. Since travel to Greece was difficult and archaeology was making a slow start, perhaps the results were predictable. But the wonderfully preserved Greek temples at Paestum near Salerno, and other equally fine monuments in Sicily, might have been expected to attract attention. They do not appear to have done so.[2] In painting and sculpture there was little to be found which was Greek and could be recognised at once as such. The few paintings which show the influence of Lucian or Philostratus, important though they may be, remain an infinitesimal fraction of what was produced. The loss of Greek music, mitigated only in the smallest degree by the preservation of some treatises on theory, had an obvious result. Though the school at Mantua had some of these texts in its library, the date at which they were first appreciated is a matter of debate. Gaffurio (1451-1522) who held a chair of music in Pavia obtained translations from Leoniceno and a competent Veronese scholar, Gian Francesco Burana. Whether these were sufficiently clear to have any practical effect has been doubted, and perhaps it was not until after Gaffurio's death that Italian musicians made more use of the Greek theoreticians.[3]

But in general the authors now added to the stock of literature brought fresh knowledge and a stimulus to further inquiry. And the small number of authors who had been known before the Renaissance came to exercise their influence in a different way. The change was longest delayed in the case of Galen; the long interval before real efforts were made to recover the original text and to read a larger number of his works is difficult to account for. No such delay affected the rise in Plato's influence once a wide range of his writings was in circulation. By offering thoughts about various political systems which were in use or under discussion in Italy he acquired a significance which could barely have been appreciated in either half of Europe in earlier centuries. Another change took place

when the Neoplatonist interpretation of his thought received support
from Ficino. This too would have seemed a strange novelty to previous
generations, not least in Byzantium, where Neoplatonism had been even
more likely to provoke ecclesiastical censure than the genuine version of
his thought. As for the author who had been termed by Dante the master
of those who know, his influence was not removed from the universities
by the rising interest in Plato. But the *Nicomachean Ethics* assumed a
greater importance than they had had in the medieval west or for that
matter in Byzantium. The scientific treatises were not immediately
brought into prominence in the way that their author would have wished;
again the fifteenth century could not advance beyond Byzantium.
Commentaries on various parts of the corpus gradually came into use,
mainly towards the end of the period. Much the same is probably true of
the *Poetics*, another text largely neglected in Byzantium. Although we
can now be sure that it had begun to circulate in the middle of the
fifteenth century, the great age of its influence may plausibly be dated
from Pazzi's translation and commentary of 1536, followed by
Castelvetro's vernacular version of 1567. It was not only in science that
the middle decades of the sixteenth century obtained inspiration from a
text which the Byzantines had preserved but could not use.

More than once in this history we have had occasion to note how
scholars expressed anxiety that yet more texts might be lost owing to the
destruction caused by wars. This fear invites the question whether in fact
the humanists of the fifteenth century succeeded in preserving
everything that had been handed down to them. One half of the answer is
to estimate how much was lost in the fall of Constantinople in 1453. On
this point there is very little evidence, but there is reason to think that
after the damage wrought by the Fourth Crusade in 1204 the Byzantines
had few if any texts that we cannot read now. The only specific report of a
loss in 1453 relates to a complete copy of the *Universal History* of
Diodorus Siculus (we now have rather less than half of it).[4] The second
half of the answer is to evaluate the occasional reports by humanists that
they possessed or knew of a copy of some work which we cannot now read.
Aurispa made such an assertion about the *Katharmoi* of the Sicilian pre-
Socratic philosopher Empedocles. The claim sounds implausible, but one
has to admit that it is not immediately clear how a confusion with
another text could have led him to make this error. He also claimed to
have Aristarchus' commentary on the *Iliad* in two volumes, but in this
case the source of his mistaken enthusiasm is obvious.[5] Similarly
Rinuccio Aretino on his return from the east in 1423 claimed to have
Archimedes, *De instrumentis bellicis et aquaticis*; probably this was a
confusion with other writers about military engineering.[6] Alleged copies
of Greek lyric poets and the orations of Hyperides are no more credible.[7]
All in all it is fair to say that the task of preserving what had been left
after 1204 was carried out with almost complete success.

Notes

Notes to Chapter 1

1 R. Weiss, *Medieval and humanist Greek* (Padua 1977) 117-18 (from an article originally published in *Rinascimento* 1 (1950) 195-226).

2 P.A. Stadter, *IMU* 16 (1973) 137-62. He seems to me justifiably sceptical on p. 157.

3 A. Pertusi, *Leonzio Pilato fra Petrarca e Boccaccio* (Venice-Rome 1964) 11-14; F. Di Benedetto, *IMU* 12 (1969) 83.

4 Pertusi, op. cit. 8.

5 Ibid. 18 n. 5; A. Diller, *CP* (1964) 270-2. The conjecture is due to E. Pellegrin, *La bibliothèque des Visconti et des Sforza, ducs de Milan* (Paris 1955) 310.

6 P.G. Ricci, *Rinascimento* 3 (1952) 159-64. Boccaccio says in his *Geneal. deorum gent.* 15.7 that he introduced Greek to Tuscany at his own expense.

7 On this delay see M. Feo, *IMU* 17 (1974) 136-7.

8 Pertusi, op. cit. 433-6.

9 Longer specimens are given by Pertusi, ibid. 169ff., 205ff.

10 The edition by J. Diggle (Oxford 1981-) reports its readings.

11 The proof that Pilato is the author of the version is due to A. Pertusi, *IMU* 3 (1960) 101-52. Its importance is not lessened by the different view that I have taken of the date of Laur. 31.10; cf. *Scrittura e Civiltà* 7 (1983) 161-76.

12 E. Garin, *Giornale critico della filosofia italiana* 35 (1956) 355-7. F. Di Benedetto, *IMU* 12 (1969) 56 n. 1, thinks that the MS used may have been Marc. gr. IV 58; it should be investigated to see if the occasional marginalia indicate Pilato's ownership. (It is probably of the twelfth rather than the thirteenth century.)

13 F. Di Benedetto, *IMU* 12 (1969) 53-112.

14 See the two volumes by R. Pfeiffer, *History of classical scholarship* (Oxford 1968 and 1976).

15 Pertusi, op. cit. in nn. 4 and 8, 189-99, 238-57, gives some examples.

16 *Anthologia Palatina* 16.29; see P.G. Ricci, op. cit.

17 Weiss, op. cit. 208-10, 216-18, 231; the first two references are to an article originally published in *La Parola del Passato* 32 (1953) 321-42.

Notes to Chapter 2

1 R.J. Loenertz, *La Correspondance de Manuel Calecas* (*Studi e Testi* 152) (Rome 1950) 64-5, 70, and see in general R. Weiss, *Miscellanea in onore di Roberto Cessi* (Rome 1958) I 349-56.

2 Letters 9.16, ed. F. Novati (Florence 1896) III 131-2.

3 Vespasiano da Bisticci, *Vite*, ed. A. Greco (Florence 1970-76) II 140-1. Palla's

own statement about the Ptolemy is conveniently available in A. Diller, *JWCI* 24 (1961) 316 (= *Studies in Greek manuscript tradition* (Amsterdam 1983) 408).

4 A. Gherardi, *Statuti dell' università e dello studio fiorentino* (Florence 1881) 365, 367-8, 370.

5 Loenertz, op. cit. 66.

6 A. Pertusi, *IMU* 5 (1964) 343-4.

7 R. Proctor, *The printing of Greek in the fifteenth century* (Oxford 1900) 34-5.

8 This information comes from Battista Guarino's *De ordine docendi*; I cite from E. Garin's edition in *Il pensiero pedagogico dell' Umanesimo* (Florence 1958) 450-3.

9 R. Sabbadini, *Il metodo degli umanisti* (Florence 1922) 18-20, drew attention to this but did not make all the legitimate inferences.

10 Letter VI of the group published by L. Bertalot, *Römische Quartalschrift* 29 (1915) 101-2.

11 He says *expositio*, but I doubt if he means a commentary, in view of what follows.

12 On the tutor in question, Demetrius Scaranus, see C.L. Stinger, *Humanism and the church fathers: Ambrogio Traversari (1386-1439) and Christian antiquity in the Italian Renaissance* (Albany, N.Y. 1977) 20.

13 L. Bertalot, *Quellen und Forschungen aus italienischen Archiven und Bibliotheken* 21 (1929-30) 210; mentioned by Sabbadini, op. cit. 23.

14 Migne, *Patrologia Latina* 122.1032.

15 See e.g. Stinger, op. cit. 102.

16 See G.J.M. Bartelink, *Hieronymus, Liber de optimo genere interpretandi (ep. 57)* (Leiden 1980), esp. pp. 3-4.

17 *Epistles* 1.6, ed. L. Mehus (Florence 1741).

18 M. Baxandall, *JWCI* 28 (1965) 191; see also his *Giotto and the Orators* (Oxford 1971) 78-96.

19 See his letter of 1424 to Antonio Loschi and the passage from his history, Muratori 19.920, both cited by H. Baron, *Leonardo Bruni Aretino, Humanistisch-philosophische Schriften* (Leipzig 1928) 125-8.

20 No. 9849; published by H. Omont, *REG* 4 (1891) 176-7, and subsequently as the frontispiece to G. Cammelli, *Manuele Crisolora* (Florence 1941), and elsewhere.

21 L. Planiscig, *Rinascita* 4 (1941) 818-26.

22 Sabbadini, *La scuola e gli studi di Guarino Guarini Veronese* (Catania 1896) 15-16, stated that the *Chrysolorina* once existed in a codex at Camaldoli, now lost, and that the least incomplete copy known to him was Harley 2580. Having looked at this MS I am not quite sure what he supposed to be missing; but it must be said that the beginning and end of the collection are not indicated. As there appears to be some additional material perhaps we should infer that the MS descends from Guarino's personal copy, in which he had inserted supplementary items. – As far as the Latin adjectives are concerned, the second and third are attested but the others may be the product of inference or confusion of thought.

Notes to Chapter 3

1 See Pertusi, *Leonzio Pilato*, 147-58.

2 Ibid. 522-4. On the date see now P. Thiermann, *RevHistTextes* 17 (1987, actually 1989) 55-71.

3 The text is printed by A. Manetti, *Rinascimento* 2 (1951) 52-5. At 52 n. 7

Manetti says the preface is a document 'che si inserisce nella polemica intorno agli antichi e moderni, viva nei primi anni del Quattrocento'. I do not myself see anything in it which is explicit enough to justify this comment.

4 It is mentioned in Letter 650 of the *Epistolario*, ed. R. Sabbadini (Venice 1914-19) II 192-4, dated 1434.

5 Weiss, op. cit. at Ch. 1, n. 1, 244-5.

6 See L. Schuchan, *Das Nachleben von Basilius Magnus 'ad adulescentes'* (Geneva 1973), esp. 62-76 and 235-42. Bruni's text is conveniently reprinted by M. Naldini (ed.), *San Basilio, Discorso ai giovani* (Florence 1984). A copy of the Greek text in Bruni's own hand is known (Urb. gr. 33), but Dr E. Berti's researches suggest that it is not the one used as the basis for the translation.

7 Letter 46 in *Epistolario* I 100-1; cf. III 46. The text was printed from Ravenna, Classense 203, by R. Truffi, *SIFC* 10 (1902) 73-94.

8 On Bruni's use of the Greek historians in his own historical writings see E.B. Fryde, *Humanism and Renaissance historiography* (London 1983) 26 and 34. I suspect that he is wrong to suggest that the influence of Plutarch was slight (ibid. 24). For a survey of the Greek manuscripts of Plutarch used by the humanists see M. Manfredini, *Annali della Scuola Normale di Pisa* 17 (1987) 1001-43.

9 D.A. Russell, *Greece and Rome* 13 (1966) 144-5. Discussion of this complex problem is taken a stage further in the article by C. Gill, *CQ* 33 (1983) 469-87, esp. 478-9. He refers to *Aratus* 51.3 as well as the *Sulla* and *Sertorius* passages. The *Aratus* was not translated by Bruni.

10 H. Baron, op. cit. at Ch. 2 n. 19, 123-5, prints the text.

11 For Bruni's version see the edition, accompanied by valuable introductory material, by M.A. Lanzillotta, *Leonardo Bruni traduttore di Demostene: la Pro Ctesiphonte* (Genoa 1986). Information is given about the other versions in J. Monfasani, *George of Trebizond* (Leiden 1976) 61-8. A specimen of Valla's version was published by J. Vahlen, *SB Wien* 62 (1869) 138ff.

12 For details see N.G. Wilson, *Scholars of Byzantium* (London 1983) 12, 132.

13 For a brief account of Lucian's influence at this date see C. Robinson, *Lucian* (London 1979) 81-95. A more thorough survey is given in the valuable monograph of E. Mattioli, *Luciano e l'umanesimo* (Naples 1980); for the earliest versions see esp. 41-7.

14 E. Berti, *RivFil* 113 (1985) 416-43, followed by his contributions in *Studi classici e orientali* 37 (1987) 303-51 and *Rinascimento* 27 (1987) 3-73. The copy of 1403 is Laur. 25 sin. 9. The Latin, along with Rinuccio's version that soon replaced it in general circulation, is printed by P. Hemeryck, *Mélanges de l'Ecole Française de Rome* 84 (1972) 129-200.

15 The date of this version is also *c.* 1400; see E.P. Goldschmidt, *JWCI* 14 (1951) 7-20.

16 The artistic evidence is treated by D. Cast, *The calumny of Apelles* (Yale U.P. 1981).

17 Nor do modern scholars normally condescend to notice them; but see A.-J. Festugière, *Personal religion among the Greeks* (Berkeley-Los Angeles 1960) 85-104.

18 L. Bertalot, op. cit. at Ch. 2 n. 13.

19 Bruni's admission of indebtedness, accompanied by the declaration that his work was a youthful jeu d'esprit, is in a letter written many years later (*Epp.* 8.4). On the *Laudatio* see H. Baron, *From Petrarch to Leonardo Bruni* (Chicago 1968) 153-68, with text on 232-63 (it is also printed by V. Zaccaria, *Studi medievali* 8 (1967) 529-54). By an unfortunate lapse he assigns Aristides' oration to *c.* 100 BC

instead of *c*. AD 160. J.E. Seigel, *Past and Present* 34 (1966) 24 n. 52, may mislead the uninitiated when he says that Bruni follows Aristides closely; I do not think it would be fair to say that the dependence is slavish.

20 J. Soudek, *Studies in medieval and Renaissance history* 5 (1968) 51-136.

21 Ed. by Baron, op. cit. 41-50 and I. Düring, *Aristotle in the ancient biographical tradition* (Göteborg 1957) 168-78. See also E.B. Fryde, op. cit. 14.

22 Seigel, op. cit. in n. 19 above, 26-7, attempts to claim that Bruni's translations of Aristotle are motivated by rhetorical enthusiasm first and foremost, with civic humanism no more than a secondary concern. This view seems questionable on two grounds: it does not consider what the purpose of rhetoric was, and it allows inadequate weight to some statements in Bruni's prefaces about the qualities of Aristotle and other authors which would have commended them to readers of the fifteenth century. One might with greater justification take this view of Bruni's *Laudatio*, in the light of his admission cited above in n. 19.

23 E. Berti, *Il Critone latino di Leonardo Bruni e di Rinuccio Aretino* (Florence 1983) 7. Bruni's autograph transcript of the Greek is now in Geneva (Bodmer 136).

24 E. Carosini ap. E. Berti, op. cit. in the preceding n. 151-3, 185-8.

25 Baron, op. cit. 3-4.

26 See Cammelli, op., cit. 122-5; D. Bottoni in R. Avesani et al. (edd.), *Vestigia: Studi in onore di Giuseppe Billanovich* (Rome 1984) 75-91; J. Hankins in *Supplementum Festivum: Studies in honor of P.O. Kristeller* (Binghamton 1987) 149-88 (I have made two slight adjustments to the translation of Guarino's rather obscure Latin).

27 Further details in N.G. Wilson, op. cit. in n. 12 above, 13, 153-4.

28 *Epistulae* 9, 4, ed. L. Mehus (Florence 1741) ii 148.

29 Baron, op. cit. 45. E.B. Fryde, op. cit. 35, notes that in this passage there is an interesting variation between the manuscripts, some making Bruni describe Plato's doctrine as *despicabilius*, others as *inexplicabilius*.

30 The relevant passages of the *De interpretatione recta* are printed by Baron, op. cit. 81-3, 88-90. Some parts are cited for a rather different purpose by M. Baxandall, *Giotto and the orators* (Oxford 1971) 23-4.

31 The matter arrises in Bruni's letters and a treatise by bishop Alfonso of Cartagena; see A. Birkenmajer, *Beiträge zur Geschichte der Philosophie im Mittelalter* 20 (5) (1922), esp. 147 and 155-210.

32 Bessarion, *In calumniatorem Platonis* 3.19.6, ed. L. Mohler (Paderborn 1927) 316-17.

33 Baron, op. cit. 77 n.

34 V. Fera in *Francesco Filelfo nel quinto centenario della morte* (Padua 1986) 93 n. 14.

35 For discussion of defects in his versions of the *Phaedo* and other dialogues see the specimens given by J. Hankins, *Plato in the Italian Renaissance* (Leiden 1990) 388-400. Bruni's view of his predecessors was discussed by E. Franceschini in *Medioevo e umanesimo: studi in onore di Bruno Nardi* (Florence 1955) 299-319. An amusing point emerges from two letters, *Epp.* 4.22 of 1423 to Demetrius (Scaranos?) and 7.4 of 1436 to Pizzolpasso (Mehus I 137-40 and II 81-90): equidem si in picturam Giotti quis faecem proiceret, pati non possem; quid ergo existimas mihi accidere cum Aristotelis libros omni pictura elegantiores tanta traductionis faece coinquinari videam? an non commoveri? an non turbari? ('Certainly if someone threw mud over a picture by Giotto, I should find it unbearable; what do

you think my feelings are when I see books by Aristotle, more elegant than any picture, defiled by such a mass of sordid translations? Calm acceptance?')

Notes to Chapter 4

1 Detailed discussion in G. Cammelli, *Manuele Crisolora* (Florence 1941) 107-22, 153-9.

2 On the young Guarino see A. Pertusi, 'L'umanesimo greco dalla fine del secolo XIV agli inizi del secolo XVI', in *Storia della cultura veneta dal primo Quattrocento al Concilio di Trento* 3/1 (Vicenza 1980) 193-200.

3 Pertusi, ibid. 207-9.

4 C. Griggio in *Miscellanea di studi in onore di Vittore Branca* (Florence 1983) III 158-9. Similar ideas are found in the prefaces to the translations by both pupils of Guarino; they are dealt with briefly by P. Gothein, *Francesco Barbaro: Früh-Humanismus und Staatskunst in Venedig* (Berlin 1932) 54-8.

5 Griggio, op. cit. 173-4.

6 A. Diller, *IMU* 6 (1963) 253-62.

7 S.G. Mercati, *Collectanea Byzantina* (Bari 1970) II 25 (from an article originally published in *Miscellanea G. Mercati* III).

8 J. Monfasani, *Collectanea Trapezuntiana* (Binghamton, N.Y., 1984) 397.

9 E.R. Dodds, *Plato: Gorgias* (Oxford 1959) 44-5.

10 For the details see F. Di Benedetto, *IMU* 12 (1969) 111 n. 2.

11 Location unknown; I was once shown a photo and asked to identify the text, which I did, but failed to make a note of the location, which at that time seemed unimportant. Efforts to trace the picture have so far been in vain.

12 For the figures see W. Spoerri, *Museum Helveticum* 37 (1980) 17-19.

13 I. Thomson, *Renaissance Quarterly* 29 (1976) 169-78, has given reasons for believing that the list of 54 volumes once thought to record the contents of Guarino's library is at best a list of what he owned late in life and probably does not relate to him at all.

14 See R. Blum, *La biblioteca della Badia Fiorentina e i codici di Antonio Corbinelli (Studi e Testi* 155) (Vatican City 1951), esp. 88, 97ff.; A. Molho in *Dizionario biografico degli italiani* 28 (1983) 745-7, who notes that a new inventory of the library will be published by S. Hough from a hitherto unknown document in the Archivio di Stato in Florence.

15 Letter 382 (ed. Sabbadini I 549-50; see also III 208).

16 For details see A. Franceschini, *Giovanni Aurispa e la sua biblioteca* (Padua 1976).

17 Franceschini, op. cit. 61-2, accepts the view of Comparetti and others that the Marciana manuscripts are meant; the alternative view is due to A. Diller, *CP* (1960) 35-6.

18 It seems to be accepted by E. Bigi in his article on Aurispa in the *Dizionario biografico degli italiani* 4 (1962) 593-5. It arises from a specific assertion in Letter 7 of Aurispa; see R. Sabbadini's edition of the *Carteggio (Fonti per la Storia d'Italia* 70) (Rome 1931). Franceschini, op. cit. 48, adds nothing.

19 Mattioli, op. cit. 49 and 56; for the last detail he cites an acute observation of E. Garin.

20 The emendation is πείσας for πεῖσαι at 48 e 4. For all these details see E. Berti, op. cit. at Ch. 3 n. 23.

21 Baron, op. cit. 127-8.

22 The texts are given in Baron, ibid. 135-8. Edgar Wind, *Heidnische Mysterien*

in der Renaissance (Frankfurt 1981) 13 n. 7, describes Bruni's judgment as 'extraordinarily prosaic', but he quotes very little of it and in the light of my summary his comment may seem a trifle harsh.

23 Listed by W.L. Newman, *The Politics of Aristotle*, vol. iii (Oxford 1902) xxii.

24 I followed the advice of E.B. Fryde, op. cit. 14 and read this letter in MS Balliol College 310, folios 120v-122r. The same points are made in the preface printed by Baron, op. cit. 73-4. On Duke Humfrey's invitation see R. Weiss, *Humanism in England during the fifteenth century* (second edition, Oxford 1957) 47-9. The details relating to the presentation copies are complex and at one time were taken as proof that Duke Humfrey had been ungenerous; some recent studies suggest that Bruni was acting in a complicated, though not necessarily dishonest, manner; see L. Gualdo Rosa, *Rinascimento* 23 (1983) 113-24.

25 The words in question are: 109 ἀτέχνως/ἀτεχνῶς, 220 πονηρός/πόνηρος, 174 κλαύσεται, 90 βαδιοίμην. I select these specimens from A.C. Cassio, *Giornale italiano di filologia* 24 (1972) 477-82; the version itself is edited by M. and E. Cecchini (Florence 1965).

26 Bruni's concern with Aristophanes had been partially anticipated by Rinuccio da Castiglione in his *Fabula Penia*, ed. W. Ludwig, *Die Fabula Penia des Rinucius Aretinus* (Munich 1975), from MS Balliol College 131. This short sketch dates from his stay in Crete in 1415-16; it exploits the first half the *Plutus* and has been thought to show some limited knowledge of Theocritus.

27 This story is given by A. Zeno, *Dissertazioni Vossiane* (Venice 1752) ii.142.

28 *Epistulae* 9.13 (vol. ii pp. 165-6).

29 Up-to-date information is to be had from C.L. Stinger, *Humanism and the church fathers: Ambrogio Traversari (1386-1439) and Christian antiquity in the Italian Renaissance* (Albany, N.Y. 1977) and the volume of conference proceedings *Ambrogio Traversari nel VI centenario della nascita* (Florence 1988); in the latter note in particular the articles by M. Gigante on Diogenes Laertius, 367-459, G. Fioravanti on Aeneas of Gaza's *Theophrastus*, 461-72, A. Fyrigos on Moschus 473-81, and P. Viti on Athanasius *Adversus gentiles*, 483-509.

30 Stinger, op. cit. 190-2.

31 See J. Gill, *The Council of Florence* (Cambridge 1959) 118 on the letter of August 10 1438 (no. 528 = 13.34), 165 on the translation of Basil (letter no. 849 = 24.6), 195 on Epiphanius, and 287 on the draft of the decree.

32 *Epistulae*, ed. L. Mehus (Florence 1759), no. 343 = 9.20; Stinger, op. cit. 73-6.

33 *Epistulae* no. 232 = 6.23, no. 286 = 8.17. See also A. Sottili in R. Avesani et al. (edd.), *Vestigia: studi in onore di Giuseppe Billanovich* (Rome 1984) 699-745, who identifies Traversari's autograph in MS Strozzi 64 and notes that it rectifies some omissions of the published version. He thinks the improvements may be due to Traversari's increasing knowledge of the language; but the other possible explanation is that Filelfo eventually made good his promise to help with the verse passages in Diogenes Laertius; see the letter no. 886 = 24.43, in which Filelfo excuses himself for delay (May 1433).

34 *Epistulae* no. 211 = 6.2.

35 *Epistulae* nos. 277-8 = 8.8 and 8.9. J. Hankins, *Plato in the Italian Renaissance* (Leiden 1990) 59-60.

Notes to Chapter 5

1 The main sources of information about Vittorino are memoirs by Sassolo da Prato, Platina, Francesco da Castiglione and Prendilacqua. These and other

pieces of evidence are conveniently reprinted in E. Garin, *Il pensiero pedagogico dell' Umanesimo* (Florence 1958) 504-718, and it is to this edition that I refer. Despite Garin's modest disclaimer his volume puts all these texts on a sounder footing. After completing a first draft of my text I read with advantage the recent monograph of G. Müller, *Mensch und Bildung im italienischen Renaissance-Humanismus: Vittorino da Feltre und die humanistischen Erziehungsdenker* (Baden-Baden 1984). One should also consult N. Giannetto (ed.), *Vittorino da Feltre e la sua scuola: umanesimo, pedagogia, arti* (Florence 1981). – The figure of forty comes from Sassolo (Garin 516), seventy from Prendilacqua (ibid. 602); both were products of the school.

2 M. Cortesi, *IMU* 23 (1980) 77-114.

3 Sassolo, ibid. 524.

4 Platina, ibid. 680.

5 Traversari, *Epist*. 24.53.

6 Castiglione, 546.

7 For Gaza's movements during the early 1440s see R. Sabbadini, *G. Aurispa: Carteggio* (Rome 1931) 168-9.

8 *Epist*. 8.49-51.

9 These treatises may not have had any effect on the teaching of music in the school; the important writer Jean de Namur (c. 1415-1473), who spent some time in Mantua and warmly acknowledged his debt to Vittorino, refers to Boethius, not the Greek authors. See C.H. de Coussemaker, *Scriptorum de musica medii aevi nova series* (Paris 1864-76) IV 345a, and more generally C.V. Palisca, *Humanism in Italian Renaissance musical thought* (Yale 1985).

10 Identified by Cortesi, op. cit., as Utrecht gr. 13. Inspection shows that it is almost certainly the work of two pupils in the school, not professional copyists.

11 This important observation was made by W.H. Woodward, *Vittorino da Feltre and other humanist educators* (Cambridge 1897) 224.

12 Guarino, *Epist*. 3.142.

13 Platina 680.

14 The exception is Vatopedi 671, written by Girard; its present location suggests that it may have been copied before the scribe left Greece.

15 M. Regoliosi, *IMU* 12 (1969) 134, with plate XIV illustrating MS Ferrara, Antonelli 545.

16 The notes are in MS Basle F-VIII-3; see M. Cortesi *IMU* 22 (1979) 449-83 with plates VI-VII.

17 Hunc primum ex poetis graecis didici a viro clarissimo Isidoro graeco iam nunc sanctae Romanae ecclesiae cardinali Tussiensi cognominato.

18 E. Gamillscheg, *JÖB* 24 (1975) 137-45, deals with this scribe and lists manuscripts so far identified as his work.

19 See plates 6 and 7 in Gamillscheg, op. cit., for the master's autograph note of donation and the page which furnishes an undated colophon.

20 J.B. Mittarellius, *Bibliotheca codicum manuscriptorum monasterii S. Michaelis Venetiarum prope Murianum* (Venice 1779) 973-4, thought that the copy seen by Traversari was the MS known now under the signature Marc. gr. VI.10.

21 This copy of 1430 is generally dated 1422, the year before Vittorino's appointment, a fact which has not prevented scholars from attributing it to the school. G. Pesenti saw the difficulty (*Athenaeum* 3 (1925) 5) and proposed a date of 1432. This still does not reconcile all the facts given in the colophon. One should assume instead that the lambda (=30) in the Greek date 6930 (= AD 1422) was written absent-mindedly as the scribe allowed the figure 1430 to pass through his head.

22 Not listed in Gamillscheg's article, but it appears in *RGK* I.

23 Text in J. Monfasani, *Collectanea Trapezuntiana* (Binghamton 1984) 405, 411.

24 A first list was drawn up by N.G. Wilson, *RevHistTextes* 4 (1974) 139-42.

25 The *Poetics* is found in Estensis gr. 100 (II D 1), Vat. gr. 1388 and 1904. The other volumes are now Laur. 72.18, British Library, Add. 14080, Paris gr. 2024, Pal. gr. 148 and Vat. gr. 2183.

26 A. Calderini, *SIFC* 20 (1913) 268-9.

27 Sabbadini, *Metodo* 73-4; A. Perosa, *Mostra del Poliziano* (Florence 1955) 73.

28 S. Lang, *Quaderni di teatro* 4 (1981) 25-6.

29 Among those published by A. Luzio, *GSLI* 36 (1888) 329-41.

30 Platina 692.

31 Ibid. 678.

Notes to Chapter 6

1 The basic source is still the pair of studies by R. Sabbadini; *Vita di Guarino Veronese* (Genoa 1891) and *La Scuola e gli studi di Guarino Guarini Veronese* (Catania 1896). His edition of the letters is also fundamental: *Epistolario* (Venice 1915-19). See also Pertusi, op. cit. at Ch. 4 n. 2; R. Avesani in *Verona e il suo territorio* IV.2 (Verona 1984) 31-6. But much work remains to be done on Guarino, and this part of my account is even more provisional than the remainder.

2 As his own lexicon is attested in what passes for a list of his books, it may seem that scepticism is out of place. But the absence of any trace of it among the surviving manuscripts is odd; note also the consideration mentioned at Ch. 4 (ii) n. 13.

3 Dr. F. Lo Monaco kindly tells me that there are references to Sophocles in the notes to Cicero's *Ad Herennium* and *Tusculan Disputations*.

4 R. Weiss, *Humanism in England during the fifteenth century* (second edition, Oxford 1957) 84-127, deals with these three among others; on Free's lecture notes see 108 n. 1.

5 Excerpts from the notes on the *Georgics* are printed by A.T. Grafton & L. Jardine, *From humanism to the humanities* (London 1986) 14-15; the source is MS Bodley 587, folio 137r. They do not comment on the error; my interpretation, if correct, has important consequences for their argument. On the teaching staff in the Ferrara school I rely on G. Voigt's work (in its Italian version by G. Zippel), *Il risorgimento dell' antichità classica ovvero il primo secolo dell' umanesimo* (Florence 1888, reprint 1968) I 555.

6 Guarino's letter is printed and discussed by M. Baxandall, *Giotto and the Orators* (Oxford 1971) 89-90, 158-60. The Byzantine source has not previously been recognised; it is printed in T. Gaisford's edition of the *Poetae graeci minores* iii (Oxford 1820) 23-4.

7 See E. Lobel, *Bodleian Quarterly Record* 5 (1926) 43-6 on MS Bywater 38. This belonged to Francesco Barbaro and some parts of it are Guarino's autograph; see A.C. de la Mare in F. Krafft & D. Wuttke (ed.), *Das Verhältnis der Humanisten zum Buch* (Boppard 1977) 106 n. 70, and C. Griggio, *Lettere Italiane* 37 (1985) 347.

8 The third Xenophon may be Laur. 55.21, written by Peter the Cretan, the scribe who worked in Mantua; in the catalogue of the Laurenziana Library A.M. Bandini (II 286) recognised the hand of Guarino in the margins, and this suggestion should be verified; the book could have reached Guarino after the death of Vittorino, if not before. There are difficulties in identifying Guarino's Greek hand: see D. Harlfinger in *Griechische Handschriften und Aldinen* (Wolfenbüttel 1978) 51, for a note on the problem and three specimens of his ex-libris. For more about his library see A. Diller, *JWCI* 24 (1961), 313-21 (= *Studies in Greek Manuscript Tradition* (Amsterdam 1983) 405-13).

9 See further J. Hankins in *Supplementum Festivum: Studies in honor of P.O. Kristeller* (Binghamton 1987) 162-76. (The suggestion that Guarino in translating two famous short epigrams by Plato (*Anth. Pal.* VII.669-70) bowdlerised them by changing the sex of the addressee appears to me to be incorrect.)

10 The text is now in Monfasani, *Collectanea Trapezuntiana* (Binghamton N.Y. 1984) 398; it was previously available in incomplete form in Sabbadini's edition of the *Epistolario* (see vol. 3 p. 343 on what he classed as Letter 707). For Corbinelli's MSS see Blum, op. cit., 102 on Laur. Conv. Soppr. 8 and 94.

11 T. Kaeppeli, *Studi romagnoli* 2 (1951) 57-65, showed that the version of *Ad Nicoclem* was made by Carlo Marsuppini and dedicated to Galeotto Roberto Malatesta of Rimini, ruler of the city from 1429 to 1432; Marsuppini was in Rimini in 1430 with other members of the Florentine establishment, who were avoiding the plague.

12 The letter was published by A. Campana, *IMU* 5 (1962) 171-8. It is with great diffidence that I venture to offer an alternative solution to the puzzle to which he drew attention. For a survey of the translations available in the fifteenth century see V.R. Giustiniani, *Rinascimento* 1 (1961) 3-62.

13 On the version of Strabo and the codices used (Eton College 141, Moscow gr. 506 and Vat. gr. 174) see A. Diller, *The textual tradition of Strabo's Geography* (Amsterdam 1975) 126-9.

Notes to Chapter 7

1 E. Legrand, *Cent-dix lettres grecques de François Filelfo* (Paris 1892). No. 56, addressed to Bessarion, contains a proof that on some occasions he used Greek in order to keep the contents confidential. In the same volume Legrand prints some of the verses mentioned below (there is an autograph copy extant, Laur. 58.15). For further information about them see D. Robin, *Renaissance Quarterly* 37 (1984) 173-206.

2 The letter is of 1441; it is printed on folios 30v-31r of the 1502 Venice edition of the *Epistolae familiares*, and has been cited with a somewhat different intention by M. Baxandall, *Giotto and the orators* (Oxford 1971) 64. – Is it conceivable that *Aeolica* is a misprint for *Ionica*?

3 A copy of the *Politics* was written for him in Milan in 1445 by Demetrius Sguropoulos (Leiden, Scaligeranus 26).

4 For an attempt to retrieve his reputation see D. Robin, *Renaissance Quarterly* 36 (1983) 202-24. G. Resta in his paper in the proceedings of the 1981 conference held at Tolentino, *Francesco Filelfo nel quinto centenario della morte* (Padua 1986), also makes generous allowance for the situation in which humanists often found themselves, but is perhaps a little too charitable.

5 Baron, op. cit. 162-3; the version of Demosthenes *On the crown* is datable 1406-7 and Aeschines *Against Ctesiphon* was done in the summer of 1412. Bruni had of course also translated the *Ethics*.

6 Filelfo's preface and translation were printed at Cremona in 1492.

7 Made from Laur. 60.18.

8 The text can be read in the edition of his speeches and other works issued in

Milan in 1483-4, folios g5-g6.

9 The text can be read in the edition of 1474.

10 The charge of ignorance was made by A. Calderini *SIFC* 20 (1913) 204-424, in a form not easy to refute, *pace* G. Resta, op. cit. 50. See further the inference drawn by R. Bianchi, ibid. 342, concerning his lectures on Cicero given at Siena.

11 From a letter of 23 January 1452 cited by C. Bianca, ibid. 213 n. 20.

12 Greek letter no. 31, in Legrand, op. cit. 61-2.

13 C. Bianca in the conference proceedings, op. cit. 215.

14 Ibid. 242-4.

15 Greek letter no. 12, Legrand, op. cit. 31.

16 Greek letters nos. 62-3, Legrand, op. cit. 110-12. In Greek letter no. 100, sent to Gaza in 1474, he discussed Cicero's rendering of the term κατόρθωμα, noting that it should not in general be equated with ὀρθόν. He contradicted Cicero on the meaning of ἐνδελέχεια at *Tusculans* 1.10 (Fera in the conference proceedings, 129).

17 On the *De ideis* see J. Kraye, *JWCI* 42 (1979) 236-49.

18 S. Rizzo in C. Questa & R. Raffaelli (edd.), *Il libro e il testo* (Urbino 1985) 231-8, with plates 1-10.

19 On Wolfenbüttel 17.21.4 Aug. 4° which is linked with Filelfo see M. Cortesi in the conference proceedings, 163-206.

20 Conventi Soppressi 181; I am indebted to Prof. V. Fera for information on this point.

21 See V. Fera in the conference proceedings, 129 on the case of *ineptus* at *De oratore* 2.17 and the *labor/dolor* distinction at *Tusculans* 2.35.

22 See V. Fera, ibid. 115-17.

Notes to Chapter 8

1 In Ficino's report the key words are *Pletonem de mysteriis Platonicis disputantem frequenter audivit*. The adverb is usually taken to mean 'often', but Ficino and most of his readers doubtless knew enough Latin to be aware that it might also mean 'in a large company'.

2 The case for scepticism has now been put very forcibly by J. Hankins, *JWCI* 53 (1990) 144-62, who suggests that the word Academy could be used figuratively to refer to Plato's works or a Latin translation of them. He also wonders whether Cosimo obtained from Plethon the Plato codex, Laur. 85.9, which he passed on to Ficino.

3 Frances A. Yates, *Renaissance and Reform: the Italian contribution (Collected essays* II) (London 1984) 8-10. On the Florentine societies see A. Della Torre, *Storia dell' Accademia platonica di Firenze* (Florence 1902) 354-64, esp. 359, 538-41.

4 M.V. Anastos, *Annuaire de l'Institut de philologie et d'histoire orientales et slaves* 12 (Brussels 1952) 1-18 (reprinted in his *Studies in Byzantine intellectual history* (London 1979)).

5 A new letter of Traversari discovered by G. Mercati, *Ultimi contributi alla storia degli umanisti, Fascicolo I, Traversariana (Studi e Testi* 90) (Vatican City 1939) 24-6, shows that Bessarion had left behind him at Modon 'Strabonis duo maxima volumina'. The date of the letter is between March 11 and April 7. At p. 25 n. 7 Mercati prints the passage of Plethon reporting geographical information received by him from 'Paul of Florence'. On the MSS of Strabo see A. Diller, *The textual tradition of Strabo's Geography* (Amsterdam 1975).

6 Text and useful discussion in Monfasani, op. cit. 39-40.

7 The basis of all modern work on Bessarion is the great three-volume study by L. Mohler, *Kardinal Bessarion als Theologe, Humanist und Staatsmann* (Paderborn, 1924-42). The article by L. Labowsky in the *Dizionario biografico degli italiani* is excellent. Valla's description comes from the preface to his Thucydides.

8 Text in *PG* 161.669-76.

9 Perhaps most notably in K.R. Popper, *The open society and its enemies* (ed. 2 London 1952). On Bessarion's discussion of Plato's proposals about marriage in the *Republic* see Anna Pontani in *Contributi di Filologia greca medievale e moderna* (*Quaderni del Siculorum Gymnasium* XVIII) (Catania 1989) 122-3, 130. See also 105 for Bessarion's attempt to rebut charges of homosexuality by referring to Diogenes Laertius 3.29-32.

10 N. Adkins, *Orpheus* 6 (1985) 149-52.

11 Porphyry, *Vita Pythagorae* 35.

12 *PG* 57.69.

13 On this see J. Monfasani, *George of Trebizond* (Leiden 1976) 102-3 and *Collectanea Trapezuntiana* (Binghamton N.Y. 1984) 199-201.

14 The text of Bessarion's account is in *PG* 161.324-8.

15 The date of the discussion was 28 December 1448 or 1449: A. Perosa, *Lorenzo Valla, Collatio Novi Testamenti, redazione inedita* (Florence 1970) xxxiv n. 64. The stages of the controversy are not entirely clear; the latest contribution is by J. Monfasani, *Collectanea Trapezuntiana* (Binghamton, N.Y. 1984) 311-12 and 574-5.

16 Bessarion's copy of Nicholas' book is MS Marc. lat. 289.

17 The text is printed, not entirely accurately, by Mohler, op. cit. III 70-87. The passages of Augustine are from *De doctrina Christiana* 2.11 and 14 (*Patrologia Latina* 34.42 and 46).

18 On all these matters see the definitive study of L. Labowsky, *Bessarion's library and the Biblioteca Marciana: six early inventories* (Rome 1979), esp. 9-15.

19 J.L. Heiberg, *SB Berlin* 1892, 59ff., esp. 65-70.

20 The text is published by L. Labowsky, *Medieval and Renaissance Studies* 5 (1961) 132-54.

21 In his copy Marc. gr. 186; observed by E. Berti, *Il Critone latino di Leonardo Bruni e di Rinuccio Aretino* (Florence 1983), 33 n. 9.

22 Examined by G.J. Boter, *The textual tradition of Plato's Republic* (Amsterdam 1986) 282-7.

23 This house of cards is the only weak point in the otherwise admirable article of E. Martini, *RhMus* 62 (1907); see p. 282.

24 According to A. Turyn, *The Byzantine manuscript tradition of the tragedies of Euripides* (Urbana 1957) 148-9, it is the best representative of the recension of Sophocles prepared by Demetrius Triclinius *c.* 1300, having been probably copied directly from the autograph of Triclinius *c.* 1465.

25 The inventory was printed and discussed by F. Di Benedetto in *Miscellanea in memoria di Anna Saitta Revignas* (Florence 1978). On Morosini's negotiations see Labowsky, op. cit. in n. 18, 27 and 124.

26 The inaugural lecture was printed as part of the preliminary material to an edition of Alfraganus (Nürnberg 1537). See P.L. Rose, *The Italian Renaissance of mathematics* (Geneva 1975) 92-100.

27 See E. Zinner, *Leben und Wirken des Joh. Müller von Königsberg genannt Regiomontanus* (ed. 2 Osnabrück 1968) and the article on Regiomontanus by E. Rosen in the *Dictionary of scientific biography*. The astrolabe is described and

illustrated by D.S. de S. Price, *Physis* 1 (1959) 26-30.

28 For more details of his career see R. Mett, *Regiomontanus in Italien* (*SB Wien* no. 520) (Vienna 1989).

29 G. Mercati, *Per la cronologia della vita e degli scritti di Niccolò Perotti* (*Studi e Testi* 44) (Vatican City 1925) 74-81, 156-8.

Notes to Chapter 9

1 *Letter* 44.23ff.

2 On these matters see F. Lo Monaco in *Lorenzo Valla e l'Umanesimo italiano* (Padua 1986) 141-64. His notes 1-4 on pp. 141-2 give the necessary bibliography on the early translations by Valla.

3 *Antidotum in Facium* IV 10.16-18.

4 See S. Camporeale, *Lorenzo Valla: umanesimo e teologia* (Florence 1972) 202-3, who cites extracts from the letters as published by J. Ruiz Calonja, *Boletín de la Real Academia de Buenas Letras de Barcelona* 23 (1950) 109-15.

5 See the edition by D. Marsh, *BiblHumRen* 46 (1984) 407-20.

6 *Letter* 11.23.

7 *IG* XIV 714; *Letter* 19.

8 συντελέσας.

9 A. Campana, *Archeologia classica* 25-6 (1973-4) 84-102, notes the first error but passes over the second.

10 See further M. Regoliosi in *La storiografia umanistica* (Messina 1989) 1ff.

11 No. 40.

12 Consulted in the edition by B. Parthenius (Treviso 1483?), which is marred by careless misprints. Valla's master copy is Vat. lat. 1801.

13 F. Ferlauto, *Il testo di Tucidide e la traduzione latina di Lorenzo Valla* (Palermo 1979), gave a useful review of the current state of the question, and the comments of D.M. Lewis, *CR* 30 (1980) 276-8, are extremely important.

14 G.B. Alberti, *Bollettino del Comitato per la preparazione dell' edizione nazionale dei classici greci e latini* 7 (1959) 65-84.

15 The idea is due to B. Hemmerdinger, *Les manuscrits d'Hérodote et la critique verbale* (Genoa 1981) 48, 180-1. But the word *acris* in Valla should be taken as a genitive reflecting the manuscript text, not as a nominative reflecting the variant. It is in any case a question whether he received information from Ciriaco.

16 Ultimately it derives from St Jerome's preface to his Four Gospels (Wordsworth-White I.1-2). Jerome also spoke of *hebraica veritas*, e.g. *Letter* 106.7.

17 The number of manuscript copies known is tiny; only three were known to A. Perosa when he published the earlier redaction in 1970; another has recently come to light: see R. Fubini in *Lorenzo Valla* ... (op. cit. in n. 2 above) 179-96.

18 *Opera* 340 = *Antidotum in Pogium* IV.

19 P. 395 in J. Vahlen's edition, *Vierteljahresschrift für Kultur und Litteratur der Renaissance* 1 (1885) 384-96.

20 The note is printed in *PG* 4.176C.

21 B. Collett, *Italian Benedictine scholars and the Reformation: the congregation of Santa Giustina of Padua* (Oxford 1985) 20 n. 45, citing J.W. O'Malley, *Giles of Viterbo on church and reform* (Leiden 1968).

22 See J.H. Bentley, *Humanists and Holy Writ* (Princeton 1983) 44-5 on this point; the whole of the chapter is worth reading.

23 S.I. Camporeale, op. cit. in n. 4 above, 307-9.

24 Pp. 76 and 82 in Mohler's edition.

25 V. Peri, *Aevum* 41 (1967) 67-90 provides an excellent survey of Maniacutia and the questions raised by his activity.

26 See A. Perosa (ed.), *Lorenzo Valla, Collatio Novi Testamenti, redazione inedita* (Florence 1970) xxiii-xxxvii on the two redactions of Valla's work, and xxxiii n. 63 for a list of passages in the second redaction which display his technique at its best.

27 R. Pfeiffer, *History of classical scholarship 1300-1850* (Oxford 1976) 37-8, dispelled the error of U. von Wilamowitz-Moellendorff, *History of classical scholarship* (English tr., ed. H. Lloyd-Jones, London 1982) 25. It should be noted in passing that in England bishop Reginald Pecock independently reached the same conclusion as Valla about the Donation, but using a quite different approach. See the fascinating study by J.M. Levine, *Studies in the Renaissance* 20 (1973) 118-43.

28 Pfeiffer, ibid. 37-8, does not do full justice to the links between the two men.

Notes to Chapter 10

1 On Trapezuntius see the two fundamental works by J. Monfasani, *George of Trebizond* (Leiden 1976) and *Collectanea Trapezuntiana* (Binghamton N.Y. 1984).

2 *Collectanea Trapezuntiana* 165.

3 Ibid. 99.

4 Ibid. 585.

5 Above, Ch. 8 (ii).

6 Op. cit. 231; cf. also 332 and 400.

7 Ibid. 232.

8 Ibid. 95.

9 Ibid. 339.

10 Ibid. 142.

11 Ibid. 406.

12 A. Pontani, op. cit. at Ch. 8 n. 9, 154 n. 7, draws attention to his extraordinary error at Plato, *Laws* 634a, where he took χωλήν 'lame' to mean χολήν 'bile'.

13 Politian, *Miscellanea* 1.90, was rightly emphasised by Monfasani (1976) 76-9; ibid. 153 n. 94 for quotations of two letters of Erasmus; cf. id. (1984), 706-7, 708-9, 724-6, 729 for the additional evidence.

14 This is known from Gyraldus, *De poetis nostrorum temporum* 2 (p. 399 in the Basle edition of his *Opera* of 1580), and from Ludovico Carbone, cited by Legrand, *Bibliographie hellénique* I (Paris 1885) xxxii n. 4. One may note in passing Legrand's quotation from Ponticus Virunius to the effect that long afterwards scholars passing Gaza's house in Ferrara would remove their hats (ibid. xxxiii n. 3).

15 See Mohler, op. cit., III 253ff., and A. Gercke, *Theodoros Gazes* (Greifswald 1903), who prints passages from MS Vat. lat. 8761. For more details of his biography see L. Mohler, *BZ* 42 (1943) 50-75.

16 S.L. Radt, *Zeitschrift für Papyrologie und Epigraphik* 38 (1980) 49, on expressions of the type οἱ περὶ followed by a proper name.

17 W. Burnikel, *Textgeschichtliche Untersuchungen zu neun Opuscula Theophrasts* (Wiesbaden 1974) 54-61.

18 Printed in *PG* 19.1167-1218.

19 One of these must have been the Elder Pliny, and it is interesting to note that Gaza remarks on the state of this admittedly very difficult text. He claims that it was close to being unintelligible until the bishop of Aleria, Giovanni Andrea De' Bussi, made substantial improvements to it.

20 The extraordinary tale is told by Strabo 13.1.54. Not all modern authorities find it incredible: see P. Moraux, *Der Aristotelismus bei den Griechen von Andronikos bis Alexander von Aphrodisias* I (Berlin 1973) 18-28.

21 Some of the corrections correspond to readings added by a second hand in Paris gr. 2069, written by Andronicus Callistus and later owned by Leoniceno. Examples cited by S. Amigues in the Budé edition of Books 1-2 of the *H.P.* (Paris 1988) xlvi-xlviii strike me as falling just within the category of notions that could occur to the intelligent critic.

22 Monfasani (1976) 154 with nn. 97-8.

23 See Ch. 9 nn. 20 & 21. The matter had also been raised by Pietro Balbi; J. Monfasani in *Supplementum Festivum: studies in honor of P.O. Kristeller* (Binghamton 1987) 189-219 has brought to light interesting material; see esp. p. 202.

24 C.L. Stinger, *The Renaissance in Rome* (Bloomington 1985) 228-34, gives a useful general survey.

25 See the text printed in Monfasani, *Collectanea Trapezuntiana*, 296.

26 They are printed by A. Wilmanns & L. Bertalot, *Archivum Romanicum* 7 (1923) 506-9, with corrections by G. Mercati, *Per la cronologia della vita e degli scritti di Niccolò Perotti arcivescovo di Siponto (Studi e Testi* 44) (Rome 1925) 34-5.

27 See Stinger, op. cit. 168-70 on the work of Piero da Monte, and his article in P.A. Ramsey (ed.), *Rome in the Renaissance* (Binghamton, N.Y. 1982) 153-69.

28 Noted by L.D. Ettlinger, *The Sistine chapel before Michelangelo* (Oxford 1965) 116-17, referring to dedication copies of versions by Lilio Tifernate presented to Sixtus IV (MSS Vat. lat. 180-3). A life of Moses by Gregory of Nyssa had been made available rather earlier in a translation by George Trapezuntius, but I am not sure how influential it was, *pace* Stinger, op. cit. 211-13.

29 *Apologeticus* 2.27, ed. A. De Pretis (Rome 1981).

30 Ibid. 2.28.

31 For some interesting details see J.H. Bentley, *Humanists and Holy Writ* (Princeton 1983) 57-9. The credit for drawing attention to it should apparently go to S. Garofalo, *Biblica* 27 (1946) 338-75.

32 It seems that Persona's MS of Agathias is no longer extant; see R. Keydell, *Agathiae Myrinaei historiarum libri quinque* (Berlin 1968) xv-xvi.

33 The most useful modern study of him is the preface to R.P. Oliver, *Niccolò Perotti's version of the Enchiridion of Epictetus* (Urbana 1954).

34 Perotti's text is printed by R. Sabbadini, *GSLI* 50 (1907) 52-4.

35 G. Mercati, op. cit. in n. 26 above, 151-5.

36 On these MSS see C. Aldick, *De Athenaei Deipnosophistarum epitomae codicibus Erbacensi Laurentiano Parisino* (Münster 1928).

37 This curiosity was cited by Burckhardt in his study of the Renaissance. The text is Gaspar Veronensis, ed. L.A. Muratori, *Rerum italicarum scriptores* III pars ii (Milan 1734) col. 1034.

38 The source is Raphael Volterranus, ap. Muratori, op. cit. XXIII (Milan 1733) 161-2.

Notes to Chapter 11

1 J. Monfasani, *George of Trebizond* (Leiden 1976) 41-53.

2 Monfasani, op. cit. 376, gives reasons for thinking him about ten years older. New evidence about his early years has been published by P. Canivet & N. Oikonomides, *Diptycha* 3 (1982-3) 5-97 (inaccessible to me); but the question has been raised whether the identification is in fact correct.

3 Shown in plate 8 accompanying D. Harlfinger's paper in I. Hadot (ed.), *Simplicius, sa vie, son oeuvre, sa survie* (Berlin 1987) 267-86.

4 The main studies are G. Cammelli, *Giovanni Argiropulo* (Florence 1941) and the article by G. Bigi in the *Dizionario biografico degli italiani*.

5 Monfasani, op. cit. 160 n. 124.

6 For Filelfo see his Greek letter no. 50, op. cit. pp. 92-3. The difference of attitudes is explored by J.E. Seigel in T.K. Rabb & J.E. Seigel (edd.), *Action and conviction in early modern Europe: essays in memory of E.H. Harbison* (Princeton 1969) 237-60. The text cited is a preface to the *De interpretatione* and *Prior Analytics* found in a presentation copy (Laur. 71.18).

7 It will appear in due course that similar procedures occur in Politian's work; see below, and see S. Rizzo in E. Livrea and G.A. Privitera (edd.), *Studi in onore di A. Ardizzoni* (Rome 1978) 759-68. The importance of the formula in ancient scholarship was recognised by D. van Berchem, *Museum Helveticum* 9 (1952) 79-87.

8 The introductory lectures are printed by K. Müllner, *Reden und Briefe italienischer Humanisten* (Vienna 1899) 3-56. The passage just cited is on p. 18.

9 See above, Ch. 3 n. 32.

10 *Miscellanea* 1.1.

11 Noted by E.B. Fryde from MS Riccardiana 120; see his *Humanism and Renaissance historiography* (London 1983) 63.

12 The letters and Gaza's essay are printed in the third volume of L. Mohler's *Bessarion*.

13 A. Field in *Supplementum Festivum: studies in honor of P.O. Kristeller* (Binghamton 1987) 299-326, is helpful on these questions.

14 See Field, op. cit. 321; E. Garin, *Rinascite e rivoluzioni: movimenti culturali dal XIV al XVIII secolo* (Bari 1975) 89-129; P. Henry, *Les Manuscrits des Ennéades* (ed. 2, Brussels-Paris 1948) 91-6. The main watermark is a letter R, a neater and smaller version of the type shown in Briquet nos. 8968-71, which range in date from 1410 to 1462; it is fairly close to the design *Lettre* 37 in D. & J. Harlfinger, *Wasserzeichen aus griechischen Handschriften* I (Berlin 1974), found in a dated MS of 1431. The other design in the Parisinus is Briquet's *fleur* 6651, dated 1452-4; it seems to me that the resemblance is exact. The watermarks therefore tend to confirm a date earlier than the activity of Ficino.

15 The MS is now Laur. Ashburnham 1439, on which see A.C. Dionisotti, *CR* 93 (1979) 341-3. It is also item 19 in S. Gentile, S. Niccoli, P. Viti, *Marsilio Ficino e il ritorno di Platone* (Florence 1984), an exhibition catalogue of great importance, as are the conference proceedings edited by G.G. Garfagnini and issued under the same title (Florence 1986).

16 He tells us this in a letter written at the end of his career: *Opera* (Basle 1576) 933-5. Some of the texts are printed by I. Klutstein, *Marsilio Ficino et la théologie ancienne* (Florence 1987). She argues that contrary to the general belief of scholars hitherto they are not the work of Ficino; if that is correct one wonders whether they can be attributed to anyone outside his circle. Under item 20 of the

exhibition catalogue (Laur. 36.35) an attribution to Janus Lascaris is considered. It may be worth noting that the Orphic *Argonautica* were translated at almost the same time by a humanist who enjoyed the patronage of Pius II, Leodrisio Crivelli. His dedication to the Pope refers to the preparations for a military undertaking against the Turks in 1463-4. See F. Vian, *RevHistTextes* 16 (1986, actually 1988) 63-82.

17 *Opera* 1537; P.O. Kristeller, *Supplementum Ficinianum* vol. 2 (Florence 1937) 87.

18 See the document described as item 140 in the exhibition catalogue.

19 The MS used is Laur. 71.33.

20 *De natura deorum* 1.107. For Bruni's observation see Baron, op. cit. 132-3.

21 *De civitate Dei* 18.37. On Ficino and 'Orpheus' see D.P. Walker, *The ancient theology* (London 1972) 22-9.

22 *Opera* 871-2 and 1537.

23 Item 43 in the exhibition catalogue.

24 Items 24 and 32 in the exhibition catalogue.

25 *Opera* 1945.

26 See e.g. R.T. Wallis, *Neoplatonism* (London 1972) 70-2. Some typical passages of Ficino are cited by R. Marcel, *Marsile Ficin (1433-1499)* (Paris 1958) 538-42, 586 n. 2. See now B.P. Copenhaver and Jill Kraye in the *Cambridge History of Renaissance Philosophy* (Cambridge 1988) 274-85, 311-12, on the results of Ficino's encounter with Neoplatonism; they bring out well the concept of magic as the art of dealing with forces inherent in natural objects, and the notion of man as a link between the temporal world and the eternal world, resulting from man's possession of an immortal soul and a mortal body.

27 Edited critically by R. Klibansky, *The continuity of the Platonic tradition during the middle ages* (London 1939, reprinted with supplementary material Munich 1981) 42-7.

28 *Opera* 868.

29 S. Gentile, *Rinascimento* 21 (1981) 3-27; see also item 46 in the exhibition catalogue.

30 Some details of chronology remain obscure; see M.J.B. Allen, *The Platonism of Marsilio Ficino: a study of his Phaedrus commentary, its sources and genesis* (University of California 1984) 210 n. 12.

31 J. Hankins, ap. Garfagnini, op. cit. in n. 15 above, 292-3. Hankins has now given us a fuller study of Ficino's Plato in his *Plato in the Italian Renaissance* (Leiden 1990) 267-359, reviewed by N.G. Wilson in *Studi umanistici* (forthcoming). One may note in particular his suggestion that the delay in printing the Plato translation may have had something to do with the astrologers' assertion that 1484 was to be a Great Year, with events of special significance for Christianity; and it also emerges that Ficino seems not to have been capable of understanding the bitter tone of the *Gorgias*.

32 S. Gentile, *Rinascimento* 23 (1983) 36-8. He notes that Ficino was willing to use the incomplete version of the *Phaedrus*, which, as we have seen, Traversari dismissed. See also J. Hankins ap. Garfagnini, op. cit. in n. 15 above, 288-9. A few soundings of my own have yielded a similar result: in the *Crito* Bruni's revised version is laid under contribution, and at *Timaeus* 30a Cicero's version was evidently useful.

33 On this see A.M. Wolters ap. Garfagnini, op. cit. in n. 15 above, 305-29, who studies the text of the draft in Florence Bibl. Naz., Conv. Soppr. E.1.2562.

34 H.-D. Saffrey, *BiblHumRen* 21 (1959) 161-84, esp. 180-1.

35 G. Resta in E. Livrea & G.A. Privitera (edd.) *Studi in onore di A. Ardizzoni* (Florence 1978) 1055-1131.

36 R. Proctor, *The printing of Greek in the 15th century* (Oxford 1900) 34-5; A. Pertusi, *IMU* 5 (1962) 323-4 with plate xxix.

37 Proctor, op. cit., 51ff., 156-7.

38 R. Hirsch, *The printed word: its impact and diffusion* (London 1978), article VI, gives a list covering the years 1469-1500.

39 N. Barker, *Aldus Manutius and the development of Greek script and type in the fifteenth century* (Sandy Hook, Connecticut 1985) 25.

40 Proctor, op. cit. 71, reports the observation made by E. Legrand. It is strange that Aldus saw fit to issue his own edition of this author in 1513.

41 Proctor, op. cit. 112-17.

42 The source is Alciato's *Opusculum*, the editions of 1515 and 1518. He had been a student in Milan in 1504-6.

43 The passage occurs on page c iii verso of the editio princeps (Venice 1522) of the dialogue *Medices legatus de exsilio*. – Considering the length of his career and the importance sometimes attributed to him, Chalcondyles is not as well known as might be expected; the standard sources are G. Cammelli, *Demetrio Calcondila* (Florence 1954) and the article by A. Petrucci in the *Dizionario biografico degli italiani*. Cammelli reproduces the Ghirlandaio fresco (facing p. 56).

44 His early career is very obscure. See B. Knös, *Un ambassadeur de l'hellénisme – Janus Lascaris – et la tradition gréco-byzantine dans l'humanisme français* (Uppsala-Paris 1945) 25. Knowledge does not appear to have progressed much since; cf. A. Pontani, *Römische Historische Mitteilungen* 27 (1985) 213-14.

45 On this aspect of his activity see E.B. Fryde, *Humanism and Renaissance historiography* (London 1983) 170-2, 182, 185-7.

46 Edited by Anna Meschini in volume III of the *Miscellanea di studi in onore di Vittore Branca* (Florence 1983) 69-113, with valuable introductory remarks.

47 For more details see N.G. Wilson, *Scholars of Byzantium* (London 1983) 240-1. Lascaris thought he was providing the still earlier version compiled by the sixth-century poet and historian Agathias.

48 Proctor, op. cit. 78-83, 168-9.

49 F. Jacobs, *Animadversiones in epigrammata Anthologiae graecae* i (Leipzig 1798) xciii; A. Meschini (ed.), *Giano Laskaris, Epigrammi greci* (Padua 1976) 12-13.

50 R. Pfeiffer, *Callimachus* ii (Oxford 1953) lxi-ii, lxxvii.

51 C. Wendel, *Abh. Göttingen* (1932, no. 1) 26-8.

52 Nos. 22-4 in the edition of A. Meschini, *Giano Laskaris, Epigrammi greci* (Padua 1976).

53 Perhaps it should be noted that Proctor, op. cit. 79, was not quite sure that the Cebes and the grammar book should be assigned to Lascaris' Florentine period, since he later employed his types in Rome and the books do not bear explicit evidence of their date. Analysis of the watermarks in the paper used settles the issue. In the Bodleian copies I found the design no. 598 in C. Piccard, *Wasserzeichen Kreuz* (Stuttgart 1981), for which the date 1496-7 is given.

54 One is not entitled, however, to give him credit for a revival in the fortunes of the Greek elegiac poet Theognis, as D.C.C. Young, *Scriptorium* 7 (1953) 3-36, did by attributing to his hand a large number of the Renaissance copies of this author. There is a general consensus among palaeographers that his identifications cannot be sustained.

Notes to Chapter 12

1 For Varus read Varius; the source is Quintilian 10.3.8, where the MSS give Varus, an error corrected in the Cologne edition of 1527. I am indebted to Prof. D.A. Russell for the interpretation of the obscure sentence in Politian's Latin.

2 This refers to the words *patrem omnis virtutis* in the *Constitutio Omnem* ad fin.; see also F. Di Benedetto, *IMU* 12 (1969) 78-99, for the Homeric citations in the *Digest*.

3 See N.G. Wilson (ed.), *St Basil on the value of Greek literature* (London 1975) 52; the passage of the so-called homily is in ch. 5.

4 Pp. 374-5 in the Gryphius edition, Lyon 1528.

5 I am grateful to Prof. A. Pontani for her help in this matter.

6 P. Desideri, *Dione di Prusa, un intellettuale greco nell' impero romano* (Messina-Florence 1978) 182, 362.

7 The episode is discussed by F.O. Menckenius, *Historia vitae et in literas meritorum Angeli Politiani* (Leipzig 1736) 419-22. Budé's version is in his *Annotationes in Pandectas*, folio 198v-199r in the Paris edition of 1533, Duaren's in his *Opera* (Frankfurt 1592) 1107. The pseudo-Herodotean life appeared in print very soon after, since it was included in the editio princeps of Homer produced in Florence in 1488.

8 The texts were published from MS Paris. gr. 3069 by L. Dorez, *Mélanges de l'Ecole française de Rome* 15 (1895) 2-32, esp. 24ff.

9 See I. Maier, *BiblHumRen* 16 (1954) 7-17. I am indebted to L. Cesarini Martinelli for her help in this matter.

10 These have now been edited with commentary by A.L. Rubinstein, *IMU* 25 (1982) 205-39.

11 The claim goes back to Sabbadini, *Metodo*, 73-4, and is repeated in A. Perosa, *Mostra del Poliziano* (Florence 1955) 73. Politian's copy is now Laur. 60.14, recently identified as being in the hand of Demetrius Damilas; see P. Canart, *RivStudBizNeoell* 14-16 (1977-79) 330. But it seems unlikely in the extreme that the three copies prepared by Girard (see above, p. 39) were not prepared for Italian scholars.

12 Attention was drawn to this by S. Rizzo, in E. Livrea & G.A. Privitera (edd.), *Studi in onore di A. Ardizzoni* (Rome 1978) 759-68. There are naturally minor variations in the formula from one commentator to the next. One may add that similar ideas are to be found in the commentaries on the grammar by Dionysius Thrax; see A. Hilgard's edition in *Grammatici graeci* III (Leipzig 1901) 3.27ff., 123.25ff. No less than 36 examples from grammarians, rhetoricians and philosophers are listed by M. Plezia, *De commentariis isagogicis* (Cracow 1949) 11-16. See above, Ch. 11 n. 7.

13 The Greek, as known to Gaza, and his renderings are as follows: (i) ἡ περὶ τοὺς παῖδας ἔκστασις: *puerorum quoque motio mentis*. (ii) ἡ πρὸ τῆς ἀφανίσεως αὐτοῦ ἐν τῇ ἑλκῶν ἔκφυσις γενομένη: *corruptio ulcerum, quae mortem interdum antecedit*. Instead of ἐν τῇ one needs ἐν Οἴτῃ.

14 See F. Garin, *RivFil* 42 (1914) 275-82.

15 This was accessible in MS Laur. 32.16, written *c.* 1280 in a hand that will have tested Politian's palaeographical knowledge to the limit. We know that he read Nonnus in Fiesole in October 1485; see A. Perosa, *Mostra del Poliziano* (Florence 1955) 84. On his use of the Laurentian codex see R. Keydell's preface to his edition, vol. I (Berlin 1959) 12*-13*.

16 Pfeiffer, *Callimachus* II (Oxford 1953) lxvii, did not quote it and very

diffidently advanced another reason for taking this view.

17 Pfeiffer fails to give him credit for this at 107, but the Latin version has *adolebit*, which is decisive. A.W. Bulloch, *Callimachus: the fifth hymn* (Cambridge 1985) is wrong on these minor details.

18 *Miscellanea* 1.78, exploiting a fragment preserved in the scholia to Apollonius Rhodius.

19 Cited aptly by A. Perosa in V. Branca et al., *Umanesimo e Rinascimento: Studi offerti a Paul Oskar Kristeller* (Florence 1980) 84.

20 See the study by A. Perosa, cited in the preceding note, and V. Fera, op. cit. in n. 26 below, 128 n. 3.

21 This fact is attested by Forteguerri's lecture on the value of Greek studies, published by Aldus in 1504. See Ch. 14 (ii).

22 Illustrated in plate V accompanying the article of F. Di Benedetto *IMU* 12 (1969) 53-112.

23 S. Gentile et al., *Marsilio Ficino e il ritorno di Platone* (Florence 1984) 185.

24 S. Rizzo, *Il lessico filologico degli umanisti* (Rome 1973) 308-17, esp. 313.

25 That one scribe, the least competent of the twelve who can be identified, was responsible for copying the three *Constitutiones* only, was noted by Th. Mommsen, *Digesta Justiniani Augusti* (Berlin 1870) I xxvi-xxvii.

26 See the edition by V. Fera, *Una ignota Expositio Suetoni del Poliziano* (Messina 1983) 224.

27 *Miscellanea* 1.84, *Epistle* 10.4.

28 Edited by A. Ardizzoni, *Poliziano, Epigrammi greci* (Florence 1951).

29 A. Perosa, *Rinascimento* 4 (1953) 11-15.

30 *Epistles* 5.6.

31 Notes taken by Bartolomeo Fonzio are in Riccardianus 153, folios 89-95.

32 Edited by V. Branca & M. Pastore Stocchi (Florence 1972) with an editio minor following in 1978.

Notes to Chapter 13

1 An impressive list is constructed by M.L. Sosower, *SIFC* 4 (1987) 140-51, partly from references in the correspondence of Palla's descendants, partly from shelf-marks indicating provenance from the library of Santa Giustina in Padua, which received sixteen Greek MSS under the terms of his will. See A. Diller, *JWCI* 24 (1961) 313-17.

2 In *RGK* IA (Vienna 1981) he is no. 377 *bis*, and is stated to have copied Themistius (Modena, Arch. II 13) and an essay of Plutarch (Laud gr. 55).

3 See M.L. Sosower, *Palatinus graecus 88 and the manuscript tradition of Lysias* (Amsterdam 1987) 46-7.

4 There is an edition by D. Geanakoplos, *Interaction of the sibling Byzantine and Western cultures* (Yale 1976) 297-304, from the MS discovered by Kristeller (Munich, lat. 28.818).

5 R.W. Hunt, *Bodleian Library Record* 9 (1973) 17-22.

6 On which see D. Marcotte, *Humanistica Lovaniensia* 36 (1987) 184-211.

7 See D.J. Geanakoplos, *Byzantina* 13 (1985) 355-72. The statement that he was the first to lecture on Aristotle in Greek needs to be qualified: Giovio says that he was the first of the Latins to do so, and Bembo in the epitaph in the church of San Francesco in Padua says that among the subjects he taught this was the first, meaning that it was his primary concern. Much of what is known about him relates to the last part of his career, after the death of Aldus, if one may make a legitimate inference from the articles of D. De Bellis, *Physis* 17 (1975) 71-93 and *Quaderni per la storia dell' Università di Padova* 13 (1980) 37-75. The most important facts which emerge are that he was one of the privileged minority allowed to borrow from cardinal Bessarion's collection, since a note by Bembo himself on MS Marc. gr. 225 of some Aristotelian commentators states that he returned the book to the library in 1531 after a loan of thirty years; and that when he published the fruits of long study of Aristotle and Theophrastus in a Giuntine edition of 1527 containing essentially biological works he improved the text in 2,000 passages, according to his own statement in the preface.

8 Among the books copied or annotated by him all three titles can be found; the Phalaris in Modena, Estensis gr. 39 (II B 2) was noted by E. Gamillscheg, *Scrittura e Civiltà* 2 (1978) 242.

9 The first view is taken by J.E. Powell in his edition of the letters in *Byzantinisch-neugriechische Jahrbücher* 15 (1939) 14-20.

10 The statement by Merula is given by C. Dionisotti, *IMU* 11 (1968) 160.

11 *Alamanno Rinuccini, Lettere ed orazioni*, ed. V.R. Giustiniani (Florence 1953), no. 31.

12 See Geanakoplos, op. cit. in n. 4 above, 242, 366.

13 See R. Kassel's note on p. 3 of his edition (Oxford 1965), referring to E. Lobel, *The Greek manuscripts of Aristotle's Poetics* (Oxford 1933) 27-31. M. Centanni, *Bollettino dei classici* 7 (1986) 37-58, who comes to a different conclusion, does not seem to give enough weight to this possibility. Callistus' conjectures in another text that is found in the same MS, the pseudo-Aristotelian *Rhetoric*, may be characterised as useful rather than outstanding; in this I agree with the judgment of M. Fuhrmann, *Untersuchungen zur Textgeschichte der pseudo-aristotelischen Alexander-Rhetorik* (Abh. Mainz 1964 no. 7) 46ff., 176ff.

14 R. Kassel, *Der Text der aristotelischen Rhetorik* (Berlin 1973) 33, 35; O.L. Smith, *Scholia metrica anonyma in Euripidis Hecubam Orestem Phoenissas* (Copenhagen 1977) xvii.

15 C. Malagola, *Della vita e delle opere di Antonio Urceo detto Codro* (Bologna 1878) 174, 480.

16 See *Sermo* 8.

17 *Sermo* 1.

18 *Sermo* 4.

19 *Sermo* 3.

20 *Sermo* 9 contains his offer. See V. Nutton, *John Caius and the manuscripts of Galen* (Cambridge 1987) 22.

21 E. Rosen, in *Didascaliae: studies in honor of Anselm M. Albareda* (New York 1961) 369-79.

22 *Sermo* 10, ad fin.; he uses the words *ornandi animi causa*.

23 For a useful account of Codro see L. Gualdo Rosa in *Dizionario biografico degli italiani* 29 (1983) 773-8. – Montfaucon, *Palaeographia graeca* (Paris 1708) 95, says that Codrus transcribed MS Regius 3302 in 1479; that MS is now Paris gr. 2776, in which I can find no evidence for his statement.

24 The best work on Leoniceno is the survey by D. Mugnai Carrara, *Interpres* 2 (1979) 169-212, and the same author's *La Biblioteca di Niccolò Leoniceno* (Florence 1991). There is valuable information about the MSS he possessed in P. Hoffmann, *Mélanges de l'Ecole française de Rome* 97 (1985) 133-8, 98 (1986) 673 n. 5, 704-08. See also V. Nutton, op. cit. in n. 20, 25-9.

25 See Politian's *Epistulae* 2.4 and 2.3 for the exchange between them.

26 D'Arcy Wentworth Thompson in *The complete works of Aristotle, the revised*

Oxford translation, ed. J. Barnes (Princeton 1984) 943.

27 Reading πρὶν for πλὴν. The phrase was deleted by the nineteenth-century critic Pikkolos.

28 P. Louis in the Budé edition (Paris 1969) vol. III, 50 n. 2.

29 For more details of this very complex question see W.F. Edwards in E.P. Mahoney (ed.), *Philosophy and humanism: Renaissance essays in honor of Paul Oskar Kristeller* (Leiden 1976) 283-305, esp. 291-9; N. Jardine in C.B. Schmitt (ed.), The *Cambridge History of Renaissance philosophy* (Cambridge 1988) 704-5.

30 The origin of syphilis is a difficult question; see A. Keaveney & J. Madden, *Hermes* 107 (1979) 499-500, K. Manchester, *The archaeology of disease* (Bradford 1983) 45-9, and M.D. Grmek, *Les maladies à l'aube de la civilisation occidentale* (Paris 1983) 199-225. Grmek thinks that there was no syphilis in antiquity and that leprosy was not known either (210, 212). (I am indebted to Heinrich von Staden for advice on these matters.)

31 The basic modern study of his life and library is by J.M. Fernández Pómar, *Emerita* 34 (1966) 211-88, which acknowledges the useful previous contribution of A. De Rosalia, *Archivio storico siciliano* 9 (1957/8) 21-70.

32 It is the first of the letters printed by J. Iriarte, *Regiae Bibliothecae Matritensis codices graeci manuscripti* (Madrid 1769) 290-1, and in *PG* 161.957-8. The date must be some time in the late seventies.

33 This essay is found in Madrid gr. 19 (4562), copied in Milan in 1464, and in Canon. gr. 83.

34 See M. Lefkowitz, *The lives of the Greek poets* (London 1981).

35 E. Legrand, *Bibliographie hellénique* I (Paris 1885) lxxxvi.

36 See N. Barker, op. cit. at Ch. 11 n. 39, 29-31, and R. Proctor, op. cit. at Ch. 11 n. 36.

37 See H. Rabe, *Prolegomenon sylloge* (Leipzig 1927) lvii-lx, lxxxvi, on Madrid gr. 137 (4687), and *RhMus* 50 (1895) 241-9, 63 (1908) 526-30 on Messina gr. 119. His reference to an old book in the library of the monastery of the Saviour at Messina containing Theodosius *De accentibus* (*PG* 161.941) presumably indicates the part of the *Canones* printed by A. Hilgard (Leipzig 1894) on pp. 362-417. Or is it the short excerpt in Madrid gr. 33 (4576)? A curiosity is the fragment of the *Gigantomachia*, an epic poem by Claudian, composed when he was a young man still living in Alexandria (Madrid gr. 141 (4691)); see A.D.E. Cameron, *Claudian: poetry and propaganda at the court of Honorius* (Oxford 1970) 14-18.

38 Details are set out by Fernández Pómar, op. cit. 245 n. 3.

39 It is worth recording that H. Rabe, *Zentralblatt für Bibliothekswesen* 45 (1928) 1-7, found in Lascaris' work little more than linguistic interpretation at a low level.

Notes to Chapter 14

1 P.O. Kristeller, *La Bibliofilia* 50 (1948) 162-78.

2 No. 45, ed. V. Branca (Florence 1943) I 60-2.

3 V. Branca ap. J.R. Hale (ed.), *Renaissance Venice* (London 1973) 228 attributes to Barbaro 'the historic founding of the world's first botanical garden at Padua', a form of words which suggests the famous garden that can still be visited; since it is generally stated to have been founded in 1545, one presumes that Barbaro is speaking of a small private enterprise. Lowry, op. cit. below n. 9, 191, avoids any misleading implications.

4 He is not so much as mentioned in A.R. Arber, *Herbals, their origin and*

evolution: a chapter in the history of botany (3rd ed., Cambridge 1986) 92-7, who passes over fifteenth-century contributions and takes as her starting point the commentary on Dioscorides by Pierandrea Mattioli (1501-1577). Mattioli in fact acknowledges the merits of Barbaro and Adriani, but prefers to use a version by a French scholar, Johannes Ruellius, which he says enjoys a wider circulation and was favoured by the medical profession. – Arber also says (p. 100) that the Padua botanic garden was founded in 1542.

5 L. Labowsky, *Medieval and Renaissance Studies* 5 (1961) 132-54 especially 137-8. The note in the *Corollarium* is on folio 6r. Recently Labowsky's argumentation has been challenged and the suggestion made that the translator is Planudes' older contemporary Maximos Holobolos. See H.J. Drossaart Lulofs & E.L.J. Poortman, *Nicolaus Damascenus, De Plantis, Five Translations* (Amsterdam – Oxford – New York 1989) 563-80.

6 The best modern discussion is by Pertusi in his contribution to *Storia della cultura veneta* 3/I (Vicenza 1980) 185-9. The two copies of the text are Harley 5628 and Ambr. N 126 sup.; the Milanese manuscript appears to be the revised and more authoritative version; a few of the corrections are in the author's hand.

7 Pertusi n. 31 cites from Dionisotti's ed. of the *Prose e rime* p. 85 to this effect.

8 Edited by F. Donadi, *Pietro Bembo: Gorgiae Leontini in Helenam laudatio* (Rome 1983). Admittedly the discussion of *logos* in Gorgias has a quite different aim.

9 On Aldus see G. Orlandi, *Aldo Manuzio editore* (Milan 1976), with a valuable introduction by C. Dionisotti; M. Lowry, *The world of Aldus Manutius: business and scholarship in Renaissance Venice* (Oxford 1979); N. Barker, op. cit. in Ch. 11 n. 39. A lively account of the academic milieu is given by D.J. Geanakoplos, *Greek Scholars in Venice* (Cambridge Mass. 1962).

10 The letter is dated 14 October 1492 and is printed on pages S vii r and v of the 1502 edition. Codrus corrected ἕνην to the Doric ἕναν and compared the Attic expression ἕνη καὶ νέα, which means 'the last day of the month', whereas the word in Theocritus means 'the day after tomorrow'.

11 The letter is printed on pages S ii r – S v r of the 1502 edition. The two passages of the *Historia animalium* are (i) 496b10-11, where in fact most MSS have the reading φρένες, as required by Codrus, and not φλέβες, and (ii) 495a20, where Codrus' proposal is very close to that of J.G. Schneider in his edition of 1811.

12 See Barker, op. cit. I confess to being not convinced by his suggestion about Musurus.

13 The definition is from Geanakoplos, op. cit. 128. Lowry, op. cit. 196-200 has a useful discussion; see also *BullJRL* 58 (1976) 381-2.

14 The volume in question contains two books issued by Callierges, the *Etymologicum Magnum* of 1499 and the Galen of 1500. It is in the Vatican Library, with the shelf-mark Stamp. Barb. AAA.IV.13. The text is most conveniently accessible in A.A. Renouard, *Annales de l'imprimerie des Aldes* (3rd edition, Paris 1834) 499-501. The identification of Forteguerri's hand is due to A. Campana. See M. Dazzi in R. Ridolfi (ed.), *Scritti sopra Aldo Manuzio* (Florence 1955) 150, who provides a plate, unfortunately too much reduced in scale to permit proper study of the notes.

15 Dionisotti ap. Orlandi, op. cit. xliii.

16 Lowry, op. cit, in n. 9 above, 200ff.

17 Dionisotti, op. cit. xlvii, while declaring it to be the clearest manifesto, does not discuss it at great length. I am not sure that he is right to assert that it

'delineava un piano di riforma radicale, sulla base della tradizione greca, classica e cristiana, dell' intiera enciclopedia, scienza e sapienza, filosofia e teologia, e proponeva il piano a Venezia'.

18 Aristides, *Panathenaicus* 322ff.

19 This observation is due to P.L. Rose, *The Italian Renaissance of mathematics* (Geneva 1975) 189.

20 See the discussion of Politian, *Misc.* 1. 84, above, p. 111.

21 The text of Forteguerri's lecture was printed by Aldus in 1504; there is a reprint in Stephanus' *Thesaurus* (Basle 1572) I i-ix. Pertusi, op. cit. above at n. 6, 184-5, deals much too briefly with it.

22 A good deal is known about printer's copy: see E. Lobel, *The Greek manuscripts of Aristotle's Poetics* (Oxford 1933) 57-9, and M. Sicherl, *Handschriftliche Vorlagen der Editio princeps des Aristoteles* (Abh. Mainz 1976 Nr. 8) (Wiesbaden 1976), together with his contributions to *RhMus* 118 (1975) 205-25 on Euripides and *IMU* 19 (1976) 257-76 on Musaeus; Lowry, op. cit. 234ff. and *BullJRL* 57 (1974) 140-4; N.G. Wilson in *Venezia Centro di mediazione tra Oriente e Occidente (Secoli xv-xvi), aspetti e problemi* (Venice 1977) II 392-6; note also L. Mendelssohn's statement in his edition of the historian Herodian (Leipzig 1883) p. viii n. **, that the Aldine does not depend on any of the three copies in Bessarion's collection.

23 On this edition se M. Sicherl, *IMU* 19 (1976) 257-76 and his contribution to D. Harlfinger et al., *Griechische Handschriften und Aldinen, eine Austellung anlässlich der XV, Tagung der Mommsen-Gesellschaft in der Herzog August Bibliothek Wolfenbüttel* (Wolfenbüttel 1978) 125.

24 See M. Sicherl's monograph cited in n. 22 above and his contribution to D. Harlfinger et al. 125-9. L. Minio-Paluello, *Opuscula: the Latin Aristotle* (Amsterdam 1972) 492-3, maintains that the use of the term Organon as a description of the works on logic derives from an epigram in the first volume of the Aldine, in which they are all printed together. Though this may be true, it is far from certain; for another view see I. Düring, *Antike und Abendland* 4 (1954) 123.

25 The date is given in the colophon as February 1495, and as Aldus was still using the official Venetian calendar, this means 1496. See Sicherl, op. cit. (1976) 10 n. 9.

26 That of Matteo Capcasa, undated, perhaps *c.* 1500. On Cavalli see M. Palma in *Dizionario biografico degli italiani* 22 (1979) 724-5.

27 It should be recorded here that J. Martin in his edition *Scholia in Aratum vetera* (Stuttgart 1974) xii-xiii is inclined to think that Musurus was the editor of part of this volume, using Estensis gr. 51 (II B 14) and other codices.

28 Book 2, p. 241 in the Yale edition (vol. 6, 1981); cited by J.S. Phillimore in the preface to his translation (Oxford 1912).

29 See the important paper by J.C.B. Lowe, *BICS* 9 (1962) 27-42; he was concerned with the text of Aristophanes, but his results are valid for dramatic texts as a whole. It is a pity that we have no means of identifying the date and authorship of the scholium on *Ajax* 354.

30 I commend the article of M. Davies, *Prometheus* 12 (1986) 19-24.

31 So H. Beckby in his edition (Munich 1969[2]) vol. i p. 88 n. 1. The Aldine has no preface; at the end a brief letter, in Greek, by Scipio Forteguerri expresses appreciation of the publisher's enterprise. An appendix corrects a number of misprints and notes variant readings from other manuscripts.

32 I would be nice to think that Aldus' publication was the source of inspiration for two of Titian's paintings for Alfonso d'Este, Duke of Ferrara. The *Worship of*

Venus and the *Bacchanal of the Andrians*, produced between 1518 and 1525, depend on Philostratus (1.6 and 25). But whoever it was who gave Alfonso the idea – the resident humanist Celio Calcagnini is as likely as anyone – we cannot be sure whether he was working from the original or a Latin version; one such version had been made by Antonio Bonfini of Ascoli in 1487. Philostratus' influence on Renaissance art is explored by R. Foerster in *Jahrbuch der preussichen Kunstsammlungen* 25 (1904) 15-48, esp. 18-21, 41-3. F. Wickhoff, ibid. 23 (1902) 118-20, recognised the source of the *Bacchanal*; the *Worship of Venus* was seen to be Philostratean by Carlo Ridolfi, *Le meraviglie dell' arte* (Venice 1648).

33 The printer's copy for Ulpian was Paris gr. 2939, written by N. Vlastos in 1484; see E. Lobel, *The Greek manuscripts of Aristotle's Poetics* (Oxford 1933) 58.

34 See the important essay of M. Sicherl, *RhMus* 118 (1975) 205-25, which inter alia disposes of the idea that Musurus was the editor.

35 Chapter 27, n. 29; noted by Wilamowitz, *Kleine Schriften*, vol. 4 (Berlin 1962) 635-9.

36 Cited by P. Orvieto in *Dizionario biografico degli italiani* 17 (1974) 785-6. The codex was probably Pal. gr. 90, which contains Gregory of Nazianzus as well and appears to have been used as the source for both authors; see N. Gertz, *Scriptorium* 35 (1981) 65-70 and *Die handschriftliche Ueberlieferung der Gedichte Gregors von Nazianz* (Paderborn 1986) 142.

37 Folios 86 and 87 of Paris gr. 3064, in the large format of 385 x 275. There is an illustration between pages 388 and 389 of Renouard, *Annales* (ed. 3, Paris 1834). See Lowry, 267 and 275 with nn. 41 and 70.

38 The modern edition is by F. Sbordone (Naples 1940). He says (p. LX) that Aldus used MS Marc. gr. 391 as the basis of his text, but we have seen that there is reason to doubt such claims. On Ficino see E.H. Gombrich, *JWCI* 11 (1948) 172. Note also E. Wind, *Die heidnischen Mysterien in der Renaissance* (Stuttgart 1981) 238 n. 58.

39 W. Bühler, *Zenobii Athoi proverbia* I (Göttingen 1987) 67, 71-2. He notes that there are some conjectures in the Aldine.

40 On the *Adages* see M.M. Phillips, *The Adages of Erasmus* (Cambridge 1964), especially pp. 62-95 (for the figure 3285 see p. 77); Geanakoplos 263-72; E. Rummel, *Erasmus as a translator of the classics* (Toronto 1985) 52-7.

41 The text of these two treatises and of the *Rhetorica ad Alexandrum* seems to derive mainly from a codex written by the prolific and intelligent scribe Andronicus Callistus, Paris gr. 2038. This book is far too clean to have served as printer's copy, so a lost transcript must have been used. According to Sicherl 79 Paris gr. 2038 was lent to the publisher by Janus Lascaris, who was by now the French envoy in Venice. This is not certain; I think the marginalia may be due to Musurus and/or Raphael Regius, and Lascaris' loan, which Aldus acknowledges, was of a copy of various rhetoricians of the post-classical period. Sicherl ap. D. Harlfinger et al., op. cit. 140 identifies the printer's copy of some of the other texts in Paris gr. 2921, 2924, 2960.

42 On him one may consult Geanakoplos 223-55.

43 H. Rabe, in the Teubner edition (Leipzig 1913) xxiv, says that the Aldine is very close to the manuscript he calls Lc (Laur. 60.25).

44 On these questions see Lowry 257.

45 His source for some of the essays was Milan, Ambr. C 195 inf. See M. Treu, *Zur Geschichte der Ueberlieferung von Plutarchs Moralia* III (Programm Breslau 1884) 22.

46 Treu, op. cit. 21 cites some critical comments. It is less surprising that for a modern editor the Aldine 'contains no new readings (only errors) and so may be generally ignored'; so B.P. Hillyard, *Plutarch: De audiendo, A text and commentary* (New York 1981) xliv.

47 They are a list of irregular verbs (pp. 116-33), Chalcondyles' essay on the rules about augments for the past tense (133-66), Book 4 of Theodore Gaza on syntax (167-265), an anonymous essay on enclitics (265-73), and a collection of *Gnomai monostichoi* (273-96).

48 One cannot entirely dismiss the feeling that Aldus' decision to reprint a text which had only just been issued smacks of sharp practice. He appears to have followed the Ferrara edition very closely. According to its editor Johannes Maciochus it derives from a manuscript belonging to Celio Calcagnini. On these editions see I.O. Tsavari, *Histoire du texte de la description de la terre de Denys le Périégète* (Ioannina 1990) 425-7.

49 The sources for the Pindar are discussed by J. Irigoin, *Histoire du texte de Pindare* (Paris 1952) 399-408.

50 Many of the texts in question had been recovered by Janus Lascaris during his trip to Greece to collect for Lorenzo de' Medici, as we learn from the preface to the 1508 volume of rhetorical manuals. The copies used by Aldus, though not sent into the printing-shop, seem to have been Marc. gr. VIII 1 and 6; see M. Sicherl in J.L. Heller (ed.), *Serta Turyniana* (University of Illinois 1974) 588-9 and M. Sosower, *GRBS* 23 (1982) 384-6. But in Gorgias' *Helen* the Aldine is very close to Madrid gr. 317 (7210), transcribed by Constantine Lascaris, as was noted by F. Donadi, *Bollettino dell' Istituto di Filologia Greca* 2 (1975) 170-84.

51 The minor texts are by Gorgias, Alcidamas, Lesbonax and Herodes Atticus. They are oddly divided between the two volumes (I say two because there are two colophons, dated April and May of 1513, but each volume appears to divide into two).

52 W. Wyse, *The speeches of Isaeus* (Cambridge 1904) liii. Similar comments have been made about the editing of the essays by Aristides; see F.W. Lenz and C.A. Behr, *P. Aelii Aristidis opera quae extant omnia* I (Leiden 1976) xcix-ci; the MSS which seem closest to the Aldine text are Paris gr. 2948 and 3006, Vat. gr. 933.

53 According to the entry in Sanudo's diary for November 4, 1508, vol. 7, 661.

54 Letter no. 1347 of AD 1523.

55 Sanudo, September 1510 and June 1512, vol. 11, 419 and 14, 414.

56 This he reveals in the letter accompanying the Aldine of 1516.

57 M. Sicherl, *Johannes Cuno* (Heidelberg 1978) 87-106; J. Irigoin in *Philophronema (Festschrift für Martin Sicherl zum 75. Geburtstag* (Paderborn 1990)) 253-62, who announces that a more detailed study by B. Mondrain is in preparation. One wonders if he may also have lectured on the *Greek Anthology*; it is known that he made a number of observations on this text. A full set of them cannot be assembled; for a preliminary attempt to sort out the confusing evidence see A. Meschini, *Bollettino dei classici* 3 (1982) 23-62.

58 G. Coggiola, *Zentralblatt für Bibliothekswesen* 25 (1908) 47-70.

59 Sanudo, vol. 19, 319 and 20, 177.

60 An outline of Musurus' life is given by R. Menge in the fifth volume of M. Schmidt's edition of Hesychius (Jena 1868) 1-88.

61 N.G. Wilson, *CQ* 12 (1962) 32-47. Musurus used at least two manuscripts of the Triclinian recension; his other sources were Estensis gr. 127 (III D 8) and the now fragmentary Sélestat, Bibliothèque humaniste 347. See M. Sicherl in B.

Haller (ed.), *Erlesenes aus der Welt des Buches* (Wiesbaden 1979) 189-231. His plate on p. 205 shows a page from the Sélestat manuscript, written by Zacharias Callierges, with the markings typical of printer's copy.

62 His words are 'veterem sermonis dignitatem atque elegantiam retinebant'. The letter is cited by H. Hody, *De graecis illustribus* (London 1742) 188-9.

63 See above, Ch. 8 n. 13.

64 Only a few of the sources used by Musurus can be identified; they include Paris supp. gr. 212 (Alciphron) and 924 (Philostratus), also a copy of Pal. gr. 134. See Sicherl in D. Harlfinger et al., op. cit. 134-6. It has been stated that for Phalaris, Brutus and Apollonius of Tyana, which had been issued by another press in Venice in 1498, Musurus simply reprinted the existing text; so Legrand, *Bibliographie Hellénique* I (Paris 1885) 53n.

65 This is the inference to be made from L.A. Post, *The Vatican Plato and its relations* (Middletown, Conn. 1934) 43.

66 G.J. Boter, *The textual tradition of Plato's Republic* (Amsterdam 1986) 295-8. But cf. Sicherl in D. Harlfinger et al., op. cit., 145-6.

67 M. Wallies, in *Commentaria in Aristotelem graeca* 2.2 (Berlin 1891) xiii-xiv, says that Musurus made minor adjustments, leaving a certain amount for future editors to do; the text as printed resembles closely that found in Paris gr. 1874. Musurus' interest in the *Organon* is attested by his transcript of the *Sophistici elenchi* Escorial Φ-II-6 (203), identified by A. Bravo García, *Estudios clásicos* 89 (1985) 291-7.

68 A. Adler, *Suidae lexicon* V (Leipzig 1938) 226.

69 U. von Wilamowitz-Moellendorff, *Euripides: Herakles* (repr. Darmstadt 1959) I 221.

70 For an example of misplaced ingenuity see the discussion of E 1203 in K. Latte, *Hesychii Alexandrini lexicon* II (Copenhagen 1966) 807. The manuscript needed no alteration except the removal of intrusive punctuation and restoration of correct word-division; but Musurus made a more elaborate change, using his knowledge of the other book he was editing at the time, Athenaeus' *Deipnosophistae* (2.43F).

71 See H. Erbse, *BZ* 61 (1968) 76, who checked a small sample of the manuscript amounting to nine pages and found sixteen attempts at emendation by Musurus which had not been recorded but deserved to be. Menge noted that in the first 2,400 entries Musurus made about 550 emendations, of which 370 are generally accepted.

72 There are three omissions in the MSS of Theophrastus at 4.4.2. The Aldine team of editors had not been aware of the secondary tradition when they prepared the editio princeps; but one can hardly blame them.

73 The sources of the edition are discussed by J. Irigoin, *REG* 80 (1967) 418-24.

74 Some other neat restorations are seen at 215A (the name of the Spartan general Pagondas, probably retrieved from Thucydides 4.93), 283C, 387F (the name of the Hellenistic writer Istros), 508B and 619B.

75 See Kaibel's Teubner edition (Leipzig 1890) I xiii-xiv.

76 On Bion see W. Bühler, *Die Europa des Moschos* (Hermes Einzelschriften 13) (Wiesbaden 1960) 14; on Callimachus Pfeiffer's edition, II (Oxford 1953) lxxv. Callierges' admirable venture soon failed. On 25 September 1516 he and his backer Cornelio Benigno, chancellor of Agostino Chigi, sold all remaining copies, 778 of Pindar and 981 of Theocritus, to Francesco Calvo, a bookseller of Pavia, for the sum of 450 ducats (only 20 of which went to Callierges). It appears that these figures include 208 copies of Pindar and 198 of Theocritus not yet sold but already in the hands of booksellers outside Rome, which presumably means that books were sent out on a 'sale or return' basis. See J. Ruysschaert, *Archivio della Società Romana di Storia Patria* 25 (1971, actually 1973) 22.

77 A. Diller, *The textual tradition of Strabo's Geography* (Amsterdam 1975) 158-61, 175; M. Sicherl in D. Harlfinger et al., 147-9.

Notes to Chapter 15

1 See R. Black, *Benedetto Accolti and the Florentine Renaissance* (Cambridge 1985) 194-201.

2 See J. Burckhardt, *The architecture of the Italian Renaissance*, ed. P. Murray (London 1985) 26-7.

3 See in general C.V. Palisca, *Humanism in Italian Renaissance musical thought* (Yale 1985).

4 Constantine Lascaris says he saw it in the imperial library; *PG* 161.918.

5 See Ch. 4 n. 17.

6 Sabbadini, op. cit. at Ch. 4 n. 18, 161-2, summarises the references to this text. He does not think the claim was fraudulent. Heiberg in his Teubner edition of Archimedes vol. 3 (Leipzig 1915) lxxxii n. 2 took a different view, and is followed by P.L. Rose, *The Italian Renaissance of mathematics* (Geneva 1975) 32.

7 N.G. Wilson, *GRBS* 16 (1975) 95-101. For some other, less important, puzzles see H. Baron, *Humanistic and political literature in Florence and Venice at the beginning of the Quattrocento* (Harvard 1955) 166-72; I. Maier, *BiblHumRen* 16 (1954) 7-17.

Indexes

(i) Antiquity (mainly authors, up to *c.* 600)

(ii) Middle Ages and Renaissance
(mainly writers, scholars and copyists)

(iii) Manuscripts

(iv) General